Harney Flats

Florida Museum of Natural History: Ripley P. Bullen Series

Harney Flats
A Florida Paleoindian Site

I. Randolph Daniel Jr. and Michael Wisenbaker

Foreword by Albert C. Goodyear

University of Florida Press
Gainesville

Copyright 1987 by I. Randolph Daniel Jr. and Michael Wisenbaker
New preface copyright 2017 by I. Randolph Daniel Jr. and Michael Wisenbaker
All rights reserved

Printed in the United States of America on acid-free paper

This book may be available in an electronic edition.

22 21 20 19 18 17   6 5 4 3 2 1

Library of Congress Control Number: 2017947612
ISBN 978-1-68340-022-6 (pbk.)

This book is a reprint of the original version published by
Baywood Publishing Company, Inc., in 1987.

Original manuscript edited by Roger W. Moeller.

University of Florida Press
15 Northwest 15th Street
Gainesville, FL 32611-2079
http://upress.ufl.edu

UF PRESS
UNIVERSITY
OF FLORIDA

Contents

Preface to the Paperback Edition   vii
Foreword   xi
Preface to the First Edition   xiii
Acknowledgments   xv

1. Research Background   1
2. Methodology   14
3. Site Stratification and Cultural Stratification   28
4. Artifact Analysis   41
5. Intra-Site Spatial Analysis   98
6. A Comparative Overview of Early Man Sites   129
7. Context of Paleo-Indian in Central Florida   145
8. Developing Models of a Band Society   162
9. Settlement Systems and Technology: A Summary Model   168

References Cited   176
Index   199

Preface to the Paperback Edition

Much Paleoindian research has been done in the Southeastern United States since the first shovelful of dirt was turned at Harney Flats in 1981. In retrospect, we see the timing of our work at Harney Flats falling on the cusp of an upsurge of Paleoindian studies in the region. Florida, in particular, has been unique in this regard because of the focus on underwater rather than terrestrial early sites. This trend in underwater archaeology, of course, speaks to the distinctive geologic nature of the Florida peninsula and its potential for inundated sites. Nevertheless, the expansive excavations at Harney Flats reminds us that significant Paleoindian terrestrial sites are still worth exploring. In the original foreword to this book, Al Goodyear remarked that the Harney Flats excavations represented a benchmark in Florida Paleoindian studies. This was largely due to the essential baseline data on Paleoindian technology and site organization that it produced. In our view, thirty years passing since the publication of *Harney Flats* (1987) has not lessened the significance of those results, and we reflect on those here.

With respect to Paleoindian technology, the substantial lithic assemblage was easily recognized as early. This was particularly apparent in the occurrence of relatively small trianguloid endscrapers as well as numerous large, less formally shaped unifacial tools with their distinctly retouched margins. To a certain extent, the presence of these tool types was not surprising, but their recovery at Harney Flats represented the first time that a clear association could be made with diagnostic Paleoindian / Early Archaic bifaces. In particular, several aspects of the lithic assemblage are worth commenting on.

First, the several dozen Suwannee/Simpson points and preforms from Harney Flats still rank as one of the largest collection of Florida Paleoindian points from excavated contexts in Florida. But even as we attempted to sort those eared lanceolate forms during our analysis, we recognized they exhibited a degree of variability that belied the traditional Ripley Bullen point typology that we relied on. More recently, two independent studies by James Dunbar (*Paleoindian Societies of the Coastal Southeast*, 2016) and David Thulman (*Journal of Archaeological Science* 39:1599–1607) have attempted to better understand the variability in what have been traditionally classified as Suwannee and Simpson points. Although both researchers used somewhat different methods, they identified patterning in the variability of basal shape, creating several possible point types. But the meaning of these proposed types largely remains unresolved (which both researchers acknowledge). Do they represent chronological or functional differences (or something else entirely)? Whatever the outcome of these or future typological studies, the excavated contexts of the points from Harney Flats will provide an important datum point to address those questions.

Second, a word of hindsight can be said about our inability to stratigraphically separate apparent Suwannee and Bolen components at Harney Flats. The Suwannee/Bolen component, of course, represents the basal cultural stratum at the site. Initially, we suggested this lack of separation was due to repeated occupations on a slowly accreting land surface during Suwannee/Bolen times. While this conclusion may still be true, it was largely reached by using rather thick (20 cm) level data rather than piece-plotted provenience data. Today a back-plot analysis using piece-plotted elevation data coupled with an artifact refitting study may yet reveal an unrealized stratigraphic separation between the Suwannee and Bolen occupations.

Third, a word of hindsight may also made regarding the presence of several seemingly enigmatic artifact classes in the assemblage. These include four relatively large and otherwise nondescript metamorphic stones (two in an apparent cache), a group of small lanceolate forms we referred to as "lozenge-shaped bifaces," and several polyhedral cores. The four metamorphic stones are the only apparent "exotic" stone in the entire assemblage. While the occurrence of nonlocal raw materials is a continental pattern across Paleoindian assemblages, their presence is virtually always in the form of knappable stone. The metamorphic stones we recovered at Harney Flats are hardly knappable. Most appear minimally shaped (if at all) and are inferred to have been used in abrading, chopping, or anvil functions. Since these functions could have been accomplished using local cherts, the presence of the metamorphic types remains puzzling (particularly one weighing 4.5 kg). The stones' origins would have been in the Piedmont, outside the state, and we speculated they arrived via intergroup exchange. So do these artifacts represent the exception (non-knappable stone) that proves the rule (long-distance exchange) with respect to the presence of exotic stone in Paleoindian assemblages? If so, we still find their occurrence unusual. Something beyond the purely utilitarian must have motivated the acquisition of these particular items.

Fourth, the lozenge-shaped bifaces and small polyhedral cores are even more intriguing. Do they represent a Pre-Clovis signature at Harney Flats? Such a possibility was anathema in the 1980s but the recovery of similar artifacts that claim Pre-Clovis status elsewhere in the East suggest this possibility today. For example, relatively small and lanceolate- to pentagonal-shaped bifaces have been reported at sites such as Page-Ladson, Cactus Hill, and Meadowcroft that are strikingly similar to what we referred to as lozenge-shaped bifaces at Harney Flats. During the analysis, we were hard-pressed to assign these forms to an existing cultural-historical type. Nevertheless, their context of recovery clearly suggests an early temporal association. We had simply assumed they were part of the Suwannee assemblage, but now we wonder if they represent a Florida Pre-Clovis point type. Likewise, the presence of several small polyhedral cores in the Harney Flats assemblage also elicits comparison to similar core forms from Cactus Hill. At Cactus Hill, such cores were associated with small, thin pentagonal bifaces recovered below a Clovis-level stratum at the site. So do the small bifaces and polyhedral cores at Cactus Hill and Harney Flats represent part of a Pre-Clovis complex in the Southeast? While we are not ready to declare a Pre-Clovis presence at Harney Flats, neither are we ready to discount it.

Turning now to the artifact distributions, we regard the spatial data generated from the block excavations as the second significant contribution of the project. Our interest in exploring intrasite spatial patterning necessitated opening large contiguous areas accompanied by piece-plotting recognizable tools. (And we did this "old school" with tapes and transits rather than total stations!) This ranked as the largest excavation of a Paleoindian site in Florida, if not one of the largest in the eastern United States. To the best of our knowledge, that fact is still true today. The results are displayed in several artifact maps in the book accompanied by SYMAP distributions of flake densities across three excavation blocks (again, produced old school via a main-frame computer). Unfortunately, discerning intra-area spatial patterning was not as straightforward as we had hoped. In short, we found that spatial patterning was more apparent between blocks than within them. Today we wonder what a reexamination of those data might reveal. With the myriad spatial analysis programs now available, new ethnoarchaeological studies to model site structure on, and a more sophisticated understanding of how postdepositional processes affect site formation, we suspect that an unrealized potential exists for interpreting the artifact distributions at Harney Flats.

Despite the gaps that our work filled in terms of Paleoindian studies in Florida, one bit of information eluded us—the chronological relationship between Suwannee and Clovis. That is still true today. While the Suwannee component represents the basal cultural stratum at Harney Flats, no apparent Clovis-age artifacts were recovered. Unfortunately, fluted points in Florida likened to Clovis have been recovered from surface contexts. Certainly, no fluted points were present in the Harney Flats assemblage. At the time we assumed that Suwannee/Simpson points represented a post-Clovis manifestation in Florida. While we still think this is the case, today other researchers suggest otherwise. Dennis Stanford et al. (*Paleoamerican Origins: Beyond Clovis*, 2005, pp. 313–353), for example, speculates that Suwannee points are Pre-Clovis in age. And if the OSL date from the Wakulla Springs Lodge (Rink et al., *Florida Anthropologist* 65:5–24) is to be believed, Simpson points may predate Clovis too. Whatever the outcome, we can only hope that it doesn't take another thirty years to resolve the typological and chronological issues related to Suwannee and Simpson points in Florida.

Finally, a word is necessary about how this reprint came to pass. At the 2016 meeting of the Southeast Archaeological Conference in Athens, Georgia, Dan Morse approached Daniel and commented on the hefty asking price that he had seen online for copies of *Harney Flats*. Indeed, that the book was selling for several times its original published price, presumably driven by the fact that it is out of print, had not gone unnoticed by Daniel. In any case, Morse observed that a market must still exist for the volume and suggested that Daniel broach University Press of Florida to gauge their interest in reprinting the book. Conversations with Judith Knight ensued, resulting in the current reprint. We don't know what the new selling price will be, but we feel confident it will be more affordable than the out-of-print version. Whatever its price, we present this reprint (slightly renamed) as testament to the enduring relevance of the Harney Flats site to Paleoindian studies in the Southeast.

I. Randolph Daniel Jr.
Michael Wisenbaker

Corrected errors should be read as follows:

> On page 1, the *Florida Department of State, Division of Historical Resources, History and Records Management, Bureau of Historic Sites and Properties* should read the *Florida Department of State, Division of Historical Resources, Bureau of Archaeological Research*.
> On page 168, *hummocks* should read *hammocks*.
> Throughout the book, *Paleo-Indian* should read *Paleoindian*, the commonly accepted term.

Foreword

With the publication of this book, great strides have been made in the study of Paleo-Indian in the Southeast. After decades of tantalizing hints at a significant presence of Early Man in Florida, provided primarily by finds of Suwannee points and Pleistocene fossils in the rivers of that state, we have in this book a full-blown study of a major site and its assemblages. Comparatively speaking, the data themselves are rather spectacular.

The excavation strategy was state-of-the-art as it emphasized the opening up of large, contiguously excavated areas with all recognizable artifacts mapped in situ. This follows in the tradition of Debert and Brand, excavations of the 1960s and early 1970s which attempted to uncover living areas. The 967 m^2 of excavated area must rank this excavation as the largest Paleo-Indian excavation in the Southeast and perhaps the entire eastern United States. The recent ethnographic fieldwork conducted among hunter-gatherers by archaeologists themselves has consistently revealed the necessity of having large areas examined to encompass the full range of settlement activity. The lack of recognizable intrasite patterning resulting from the expansive excavations at Harney Flats, however, while at first glance is frustrating, is in reality a vindication of the excavation method. What the spatial distribution at Harney Flats may be telling us is that Paleo-Indian settlement behavior in peninsular Florida is significantly different from that of systems to the north. For those interested in modeling variability in Paleo-Indian cultural systems by latitude, we now have a well-analyzed and thoroughly reported body of data on the southern extreme. This is doubly significant as Harney Flats is also situated on the southern end of the natural occurrence of chert on the eastern seaboard. The chert-bearing Tertiary limestones which begin in South Carolina cease to occur in the area of Tampa Bay.

The strategies of lithic analysis employed by the authors are also appropriate for the kinds of theoretical interests that characterize prehistoric hunter-gatherer studies today. Techno-functional analysis, coupled with wear analysis by polish and experimentation, is the strongest approach currently available to the archaeologist. When information gathered from studies of tool production and use are related to theoretical concepts about the organization of hunter-gatherer technologies, prehistorians can be said to be conducting paleoanthropology.

Within the raw materials represented, the lack of exotic cherts among the chipped stone tools is significant and forms another feature which distinguishes Harney Flats from other Paleo-Indian sites in the East. An obvious implication of this finding is that Paleo-Indian folk in peninsular Florida may have been less geographically mobile than their northern counterparts living in colder and more seasonally pronounced climates. In Florida, the near absence of fluting among Suwannee points, the near absence of gravers, the infrequent occurrence of hafted teardrop-shaped endscrapers, and the domination of assemblages by large, well-made plano-convex unifaces are all technological signals that a substantially different adaptation may have been taking place. While technologically it is not difficult to class these people as "Paleo-Indian," it is evident that we must regard the makers of Suwannee points in Florida on their own terms. The publication of this book allows us to begin doing that in a way that is thorough and precise, and as such, it is a benchmark in Florida archaeology as well as Paleo-Indian studies in the East.

Albert C. Goodyear

Preface to the First Edition

The investigations at Harney Flats are important for several reasons. First, the data from the site fill a major gap in our knowledge of early man in the Southeast in general and Florida in particular because of the paucity of previously excavated early sites. Paleo-Indian studies in the state have largely been associated with a diagnostic projectile point style, a vague idea of other lithic artifacts, and inferences from early sites in other areas. Almost all other aspects of the Paleo-Indian culture including its temporal position within the Southeast have remained unknown. While we emphasize the early occupation at the site, the importance of the younger component and the stratified sequence should not be overlooked. Although the relative chronology defined by diagnostic projectile points has not modified the established sequences based on typological comparisons to sites elsewhere (see Bullen, 1976:33; 1975: 1–4), such a sequence, with the Suwannee point manifesting the basal cultural stratum, can now be demonstrated in central Florida.

Perhaps the most significant aspect of the fieldwork was the emphasis on opening large contiguous areas and mapping individual artifacts to study internal site structure. Broad-scale patterning includes a living area and activity areas. Although fine-scaled patterning within each area is still unclear, the existence of spatial structure has been demonstrated in deep sand lithic sites in central Florida.

Another important aspect of the project is the perspective from which the lithic analysis was approached. In examining the organization of the technology, we went beyond the traditional techno-functional stone tool study to understand the role of the lithic assemblage in the overall settlement system adaptation. This was particularly successful due to the unique nature of the site and its stone tool assemblage. Aiding the analysis was the tool replication and use-wear study (Ballo, 1985), the most comprehensive study on Florida cherts to date. This study has helped to reveal the generalized nature of the implements and indicates that tool form and function are not necessarily independent variables.

Upchurch (1984) conducted a study to document Paleo-Indian lithic raw material selection in central Florida and trace mobility patterns as revealed by the use of chert from particular quarry areas. Further work is needed for proper evaluation, but results to date suggest that some preferences existed for the selection of more homogeneous limestone replaced cherts—a pattern similar to Paleo-Indian use of cryptocrystalline stone elsewhere. No exotic lithics (i.e., chert types found outside of the Tampa Bay region) were observed in our sample. These findings are consistent with a previous study (Goodyear et al., 1983) and suggest that the mobility of Paleo-Indian groups in central Florida may have been limited.

Finally, a strong foundation for a model of Paleo-Indian settlement systems has been made. Refinement of this model using more detailed spatial analysis, tool refitting, and use-wear studies must be encouraged for us to understand the adaptation of early man in Florida and in other portions of the Eastern United States.

Acknowledgments

A project of this size and duration is never completed without the assistance of many people which we would like to acknowledge here. First of all, the Federal Highway Administration and the Florida Department of Transportation (DOT) provided the funding for the project as part of the I-75 Highway Salvage Program. The assistance provided to us in the field by the Temple Terrace Office of the DOT is particularly appreciated.

Thanks are also due to several local residents. Son Anderson, Brian Evensen, and Tony Polydori all allowed us to view their artifact collections. Gene Bartolotti answered our questions about the land alterations which have occurred in the vicinity of Harney Flats during the recent past. We would also like to thank Ben Waller who allowed us to examine his extensive collection of Suwannee points.

A special thanks goes to Charlie Poe who served as a field supervisor during the Phase III excavations. The crew consisted of the following people:

Mindy Lytle	Allen Cooper
Michael Norton	John Mitchell
Lisa Burns	Ed Cannette
Bill Johnson	Susan McDonough
Gary Rutt	Randi Rossman
Bill Huser	Curtis McKinney
Dave Pohl	Wanda DeMontmollin
Ken Brown	Jay Hardman
Jane Schneider	Katharine Bierce-Gedris
Mark Worthen	Paul Swofford
Joy Suarez	John King
Linda Churchill	Mark Obarka
John Welch	Cheryl Elkins
Greg Girard	Jerry Westphal

The cooperation of the Department of Anthropology at the University of South Florida is greatly appreciated. All of the artifacts were accessioned by students in the Anthropology Department. The laboratory was directed by George R. Ballo under the supervision of Roger T. Grange.

We are also grateful to many people who helped with the analysis and preparation of the report. This includes many staff members and other employees of the Florida Bureau of Archaeological Research. Katharine Bierce-Gedris participated in many phases of the analysis. George R. Ballo conducted our lithic use-wear analysis. Sam B. Upchurch was the project geologist and conducted our chert provenance analysis.

Credit for the illustrations goes to several people. Roy Lett performed the artifact photography. Randy V. Bellomo and Charles Poe drafted the figures. Elizabeth J. Misner drew the artifact illustrations. Randy Bellomo also generated the computer SYMAPS.

A special thanks is also extended to Albert C. Goodyear who served as archaeological consultant for this project and provided helpful advice on many phases of the analysis.

The authors would also like to express their special gratitude to B. Clavin Jones who recognized the importance of Harney Flats and was instrumental in seeing that this project came about. Without his support and concern there simply would have been no Phase III excavation.

The metamorphosis from report manuscript to book is a unique process. Credit for this transformation is due to Roger W. Moeller for editing the manuscript into book form and to the production staff at S. L. EDCO.

Finally, the senior author would like to express his gratitude to his wife Becky, who probably thinks she will never hear the end of Harney Flats.

Harney Flats

CHAPTER 1
Research Background

THE I-75 PROJECT

This volume provides comprehensive results of excavations conducted at Harney Flats—one of the archaeological sites of the I-75 Highway Salvage Program investigated by the Bureau of Historic Sites and Properties (now the Bureau of Archaeological Research). The Florida Department of State, Division of Historical Resources, History and Records Management, Bureau of Historic Sites and Properties has maintained a cooperative agreement with the Florida Department of Transportation since 1966 to allow the Bureau to assess impacts of highway construction on cultural resources within the state of Florida.

Under this program a Phase I survey was conducted in 1978 by B. Calvin Jones over 66.3 km of the proposed I-75 right-of-way through Hillsborough County. A total of thirty-one archaeological sites was recorded during the survey by means of subsurface testing of selective topographic features including ridge tops, slopes,

Table 1. Archaeological Sites in Hillsborough County Investigated in Conjunction with the I-75 Highway Salvage Project

Site	Phase II Test Excavations Reference	Phase III Excavations Reference
8Hi99	K. Hardin (1982)	
8Hi393c	K. Gagel (1981b)	
8Hi393c/uw	J. Palmer et al. (1981)	
8Hi450	Daniel and Wisenbaker (1981)	
8Hi471	M. Almy (1982)	
8Hi472	J. Haviser (1983)	B. Johnson (1985)
8Hi473	M. Chance (1982)	M. Chance (1983)
8Hi476	B. Wharton (1983)	M. Chance (1982)
8Hi480	M. Almy (1981)	
8Hi483A	R. Daniel (1982)	
8Hi483B	K. Gagel (1981a)	
8Hi507	(This volume)	(This volume)
8Hi510	K. Gagel (1984)	
8Hi521	K. Gagel and I.R. Daniel, Jr. (1985)	
8Hi522	K. Gagel and I.R. Daniel, Jr. (1985)	

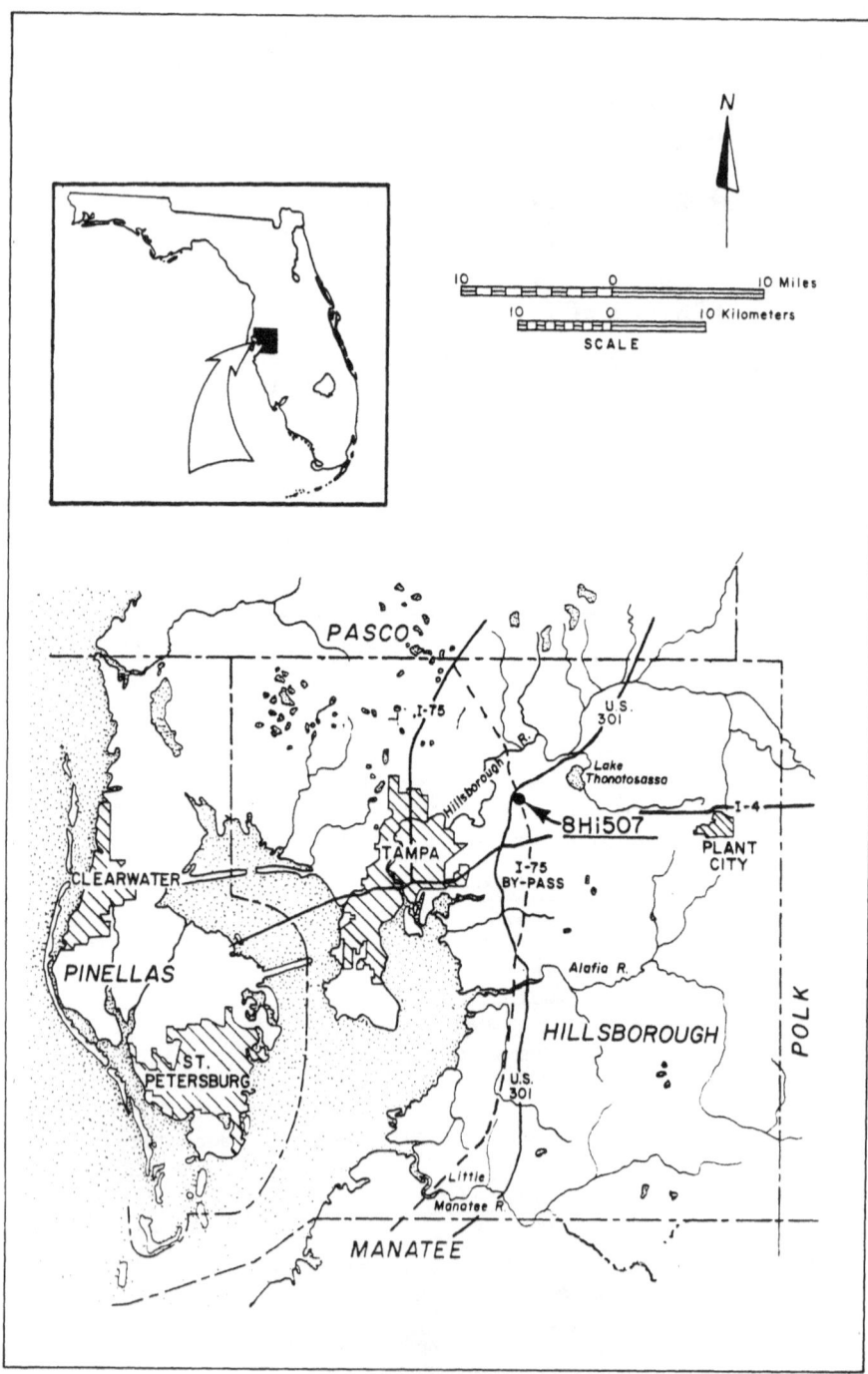

Figure 1. I-75 Right-of-way through Hillsborough County, Florida.

RESEARCH BACKGROUND / 3

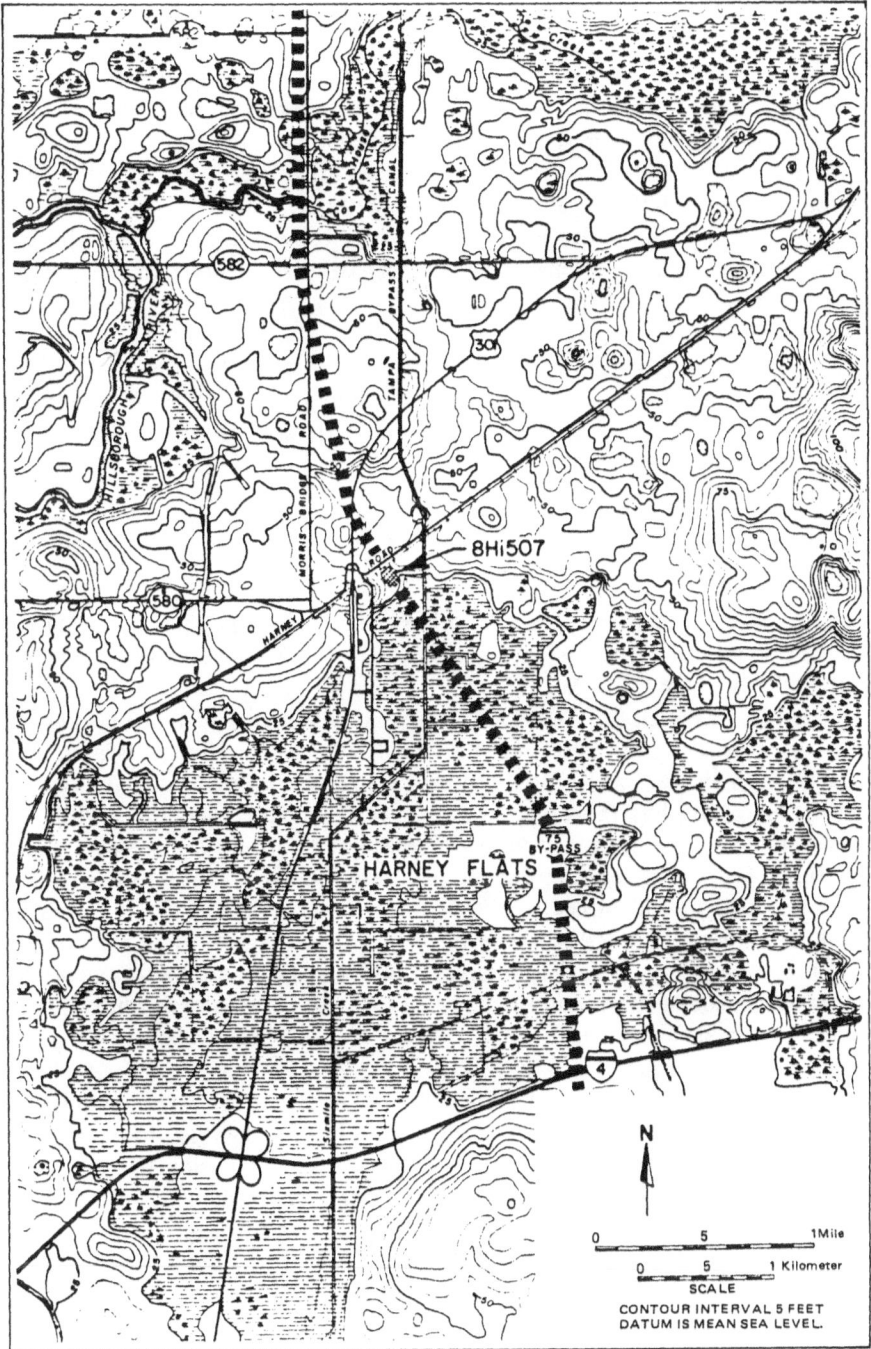

Figure 2. Topographic map of Harney Flats.

plateaus, river terraces, and natural levees transected by the right-of-way. In addition to the test pits, visual surface inspection was conducted over the entire corridor. Thirteen of the thirty-one sites were chosen for Phase II testing. While testing was underway, four of these sites were deemed significant enough to warrant Phase III mitigative salvage excavations (Jones and Tesar, 1982).

Table 1 lists Phase II excavations and Phase III salvage projects in the Hillsborough County I-75 corridor (Figure 1). With the exception of 8Hi471 and 8Hi480, both of which manifested major ceramic components, the sites in the corridor contained Archaic (primarily Middle Archaic) period cultural materials. However, there were suggestions of Paleo-Indian remains at some sites. Ten weeks of Phase II test excavations corroborated Jones' belief that the Harney Flats site contained significant quantities of Paleo-Indian lithic materials. Because no major land sites of this time period had been excavated in Florida, we decided to conduct an extensive Phase III mitigative salvage excavation at Harney Flats (Figure 2).

SITE SETTING

Physiography

The Harney Flats site is located in Hillsborough County just south and east of the intersection of Harney Road and U.S. 301. (USGS Thonotosassa Quadrangle; 1974, SE1/4 of NW1/4 of Section 19, Township 28 South, Range 20 East) about 3.2 km east of the city of Temple Terrace (Figure 3).) The site is bounded by private property along the north, northeast and west, and the Tampa Bypass Canal and levee to the east and south. The area tested was approximately 360 m long (north and south) by 100 m wide (east and west) and covers about 4 ha. Although some of the site's surface had been disturbed prior to testing, there were several recognizable zones of vegetation within the Phase II test area. The northern third of the site, a well-drained hillside, was covered with xerophytic flora. South of this dry zone, seven-year-old pines had been planted in diagonal rows from northwest to southeast. Mesic vegetation was observed down slope south and east of the planted pines on the southeastern portion of the right-of-way. The extreme southern parts of the proposed road corridor were covered with marsh-like vegetation on the west and a hydric hardwood swamp to the east.

Harney Flats, between 5 and 10 m above sea level and covering more than 180 km^2, is a plain that slopes gently upward from Hillsborough Bay to the adjacent Polk Upland (Figures 3 and 4) at well over 30 m in elevation (Deulering and MacGill, 1981; Knapp, 1980; White, 1970). The plain is a former bay bottom which was submerged sometime during the Pleistocene and was part of an estuary larger than the present Hillsborough Bay (MacNeil, 1949; Motz, 1975). This low, swampy plain in the Hillsborough River Valley, a secondary landform of the Gulf Coastal Lowlands physiographic region (Wright, 1973), is intermittently rimmed by a scarp, on the northern rim of which is located the site (Figure 2). The scarp is what remains of the Pamlico shoreline (Healy, 1975) and represents an advance of the sea to an altitude of about 8 m (Alt and Brooks, 1965; MacNeil, 1949).

RESEARCH BACKGROUND / 5

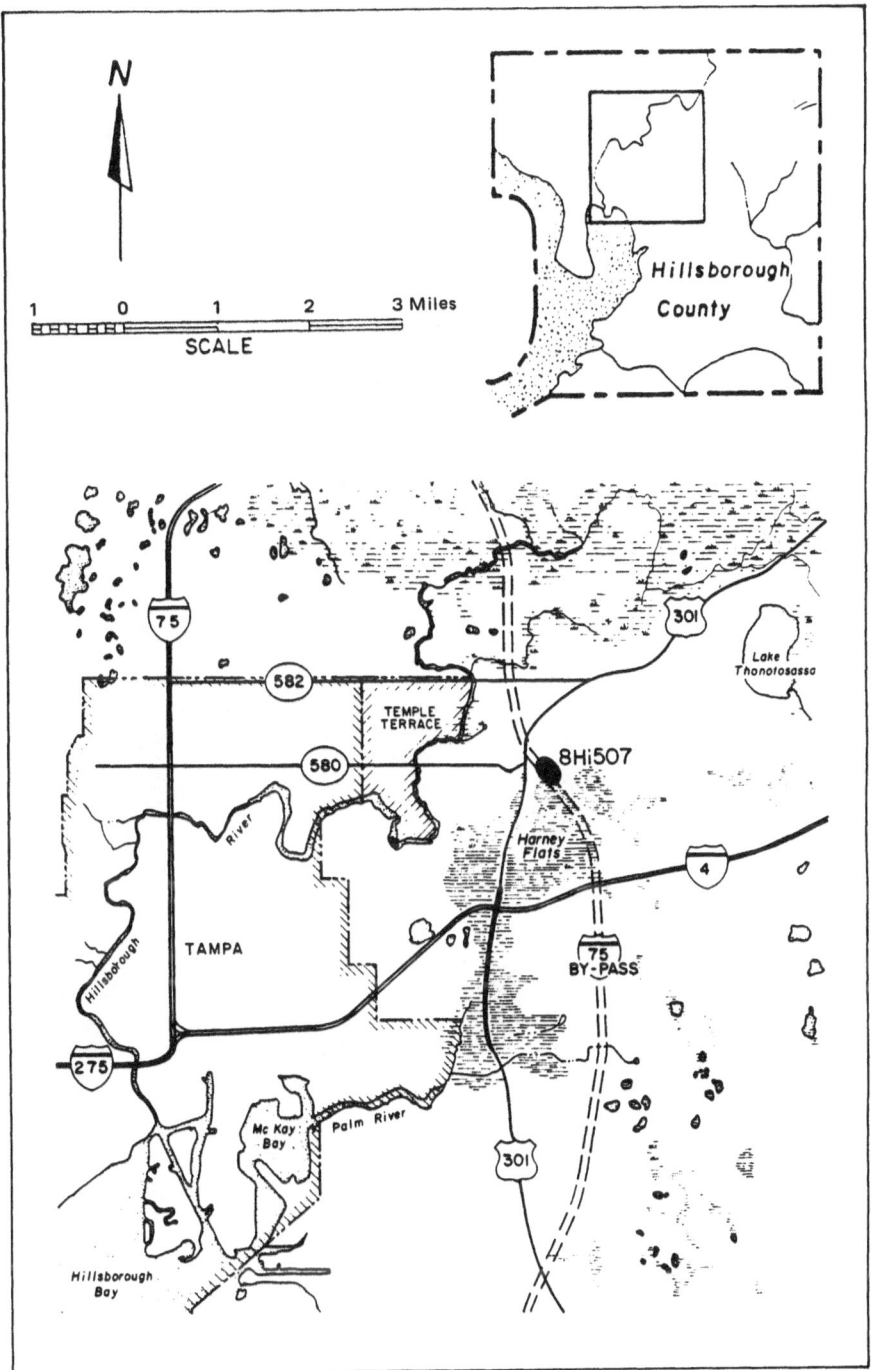

Figure 3. Site location map.

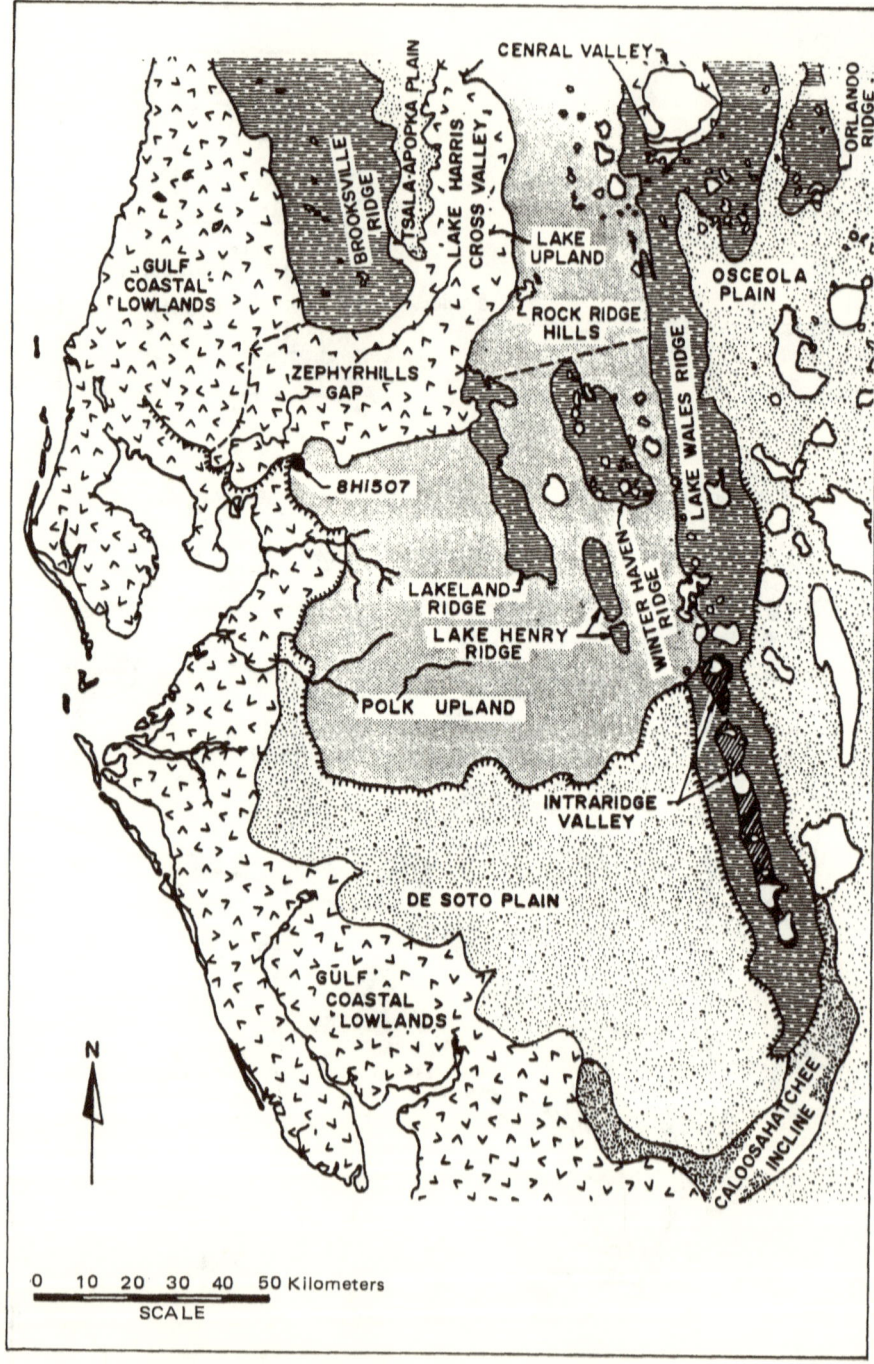

Figure 4. Physiographic map of West-Central Florida.

Soils

Surface sand is a common component of Florida's soils and several plausible explanations have been offered to account for its presence. In the past, sand was considered Pleistocene in age and inferred to be of marine origin. Florida sands, however, result from numerous phenomena including relict beach deposits, lagoon bottoms, dunes, erosional activities, and from soil forming processes which have concentrated them from underlying Tertiary rocks containing quartz (White, 1970:152). The latter source was probably affected by the length of time the particular terrain was dry. In areas above the Wicomico terrace (30 m elevation), denudation was extensive, indicating that areas not submerged by Wicomico seas were subaerially exposed to erosion for a much longer time than those regions which were inundated. Nevertheless, much of the soil in Hillsborough County was formed from higher stands of sea which left a mantle of quartz sand over earlier deposits (Leighty *et al.*, 1958:51).

At the Harney Flats site three discrete soil types are present. A gently undulating phase of Lakeland fine sand covers the northwest (all directions are in reference to grid north, ca. 40° west of magnetic north) portion of the site, and a brown layer phase of Blanton fine sand is in the southwest. The remainder of the site, where the bulk of the Phase III excavations took place, is composed of Leon fine sand, with the exception of extreme southeastern portions where soils are unclassfied.

Leon fine sand is a member of the intrazonal soil order, formed under the influence of local relief and parent material. This soil type, however, also belongs to the groundwater podzol soils group which is developed as a consequence of humid climatic conditions. This is the most prevalent soil type in Hillsborough County. It is developed from thick beds of unconsolidated sand, and occurs on level to gently sloping land with somewhat poor drainage. The soil is highly acidic and this has resulted in the decomposition of bones and wood that otherwise might have been preserved at the site. It is similar to other podzols in having a pan layer 35 to 75 cm below surface made of organic matter and minerals in the subsoil at the top of the water table. The hardpan perches water during periods of heavy rainfall (Leighty *et al.*, 1958), but was formed subsequent to the deposition of preceramic cultural materials at the site (Hunt and Hunt, 1957).

Although the brown layer phase of Blanton fine sand is most often found in flatwoods, it sometimes occurs, as at Harney Flats, on low ridges or slight knolls that are surrounded by soils of the Leon series or between areas of Leon and Lakeland soils. This series of Blanton soil is not as well-drained as other Blanton soils and surface runoff is slow. It is moderately acidic but, unlike Leon fine sand, lacks an organic pan (Leighty *et al.*, 1958).

The gently undulating phase of Lakeland fine sand on the northwestern portion of the site is made up of moderately thick beds of unconsolidated sand, is found on high ridges, and is often associated with Blanton soils. This type of soil has medium to rapid surface runoff and is extremely acidic. Lakeland fine sands are similar to Blanton soils in lacking an organic hardpan (Leighty *et al.*, 1958).

The soils in the extreme southeastern portion of the site are not classified since few true soils may be identified in such environs. The area is a level-to-depressed freshwater swamp with standing water during much of the year, and where the water table is either near, at, or above the land surface throughout the year.

Hydrology

A segment of the Hillsborough River is located less than 2.3 km northwest of the Harney Flats site. The river drains 1790 km^2 of land in Hillsborough, Hernando, Polk, and Pasco counties (Conover and Leach, 1975), rises in the Green Swamp area of central peninsular Florida, and flows 87 km southwestward to Hillsborough Bay at Tampa (Menke et al. 1961). During the nineteen-year period from 1940 to 1958, the discharge of the stream at the gauging station at Hillsborough River State Park where it drains approximately 570 sq. km of land, was 760 millions of liters per day (mld) (Menke et al., 1961). The flow of the river is sustained by an average discharge (1923-74) of 145 mld from Crystal Springs which enters the Hillsborough River in Pasco County (Rosenau et al., 1977). Usually the monthly flow of streams in this region is highest in late summer or early fall and lowest in the spring and early summer (Kenner, 1969).

A comparison of the Hillsborough River with that of a comparable segment of the Withlacoochee River, below Dunnellon, suggests that the ancestral drainage of the Withlacoochee was via the Hillsborough. The Hillsborough River valley has certain attributes which indicate it is an old drainge: 1) The river flows into Tampa Bay, which is the largest estuary on the west coast of peninsular Florida, whereas, the Withlacoochee enters the sea abruptly with no embayment at all; 2) The Pamlico terrace (Pleistocene age) turns up the valley walls of the Hillsborough but not the Withlacoochee; 3) The Hillsborough River follows a broad swampy floodplain or possibly a filled estuary, whereas the Withlacoochee flows into a narrow channel in limestone bedrock—suggesting the initial stage of a fluvial cycle (White, 1958; 1970:144).

The Harney Flats site is less than 650 m northeast of the head of Sixmile Creek which arises in Harney Flats and flows 11 km southward to the Palm River (Motz, 1975). Sixmile Creek is the primary tributary of the Palm River and in its upper reaches has been "improved" by straightening and dredging as part of the Tampa Bypass Canal. During periods of high rainfall, the creek overflows and inundates the prairie. Much of the dry season flow of Sixmile Creek emanates from springs. The Palm River, which formerly drained about 104 sq. km of land in Hillsborough County, is approximately 3.2 km in length and flows southwestward before emptying into McKay Bay (Menke et al., 1961).

In addition to the river basins, both artesian and water table springs are present in this region of Florida. The water table or nonartesian spring forms as a result of rainwater percolating through permeable sediments, such as sand, until the water reaches an impermeable bed such as clay. The water moves down gradient along the top of the impermeable bed to an opening where it emerges in the form of a spring or seep. These water table springs normally have a small and variable flow because of rainfall variation. Thus most nonartesian springs depend on local rainfall for replenishment and may even cease flowing during dry periods as a result of the low storage capacity of their aquifers. On the other hand, where water is confined within permeable sediments, sealed beneath confining beds, and is under sufficient hydrostatic pressure to rise to the surface through openings in the confining beds, an artesian spring is formed. Most of Florida's large springs are of this type. Annual rainfall is sufficient in the recharge areas of the Floridan aquifer (southern portions of Alabama, Georgia, and South Carolina as well as parts of Florida) to maintain a perennial flow at most artesian springs, even with low levels of precipitation (Rosenau et al., 1977). Thus, the primary advantage of artesian aquifers for man is that they represent a dependable and constant source of water at their discharge point(s) (Cherry et al., 1970). Studies conducted after the construction of the Tampa Bypass Canal, however, indicate the potentiometric surface in this vicinity has dropped between 91 and 152 cm from 1975-1976. As a consequence of this decline, flow from springs in Harney Flats has been reduced and has stopped in some instances (Causseaux and Rollins, 1979; Dew and Stewart, 1980).

In addition to these rivers, springs, and lakes mentioned above, a small water table pond was once located less than 400 m north of the site, although it was drained sometime prior to 1948. A sinkhole east of this location is less than 540 m northeast of the site, now in the middle of the Tampa Bypass Canal. And at the time of excavation, a dredged water hole was present just southeast of the site.

Climate

In Hillsborough County, the climate is humid subtropical with an average summer temperature in Tampa of 27.4°C. From 1899 to 1955 records indicate an average annual temperature of 21.9°C (Leighty et al., 1958). Interior portions of central Florida are in the Plant Hardiness Zone designated as 9B, indicating an average minimum temperature of −4°C (Little, 1978:5).

Over the past eighty years, the average annual precipitation at Tampa has been 131 cm. Total yearly precipitation, nevertheless, fluctuates considerably (Hughes et al., 1971). The highest amount of annual precipitation recorded was 194.48 cm in 1959 and the lowest annual precipitation was 73.38 cm in 1956. In this region of Florida, rainfall exceeds potential evaporation by 7.5 to 15 cm (Visher and Hughes, 1969). The Tampa Bay area normally has two rainy seasons, one in summer and the other in early spring. A high percentage of this rainfall occurs from June through September as a result of thunderstorms and tropical disturbances such as hurricanes (Wright, 1973:17). There are normally eighty-one to ninety thunderstorms per year in the Tampa area. Low areas with poor drainage in Hillsborough County are periodically flooded during the rainy season (Leighty et al., 1958:2).

Flora

Because of Florida's geological history involving periods of higher sea level, as well as many other variables, the state contains many areas of unique vegetation (Fernald, 1981:66). Florida has more native trees than any other state except Hawaii; a large number of trees found in no other state (Little, 1978) are included in the more than 3,500 species of vascular flora (Ward, 1978). In central Florida, plant species from both northern and southern Florida are found. Species of flora found in peninsular Florida are remarkably more cold tolerant than those of other humid subtropical climates, mostly as a consequence of sporadic, but severe, spells of winter cold from -15 to $-10°C$ (Butzer, 1971:70).

The interaction of soils, geomorphology, drainage pattern, fire, and other ecological factors plays an important role in the formation of plant communities and plant associations. Seven important and obvious plant associations have been defined for the Tampa Bay area and are listed here (Lakela et al., 1976):

1. *Pine flatwoods* are open woodlands dominated by pines; Cypress and saw palmetto may also occur. Small hardwood hammocks, bayheads, swamps, marshes, and grasslands are often scattered throughout the flatwoods.
2. *Xerophytic pine-oak woodlands* or *Sandhill Communities* (Davis, 1967; Florida Department of Natural Resources, 1975) are characterized by woodlands of slash or longleaf pine and scrub oak (turkey and sand live oak) associations, and are found in well-drained uplands.
3. *Mangrove association and coastal marshes* are present in tidal areas that vary from saline to brackish and are characterized by mangrove and grasses.
4. *Coastal strand* is made up of dune formations and sandy soils beyond the reach of high tide, with vegetation consisting of many herbs and shrubs.
5. *Swamps and bayheads*—the latter are composed of large shrubs and trees, many of which have broad leathery evergreen leaves (Clewell, 1971)—occur on low flooded grounds, with cypress swamps consisting of cypress and various other species such as red maple. The hardwood swamps or bayheads are characterized by red bay, black gum, loblolly bay and sweet bay. These groupings are frequently mixed and variable and are usually found bordering wet areas.
6. *Sandpine scrub woodland* is not common in the Tampa Bay area. Representative species are sand pine and rosemary. This type of vegetation is found on excessively-drained, deep sandy soils such as relict sand dunes.
7. *Grasslands* are wet prairies on seasonally flooded lowlands, whereas dry prairies are less frequently flooded areas within the flatwoods. Both are characterized by grasses and sedges, but wet prairies also have a number of aquatic species present.

Although Lakela et al. (1976) does not mention hammocks as a separate community, these clusters of broadleafed, often evergreen trees found growing on relatively rich soil are common in Florida (Department of Natural Resources, 1975: 110). They are the climax vegetation of most areas of central and peninsular Florida usually occurring in sandy soils where limestone is near the surface. Characteristic trees of the central Florida hammocks are Southern magnolia, laurel oak, and American holly. Live oak-cabbage palm hammocks are a common type.

Pine flatwoods, xerophytic pine-oak woodlands, swamps and bayheads, and grasslands are well within the catchment area of the Harney Flats site. Much of the Tampa Bay vicinity has undergone extensive alterations caused by land clearing, agricultural activities, construction, dredging, filling, and waste disposal. These disturbances have greatly modified many areas where plant and animal life were once abundant (Lakela *et al.*, 1976).

Fauna

Stevenson (1976) enumerates 880 species of vertebrates in Florida which are subdivided as follows: 208 freshwater fishes, 53 amphibians, 98 reptiles, 428 birds, and 93 mammals. Of cold-blooded animals—amphibians, fishes, and reptiles—Florida has more species than any other equal area of the world. Another factor contributing to this diversity is that fresh waters of Florida have more marine fishes than those of any other part of the United States (Carr and Goin, 1955).

HISTORICAL IMPACTS

A number of historical events which occurred in the vicinity of Harney Flats had a direct impact on landforms and drainage patterns in the area.

The first recorded events occurred in conjunction with activities taking place at Fort Brooke, which came into being as a result of the Seminole Treaty of 1823. The Seminole Indians agreed to move onto a reservation which was to be located in the south central part of the Florida peninsula. Commissioners representing the United States government in negotiations suggested that such a military post be placed at Tampa Bay to "protect" the Indians from outside elements (Covington, 1952).

Colonel James Gadsden, one of the treaty commissioners, was appointed to oversee the survey of this new reservation. He warned Secretary of War John C. Calhoun that the Seminoles would not move onto the reservation if the United States Government neglected to show power and disposition to compel obedience. Gadsden suggested that a military post be immediately established at Tampa Bay (Covington, 1952). As a consequence, the reserve was established supposedly to be used only for military purposes (cf. Carter, 1962:657).

The military post was eventually located at the mouth of the Hillsborough River and played an important role in the settlement of Florida's west coast. Actual construction began in 1824. The fort served as a base of operations during the Seminole Wars and many famous military figures (e.g., Lt. George McCall, LtC. George M. Brooke, Brevet Brigadier General Duncan Clinch, General Edmund P. Gaines, Major Francis L. Dade, John Lee Williams, General Winfield Scott(?), Coacoochee, and Col. William Jenkins Worth) were stationed there during the middle of the nineteenth century. Due to the trade and protection offered by Fort Brooke, Tampa began to grow slowly during the days before Tampa Bay was discovered by the tourists and cigar manufacturers (Covington, 1952).

In conjunction with an 1852 land survey of the Fort Brooke Military Preserve by Charles Hopkins, the area of land on which the Harney Flats site is located was parceled into thirty-two and thirty-six ha. tracts for no recorded reason. On his map the Fort King Road passed through the northwest corner of Section 19, which includes the Harney Flats site, although according to Robinson (1928:18) the road was nothing more than a trail. The Fort Brooke Military Reserve comprised 66,300 ha, with Fort Brooke in the geographical center (Jefferson Davis War Department Map, 1856). The site, located near the northeast corner of the reserve, more than 16 km from the fort apparently suffered no significant adverse impact from the military reserve.

The construction of the Tampa and Thonotosassa Railroad in 1894 and the highway (Harney Road) significantly altered the drainage patterns in this vicinity. Before construction could take place, the area was elevated with fill material (much of which probably came from a borrow pit on the northeastern edge of the Interstate right-of-way). There still must have been problems with drainage, even after the road and railroad had been completed, because a ditch was dug from the pond through the borrow pit and then along the eastern extremity of the site to an existing canal in Harney Flats some time between 1943 and 1948 (Leighty et al., 1958; USGS Thonotosassa Quad, 1943). Another ditch about 2 m wide and 1 m deep ran parallel to the first across the lower southern quarter of the site to carry water into the Tampa Bypass Canal.

By 1943, four houses and several dirt roads were constructed west of the Harney Flats site (USGS Thonotosassa Quad, 1943). One of the roads was located west of the site baseline and was found when Phase II test excavation units yielded shells (apparently used as fill) near the surface of the ground. Some citrus farming has taken place to the north and west of the site since around 1943.

In the early 1960s a concrete block house was built on the site and practically delimited the northern boundary of the Area I excavation location. Based on the amount of ruderal vegetation near the house, it was obvious the land surface had been somewhat disturbed, probably as a result of plowing. In addition, the residents of the house buried garbage (including an entire car frame) in their back and side (east) yard. Although some Phase II test units were abandoned due to these disturbances, most of the site had not been disturbed except within a few centimeters of the surface.

One other minor disturbance of note was a triangular-shaped patch of seven-year-old planted pines with the northernmost row being about 20 m south of and parallel to the south side of the house. There were approximately eighteen rows of pines spaced about 6 m apart; all of which were removed as the excavations progressed.

The major changes in the vicinity of the site, however, took place within Harney Flats itself. According to a local informant, Mr. Gene Bartolotti, the headwaters of Sixmile Creek were drained by a series of canals in 1925, and, as a consequence, the water table at Harney Flats was lowered. Before this, the flats were characterized as being a huge swamp. After drainage, portions of Harney Flats were farmed between 1934 and 1940 as a part of the W.P.A. program. Truck farms for growing various types of vegetables were established in the area during this time (Bartolotti, personal communication, 1983).

Probably the most drastic impact on the area of Harney Flats has been the Tampa Bypass Canal. The canal corridor which averages more than 300 m in width is less than 75 m east of the Interstate right-of-way on which the site is located, with the canal itself at least an additional 75 m farther east than the western boundary of canal properties. Construction on the 43 km long Tampa Bypass Canal was begun in 1976 as part of a flood-control project east of the city of Tampa by the U.S. Army Corps of Engineers. It was designed to divert floodwater from the Hillsborough River above Tampa through a canal to McKay Bay (Causseaux and Rollins, 1979:1).

The canal has had marked effects upon the hydrology of the area by causing a drawdown of the potentiometric surface of the Floridan aquifer and a diversion of flow from other parts of the hydrologic system. This has increased the head difference between the overlying perched water table aquifer and the Floridan aquifer (Motz, 1975), which permitted water from the perched water table aquifer to seep into the Floridan aquifer causing a lowering of water tables as well as a decrease in their storage capacities. Thus, swampy regions along certain portions of the canal, such as along the southeastern fringe of the Harney Flats site, have dried up since construction of the canal. If not for the construction of the canal, much of the Paleo-Indian component at the Harney Flats site would have been inaccessible.

CHAPTER 2
Methodology

PHASE I SURVEY

Harney Flats (8Hi507) was one of two sites within the I-75 right-of-way that the Phase I surveyor, Calvin Jones, believed might yield Paleo-Indian materials. Although no such artifacts were recovered during the survey, Jones discovered Suwannee points, uncovered when the Tampa Bypass Canal was being dug through Harney Flats, in amateur archaeologists' collections.

PHASE II TESTING

Beginning in early August, 1981, nine field workers spent ten weeks conducting preliminary test excavations at the Harney Flats site to locate and delimit artifact concentrations within the right-of-way and to recover diagnostic artifacts. A permanent baseline that generally corresponded to the proposed highway centerline was used for grid north (41°16'30" west of magnetic north). The key stake (0,0) was placed near the northern edge of the site just south of Harney Road. Additional stakes were set along the baseline from the key stake to the 350S line at 30 m intervals. At each of the thirteen stations along the baseline, east-west lines were established perpendicular to the baseline, with stakes placed at 45W, 30W, 30E, and either at 45E or 60E—depending on the width of the right-of-way. This provided a total of sixty-five potential testing stations systematically distributed across the site. Relative elevations were taken at each station and at obvious breaks in the terrain.

Since only ten weeks were allocated for testing more than 4 ha., and since deep deposits (ca. 2 m) were anticipated, a backhoe was used to dig short trenches that a worker could enter. Fifty cm^2 columns were excavated by 20 cm arbitrary levels to a depth of 2 m in the walls of these trenches. All of the dirt was screened through .25 in mesh hardware cloth with the recovered artifacts being assigned a separate provenience for each level at each station.

Because of the high water table at the southern edge of the right-of-way, test pits south of the 270S line were excavated differently. A volume fill from the backhoe trench equivalent to a 50 cm × 50 cm column was screened for artifacts and only a very general idea of level provenience was determinable. Total artifact counts (predominantly lithic debitage) from fifty-six of the test pits are listed by provenience in Table 2.

Table 2. Lithic Artifact Totals Recovered from 50 × 50 cm Test Units

Location	Number of Artifacts	Location	Number of Artifacts	Location	Number of Artifacts
0S/45W	8	120S/0	51	240S/30W	37
0S/30W	9	120S/30E	91	240S/0	119
0/0	6	120S/59.58E	26	240S/30E	84
0S/30E	20	150S/45W	36	240S/60E	12
30S/45W	17	150S/30W	39	270S/30W	35
30S/30W	18	150S/0	48	270S/30E	17
30S/0	11	150S/30E	48	270S/60E	0
30S/26E	65	150S/60E	102	270S/0	7
60S/45W	50	180S/45W	30	300S/45W	11
60S/30W	36	180S/30W	25	300S/30W	6
60S/0	13	180S/0	35	300S/0	15
60S/30E	67	180S/30E	47	300S/30E	1
90S/45E	32	180S/60E	76	330S/45W	10
90S/30W	15 (1 sherd)	210S/45W	53	330S/30E	5
90S/0	46	210S/30W	78	330S/0	12
90S/30E	50	210S/0	78	330S/18E	15
90S/45E	47	210S/30E	43	351S/0	24
120S/45W	30	210S/60E	23	351S/30W	0
120S/30W	26	240W/45W	29		

On the basis of these results several 30 m sq blocks east of the baseline and between the 120S and 240S lines were selected for additional sampling. This sampling was done by manually excavating randomly selected 1 × 1 and 1 × 2 m test units by 20 cm arbitrary levels using standard archaeological techniques. Because of a rise in the water table during the later stages of the project, test units in the central and southern portions of the site could not be completed and our efforts were directed to drier areas of the right-of-way above the 8 m contour. A total of 72 m² of test units was excavated in this manner.

To clarify stratification of geological/archaeological deposits, five backhoe trenches totaling approximately 177 m in length were excavated to explore areas along the eastern edge and center line of the right-of-way.

Due to drier conditions during the excavation of the 50 × 50 cm test pits, excavations usually reached depths of 2 m, but generally no artifacts occurred in the last one or two levels (i.e., levels 9 or 10). During the latter part of the excavations of the 1 × 1 m test units, however, water was encountered at about level 8 or 9 preventing further excavation. Cultural material was found to occur from the surface to between 1.60 and 1.80 m below the surface.

Most of the Paleo-Indian component was isolated in a 60 cm band within a sandy zone located in levels 6, 7, and 8 (i.e., 1.00-1.60 m below the surface), but it appeared to be concentrated in levels 6 and 7. This was most clearly demonstrated in the more level areas of the right-of-way. Farther down slope the depth of this component decreased, although it was consistently found below the hardpan zone across the site. A Middle Archaic component was present in levels above the early component demonstrating the stratified nature of the site.

Although no conventional features (e.g., pits and hearths) were identified, some test units revealed clusters of artifacts believed to be in primary archaeological context. These included a pair of sandstone abraders, and "exotic" metamorphic rocks, a hammerstone and core fragments, a pair of unifaces, and some other stone tools. All these tools came from the lower levels, below the hardpan. The identification of this component as dating to the Paleo-Indian period was made on the basis of the recovery of associated Suwannee and Simpson lanceolate points and preforms (Bullen, 1975:75-76).

In summary, the Phase II testing not only demonstrated the existence of deeply stratified *in situ* deposits of Paleo-Indian cultural material, but also isolated significant areas of the component within the right-of-way.

Since the site had the potential to greatly add to our highly limited understanding of early man in Florida, a proposal was submitted and accepted for a crew of twenty-six to spend seventeen weeks doing additional fieldwork.

PHASE III EXCAVATION

Research Problems

Since little was known about upland Paleo-Indian sites in the state, the goal of the Phase III excavation was relatively simple—to investigate intra-site structure at the Harney Flats site. The strategy was to excavate large contiguous areas that, when combined with the accurate recording of the horizontal and vertical provenience of artifacts, would provide data on spatial organization. By analyzing the spatial distributions of tools and debitage, we planned to isolate activity areas and classes of stone tools. In gathering these data we would also have the opportunity to examine a large Paleo-Indian stone tool assemblage from the context of a single site.

Field Procedures

The Phase III fieldwork began on November 20, 1981, and continued through March 26, 1982. Phases II and III were supervised by Randy Daniel with the assistance of Mike Wisenbaker and Charlie Poe.

Based on the Phase II results, three areas totaling about 10,000 m^2 were initially selected for further sampling. However, since much of the 40,000 m^2 right-of-way had not been adequately tested due to the high water table, additional test pits were excavated before a final choice of excavation areas was made. Also, a total of 77 1 X 1 m test pits were placed approximately every 10 m in the eastern half of the right-of-way between the 100S and 250S lines. Based on the qualitative (tool types) and quantitative (density of artifacts) data obtained from these units and the Phase II results, we selected the three large areas to be excavated. The three areas comprised 283 m² in Area 1, 380 m² in Area 2, and 196 m² in Area 3 (Figure 5), including some units previously excavated during Phase II. The total area comprised 976 m² within the portion of the right-of-way to be tested. Of this total 967 m² were excavated within the area of the early component. An additional thirty-five 50 × 50 cm test pits were excavated elsewhere.

The problem of sample size occurs on two levels at the Harney Flats site: the site as a whole and the individual areas. Only the sample of the site (i.e., the early component) as a whole is of concern here. The sampling of the individual areas will be discussed in Chapter 5.

The size of the early component within the right-of-way is estimated to be approximately 1.35 ha, but the site extends an unknown distance beyond the limits of the right-of-way making determination of the total site size difficult. Nevertheless, it is our opinion, based on test pit results, that the vast majority of the site lies within the excavated portion of the right-of-way. Our work, then, resulted in excavation of approximately 7.2 percent of the known site.

Two additional exploratory trenches, excavated with heavy machinery, were placed in the northwest portion of the right-of-way to examine that area for evidence of a prehistoric cemetery. Based on the preliminary results from Phase II and experience with other early sites, Calvin Jones thought that the Harney Flats site might have been a base camp or large residential area. If this were true, a prehistoric cemetery might have been associated with the site. Moreover, if a cemetery were present in the right-of-way, Jones thought it would be on the top of the sand ridge to the northwest. Since preservation of bone remains is highly unlikely in deep sand sites in central Florida, Jones felt the primary indication of the cemetery would be clusters of stone tools left as grave goods, as found at the Sloan site (Morse, 1975). If indications of a cemetery were uncovered, then the location and length of the fieldwork would be adjusted. However, the trenching not only revealed no signs of a cemetery, it also demonstrated the absence of the early component in that area, and thus helped to define the northern limits of the site.

Surface elevations were taken at 3 m intervals before excavation. About 1 m of topsoil in each of the excavation areas was then removed with heavy machinery to facilitate the opening of large contiguous areas. Permanent transit stations were established adjacent to each area for precise vertical control.

Each area was gridded into 4 × 4 m blocks designated by their southeast corner stake. The blocks were subdivided into 1 × 1 m squares and assigned letter designations, beginning with the letter A in the southeast corner and ending with S in the northeast corner.

The primary reference for the 16 m sq block, 124S/36E, would be followed by the secondary or specific reference for each of the 16 1 m squares within the block. For example, unit A would be referred to as 124S/36E "A." The letters (excluding I, O, and Q to prevent confusion) for each of the units were arranged in alphabetical order. This system reduced the potential for error in recording provenience

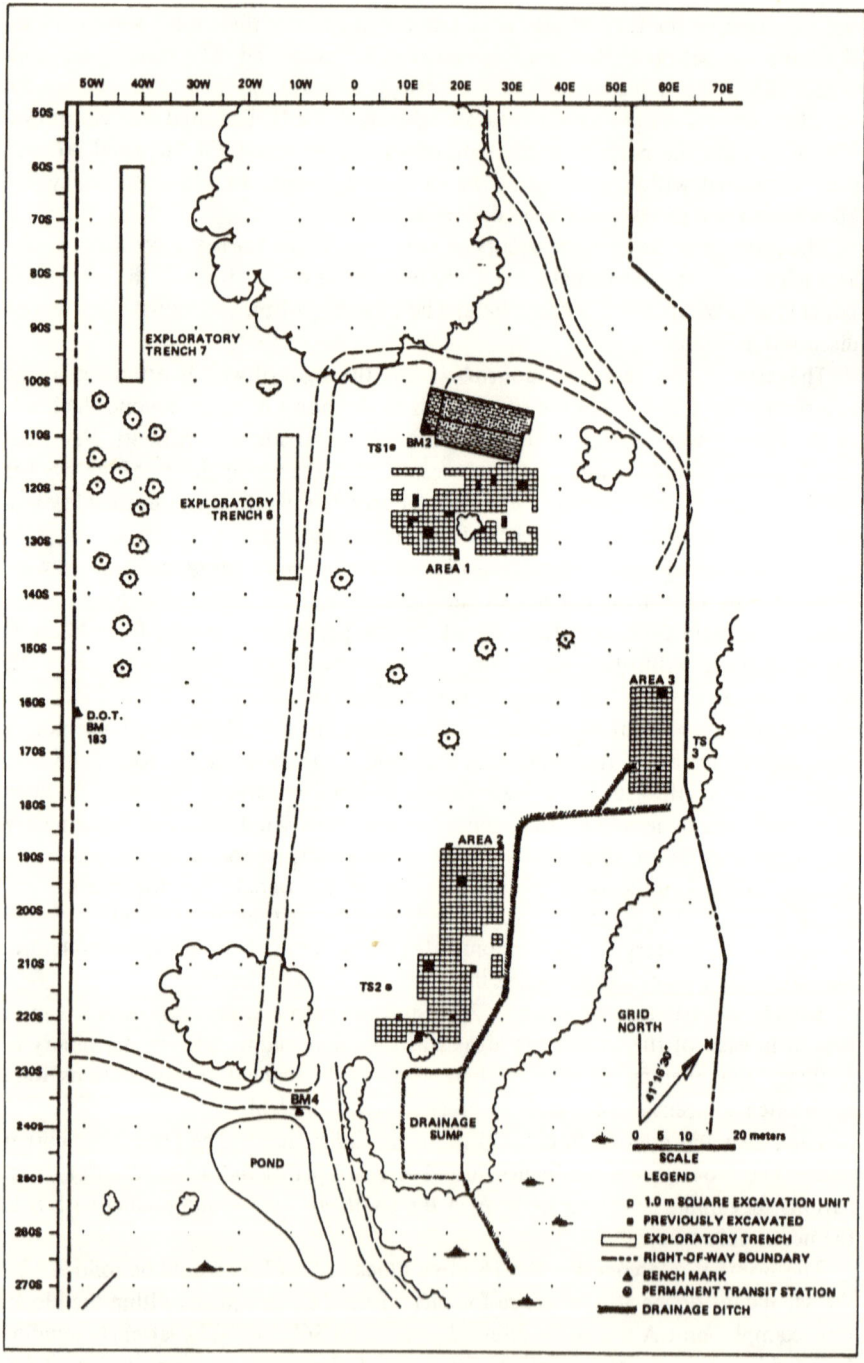

Figure 5. Phase III excavation areas.

information from more than 900 excavated units. The elevation of the southeastern corner of the 16 m sq block was calculated and used as a reference point for all sixteen squares in a single block.

Excavation Techniques

The principal excavation technique used at Harney Flats was flat shovel-skimming or schnitting through 20 cm arbitrary levels. Coupled with hand troweling when suspected tools or large artifacts were encountered, this served as an efficient means of soil removal while providing a precise method for uncovering *in situ* artifacts. Any tool forms that were recognizable and identifiable using conventional terminology (e.g., projectile point, biface, uniface, core, modified flake tool, hammerstone) were accurately plotted, bagged, and labeled by horizontal and vertical provenience immediately after being uncovered.

Artifacts assigned to general level proveniences consisted primarily of lithic debitage, although some small tool fragments that were not detected *in situ* were also included. Soil samples were collected for both phosphate analysis and flotation.

Excavators generally worked in pairs in a single 1 m square within the larger block described above; one dug while the other screened. For example, within each block one team would excavate units A, B, G, and H while another team would simultaneously excavate units L, M, N, and P. When these were finished the remaining eight units would be similarly excavated, completing a block of sixteen 1 X 1 meter units (Figure 6).

After excavating a unit level, each team was required to complete a form with pertinent information such as types and quantities of artifacts, soil descriptions, possible disturbances, and appropriate field specimen numbers. In addition, individual floor maps showing plotted artifacts for each level and unit profiles were drawn.

Some more experienced crew members were assigned special functions. One or two people, under the direction of the field supervisor, were assigned the task of mapping the long profiles (Figures 7-9). Another crew member maintained a running inventory of field specimens. This consisted of general level artifacts, piece-plotted specimens, and soil samples. Field specimen numbers were also given to some isolated pieces of charcoal and thermally altered lithic specimens. Although none of these specimens could be assigned to any cultural feature, they were collected for C^{14} and thermoluminescent dating of the early component. In addition an artifact map on which all piece plotted artifacts were accurately diagrammed was maintained for each area.

The first portion of the Phase III fieldwork, consisting of excavating isolated test pits, was finished by about the third week of December, 1981, and efforts were shifted to begin the block excavation in Area 1. Initially, the entire crew was assigned to work in one area so that they could become familiar with the procedures involved in excavating a large contiguous area.

By the end of January excavation in Area 1 ceased and efforts were directed to Areas 2 and 3 (Figure 8). By this time everyone was familiar with all field procedures, and it was possible to divide the crew between the two areas during the

20 / HARNEY FLATS

Excavation of 16 m square unit in progress, Area 1.

Excavation in progress, Area 3.

Figure 6.

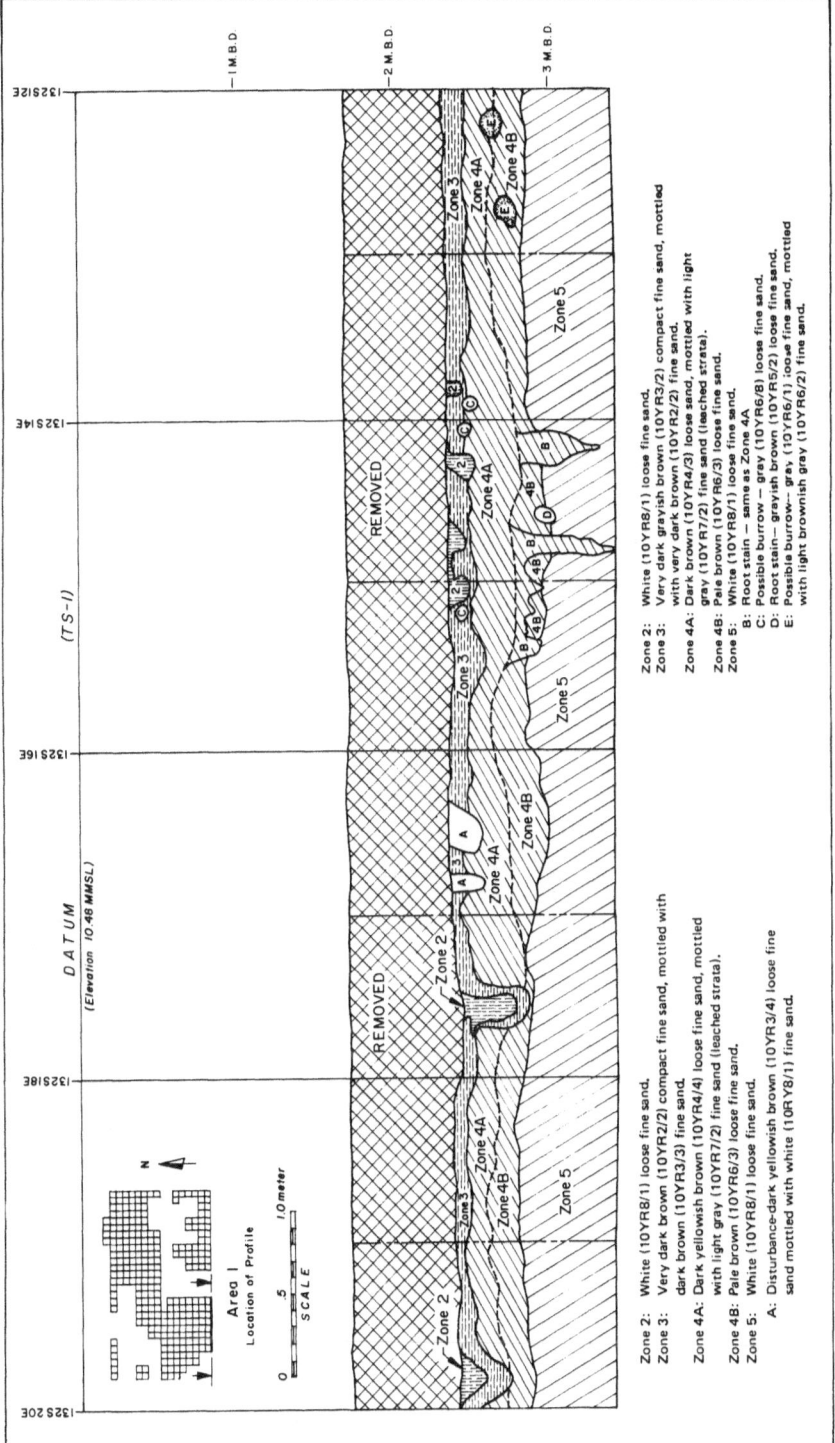

Figure 7. Area 1: East-West Profile at 132S.

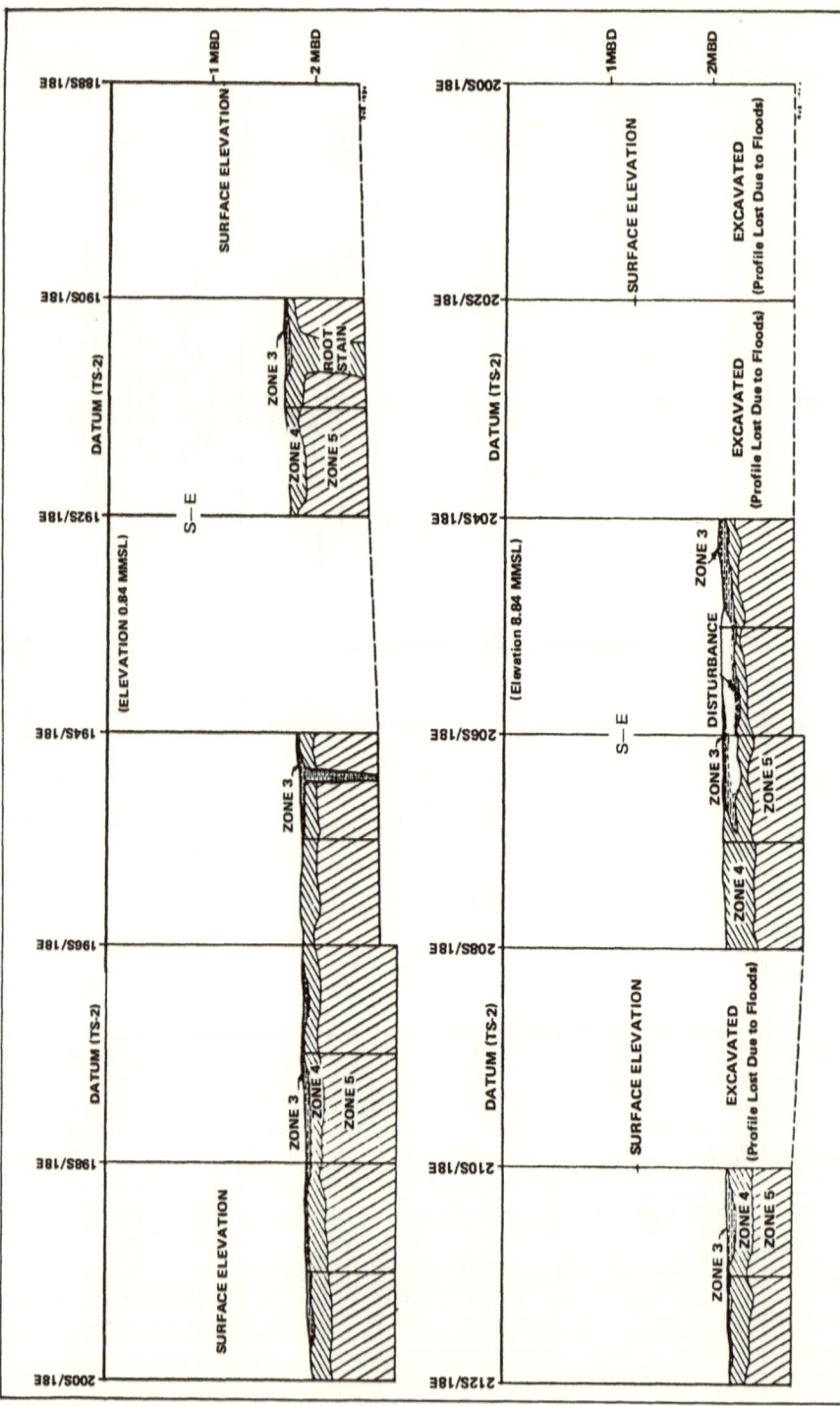

22

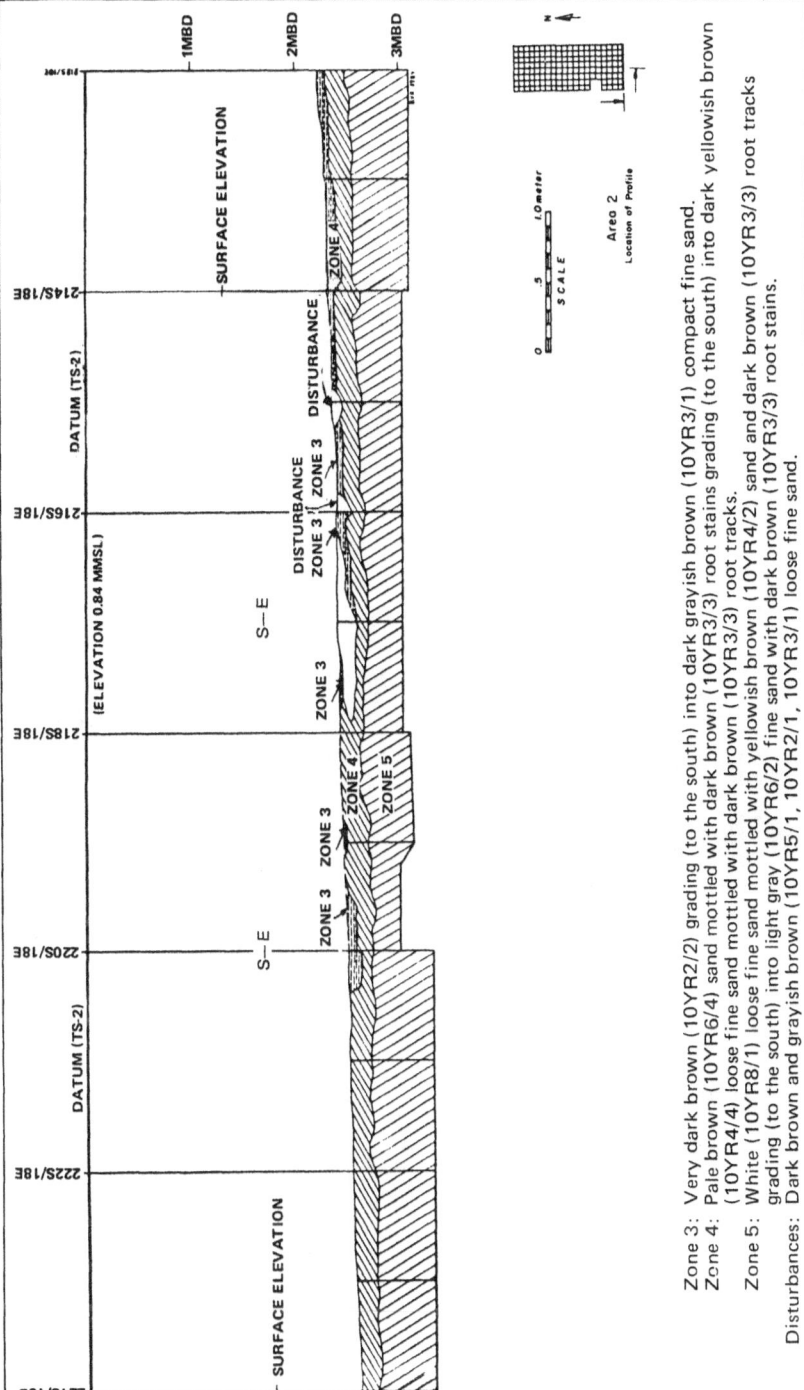

Figure 8. Area 2: North-South profile at 18E.

Zone 3: Very dark brown (10YR2/2) grading (to the south) into dark grayish brown (10YR3/1) compact fine sand.
Zone 4: Pale brown (10YR6/4) sand mottled with dark brown (10YR3/3) root stains grading (to the south) into dark yellowish brown (10YR4/4) loose fine sand mottled with dark brown (10YR3/3) root tracks.
Zone 5: White (10YR8/1) loose fine sand mottled with yellowish brown (10YR4/2) sand and dark brown (10YR3/3) root tracks grading (to the south) into light gray (10YR6/2) fine sand with dark brown (10YR3/3) root stains.
Disturbances: Dark brown and grayish brown (10YR5/1, 10YR2/1, 10YR3/1) loose fine sand.

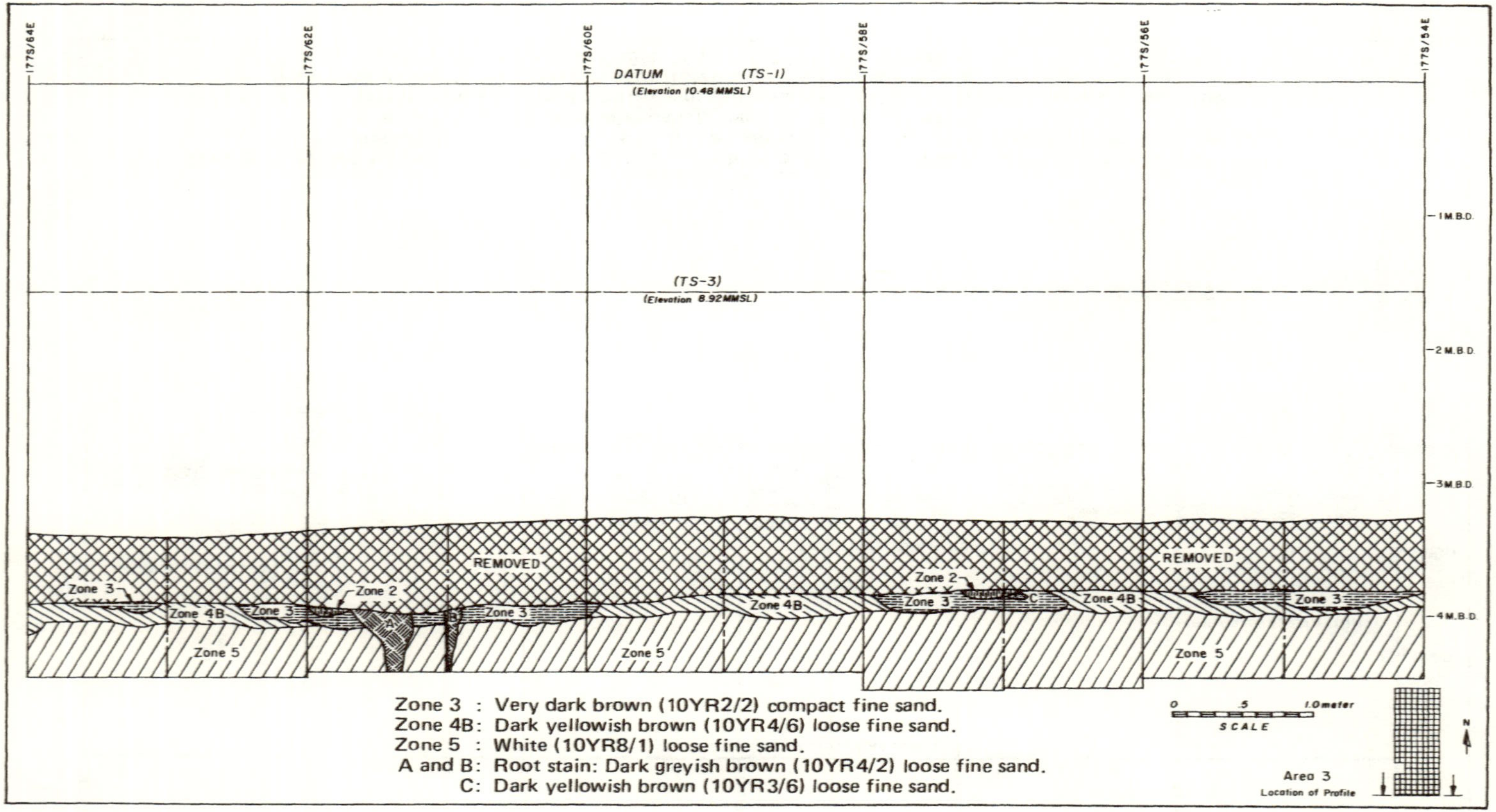

Figure 9. Area 3: East-West profile at 177S.

remaining field time. Each of the assistant supervisors directed approximately half of the field crew as they worked in either Area 2 or 3, while the field supervisor made adjustments and coordinated work in both areas as needed. Because Area 3 was about half the size of Area 2, excavations there were completed sooner. By late March, the entire crew was working in Area 2.

It became apparent that with the time remaining a block of excavation units in the southern portion of Area 2 could not be connected to the excavated units in the northern portion of the area unless a change was made in the excavation procedure. To connect the two excavations, intervening units were excavated by shovel

Table 3. Unscreened Excavation Units

Area 1:

124S/28E	K, J	entire unit

Area 2:

192S/26E	C, D, E, F	entire unit
192S/30E	C, D, E, F	entire unit
196S/26E	J, K, R, S	entire unit
196S/26E	C, D, F	entire unit
196S/22E	C	entire unit
204S/22E	J, R, S	entire unit
222S/22E	J, K, R, S	entire unit
196S/30E	C, D, E, F	entire unit
216S/22E	A, B, G, H	entire unit
200S/30E	C, D, E, F	entire unit
220S/18E	A, B, G, H	entire unit
224S/18E	J, K, R, S	entire unit
200S/30E	L, M, N, P	entire unit
204S/30E	L, M, N, P	entire unit
216S/18E	C, D, E, F	entire unit
216S/18E	L, M, N, P	entire unit
204S/26E	A, B, G, H	entire unit
204S/26E	C, D, E, F	entire unit
220S/22E	C, D, E, F	entire unit
220S/22E	L, M, N, P	entire unit

Area 3:

161S/58E	C, D, E, F	Level 7
161S/58E	C	Level 6
165S/58E	D	Level 7
165S/58E	E	Level 7
165S/58E	F	Level 6
169S/58E	C	Level 7
169S/58E	E	Level 7
161S/62E	M, N	entire unit
173S/62E	D, E, F	entire unit

shaving and troweling as before, but screening was eliminated. All recognizable tools were plotted as before, but almost no debitage was recovered. Some small tool fragments were undoubtedly overlooked in the process. A list of all units that were excavated in this manner is given in Table 3. This list also includes some other units excavated in this manner because they had been damaged by water.

In all three areas efforts were directed toward connecting previously excavated test pits to one another and excavating as much of the stripped area as possible by following apparent artifact concentrations. Although qualitative differences in artifact types between areas were discernible in the field, it soon became apparent that "clusters" of artifacts were not distinct.

Contingencies

Although the excavations proceeded relatively smoothly, two particular problems were encountered. As a result of heavy rain, some units of Areas 2 and 3 were eroded and suffered cave-ins of unit walls. When this occurred, affected units were excavated as quickly as possible and then filled with sand to prevent damage to adjacent units. Rain also prevented us from reaching culturally sterile levels in some units. This problem was corrected to a certain degree by the excavation of a backhoe trench along the southern edge of Area 3 and the eastern edge of Area 2 (Figure 5). While for the most part this trench served to efficiently drain excess water from the two areas, there were several occasions when levels could not be excavated because units especially in Area 3 were saturated. Nevertheless, we contend that the major portion of the early component was excavated in these units.

The second major problem was vandalism. Artifact collecting has been widespread in the Tampa Bay area for many years and numerous instances of unauthorized digging have occurred. For this reason a security guard was posted at the site during the weekend daylight hours—the time we thought the site was most susceptible to pot hunting. Unfortunately no allowances were made for the few daylight hours remaining after regular work hours. On at least two occasions we returned to work in the morning to note disturbances to the site. The first occurred early in Phase III and resulted in some disturbances to test pits (stakes pulled and walls collapsed), while the second happened much later in the project and included digging into walls and floors of some units in Area 2. Although none of the vandalism appeared to result in any serious damage, it caused a certain amount of concern for site security in our absence.

The final field day was spent scraping the remaining unexcavated portions of the three areas with heavy machinery in hopes of quickly locating possible caches of artifacts or features. Unfortunately (fortunately?), none were uncovered, although some additional artifacts were located and recorded.

Artifact Processing

Periodically during the excavation, all field specimens were taken to the University of South Florida, where a field archaeology laboratory had been established for the I-75 Highway Salvage Project. There, all artifacts were cleaned, accessioned, and roughly sorted according to type. Subsequently, all artifacts were sent to the Division of Historical Resources, History and Records Management (FDHRHRM) in Tallahassee, Florida, where the primary analysis was undertaken. Ninety-five weeks were budgeted for this analysis and report preparation.

Copies of all field notes, maps, and photographs pertaining to the excavations are stored at the FDHRHRM. All artifacts, analysis notes, and data on computer tapes are also available to other researchers (FDHRHRM Accession Numbers 81-158 and 81-163).

CHAPTER 3

Site Stratification and Cultural Stratification

We divided the Leon fine sand, which covers much of the Harney Flats site, into six different natural zones. The uppermost zone (Zone 1) consists of gray sand with modern duff and humus. This is underlain by a white, loose fine sand (Zone 2) permeated with small roots and root stains. Often these two zones simply grade together making distinctions between the two difficult. Zone 3 is a very distinctive hardpan consisting of a very dark brown to black, compact fine sand cemented with organic matter. Beneath the hardpan are two sandy zones which contain the early cultural component. Zone 4 is a yellowish brown sand that is primarily the result of leaching from the overlying hardpan stratum and grades into a zone of very pale brown loose fine sand (Zone 5). Rather than two zones, the sand underneath the hardpan could also possibly be seen as a single sandy zone; the uppermost portion of which contains material leached from the hardpan. Since the degree of leaching varies across the site, distinguishing between Zones 4 and 5 is sometimes difficult. We preferred, however, to make a distinction between the two zones during the fieldwork. The last zone encountered during excavations (Zone 6) is a very compact layer of greenish-blue clayey sand, believed to have been deposited over the existing Tertiary carbonates sometime during the middle to late Miocene epoch (Davies and LeGrand, 1972).

Zone 1 extended from the ground surface to between 10 and 20 cm below surface, while Zone 2 extended to approximately 45 or 55 cm below surface. The hardpan zone varied in depth and consistency across the site. In the flatter areas of the site (i.e., above the 8 m contour), it occurred as a 10-15 cm thick band between 50 and 60 cm below surface, while farther south it was slightly deeper, starting between 70 and 90 cm below surface. This type of hardpan generally occurs in a 10 cm band in Leon fine sand throughout Hillsborough County at a depth of 55 to 65 cm below surface. Zone 5 was found to extend below the hardpan to a depth of about 2 m before water was encountered. The exception to this was near the eastern edge of the right-of-way where Zone 6 was encountered as deep as 140 cm below the surface. This zone was culturally sterile. Test pits (both .50 X .50 m and 1 X 1 m) excavated into 20-40 cm of clay yielded no cultural material.

The Lakeland fine sands encountered on the northwestern portion of the site, including the western extremity of Area 1, were divided into four separate (but more or less homogeneous) stratigraphic zones. The uppermost horizon (Zone 1), from ground surface to about 15 cm below the surface, was a dark gray to grayish brown loose fine sand intermixed with a slight amount of organic matter. Zone 2 (about 15-30 cm bs) was similar, but lacked organic staining. Zone 3, which extended from approximately 30-75 cm below surface, was a yellowish-brown loose fine sand. Zone 4, which extended to 200 cm bs, was similar to the overlying stratum, but was brownish-yellow.

Although Blanton fine sands are located on southwestern portions of the site, they were not found within any of the three large excavation areas. From the surface to 10 cm Blanton fine sands appear as a gray to dark gray fine sand. The underlying layer (10-55 cm) has the same consistency as the first zone, but is browner (hence the name—brown layer phase of Blanton fine sand). The deepest zone of this soil type (55 to 200 cm bs) is lighter in color than the overlying horizon and is marked by occasional patches of pale yellow soil.

SOIL ANALYSIS

Soil samples from levels 6, 7, and 8 of the test pits were analyzed for phosphate content. This work has been an on-going part of the analysis for most of the Highway Salvage sites (Almy, 1982; Chance, 1982; Gagel, 1981; Daniel and Wisenbaker, 1981). Unfortunately, the results are not very informative. The assumption has been that certain locations within sites should have higher levels of phosphate resulting from the decay of organic refuse due to human occupation. Thus far, the samples from these sites can be interpreted as having naturally occurring levels of phosphate, except in the upper levels where modern agricultural practices have increased the natural amounts of phosphate.

Figure 10 is a phosphate contour map of the test pit data. One count for each unit was obtained by averaging the totals of the combined levels from the early component. These averages range from 8-395 parts per million (ppm). The contour map shows three areas of relatively high phosphate concentration (i.e., greater than 50 ppm). However, since the higher counts consistently come from a single level (generally level 6) where the sample is associated with the hardpan formation, these high readings may be associated with the natural formation of the hardpan and not with prehistoric human activity. This correlation has also been reported from at least one other Highway Salvage site (Almy, 1982:169). Soil samples from within the area excavations have also been analyzed. Phosphate concentrations were usually low, less than 50 ppm, but greater amounts tended to occur in association with the hardpan.

The soil analysis does not indicate any results that can be confidently interpreted to be a consequence of early occupation of the site. Because of the negative results from all the sites as well, we suggest that a reevaluation of soil analysis on deep sand lithic sites is necessary.

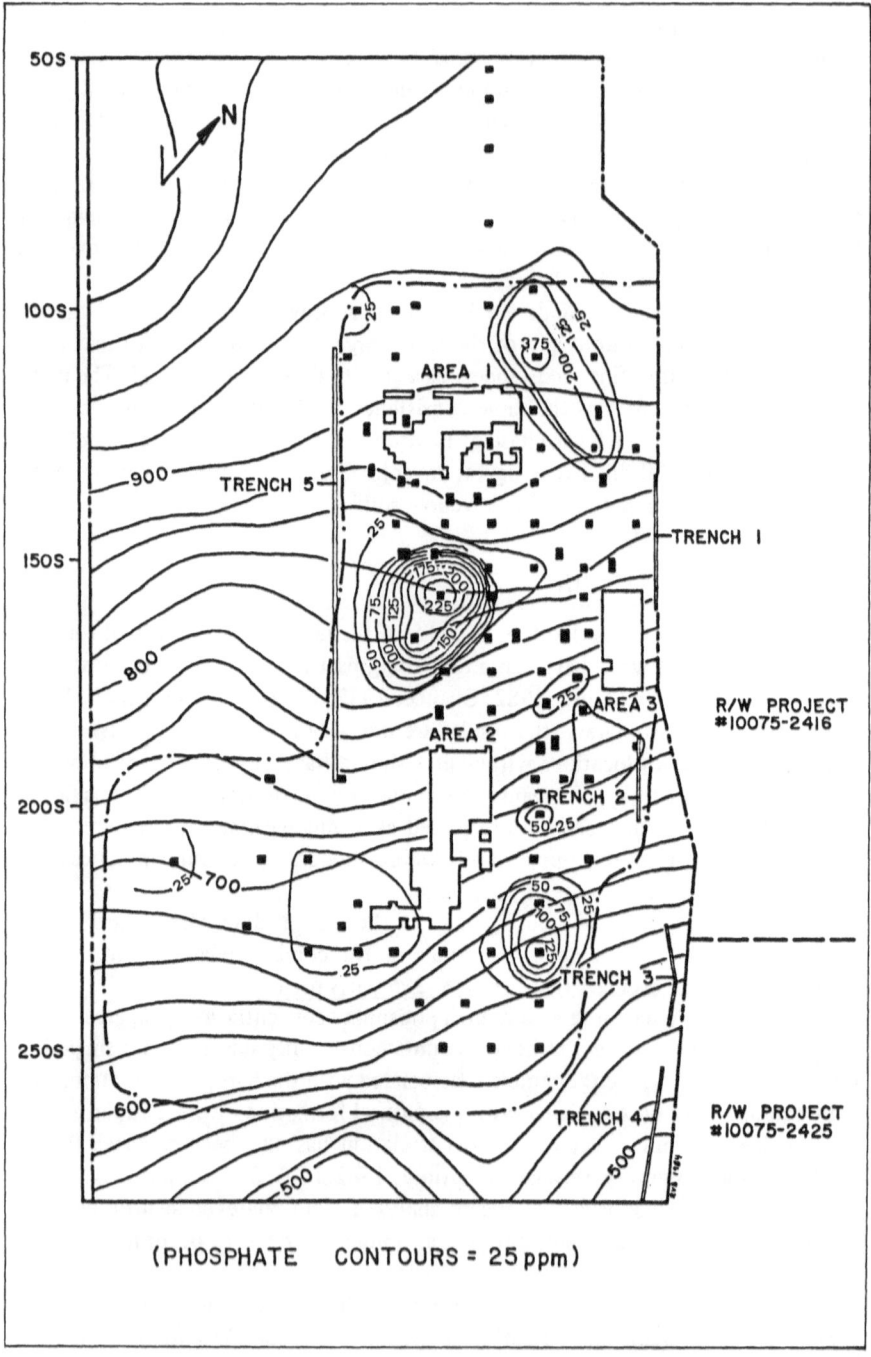

Figure 10. Test pit contour map of soil phosphate analysis, 8Hi507.

HYDROLOGY

The primary reason no identifiable faunal or floral remains were preserved at Harney Flats is the highly acidic soils. The acid soils, along with a constantly changing water table and oscillating humidity, served to accelerate the decomposition of organic matter. Similarly, the strongly acid soils and ground water leaching served to eliminate any signs of cultural features, such as pits and hearths, that might have been present at the site.

One other natural process which probably had a significant impact on the site's surface was the movement of large quantities of water across it. A water table pond was located about 400 m north of the site. Prior to the construction of Harney Road (which permanently altered the drainage pattern in the area by elevating the surface of the land between the pond and the site) and the railroad which ran immediately parallel to Harney Road, prolonged or moderate-to-heavy rainfall occurring over the past 5,000 years would have flooded the 16 ha body of water and would have caused it to overflow across and through eastern portions of the Harney Flats site.

The amount of rainfall necessary to flood the pond was estimated at slightly over 5 cm by measuring the area of the pond's drainage basin (ca. 315 ha) and then calculating the volume of water needed to raise the water level in the pond above the 31 ft contour (since no point along the drainage corridor passing through the site was more than 31 ft in elevation). This estimate was based on an initial water surface elevation of 29 ft and the assumption that the sinkhole just east of the pond was filled to capacity and no longer discharging into the Floridan aquifer. We also disregarded factors such as evapotranspiration, interception, and surface detention (Strahler, 1971) that would increase the amount of rainfall needed to cause flooding.

Flooding appears to have had several effects on the site. This may have been why as much as 40-50 cm of topsoil were missing from Area 3, since this is the place where most of the water from the pond would pass under flood conditions and although artifact concentrations in Area 3 began at higher levels than in other portions of the site (e.g., from 60-80 cm bs rather than 100-120 cm bs), Paleo-Indian artifacts were consistently found in context below the hardpan. Erosional damage seemingly did not affect the provenience of artifacts in the lower levels.

Water passing through the eastern portion of the site may also account for a series of long, linear disturbances—ca. 12 m long and 20 cm in diameter—which were circular in cross-section and resembled tree roots or rodent burrows, but were patterned too regularly to have been either. These disturbances, which ran normal to the slope, were composed (except for the center which was white sand) of the same soil type as the hardpan, and were at the same depth below surface. Although we approached a number of soil scientists and geologists with this problem, they were unable to offer any plausible explanations. In our opinion these unusual formations resulted from lateral underground drainage of runoff when excess water saturated the sandy soils in the area of the drainage basin north of the site.

Flooding across the site may have played a part in the formation of Leon soils. Three soil types occur in the immediate vicinity of the water table pond just north of the site (Leighty et al., 1958). The soils on the bottom of the pond (below 5 and 8 m) are classified as shallow pond sands usually found in depressions covered by water for much of the year. Plummer fine sands, characterized by slow surface runoff and occasional ponding, constituted the next higher tier of soils between the 8 m and 9 m contours. The uppermost tier in this pattern consists of the Leon fine sand that encircles the Plummer fine sands. The Leon fine sands continue down into the drainage corridor and onto eastern portions of the Harney Flats site. Since water tables conform to surface topography (Strahler, 1975:218), a hardpan must have eventually formed along flood prone areas, such as through the corridor, and acted as a stimulus in the formation of Leon fine sands and their associated organic pan layers on this portion of the site.

CULTURAL COMPONENTS

The cultural sequence at Harney Flats is best seen in Area 1 where the majority of the Phase II test units were dug from the original ground surface down to culturally sterile or near-sterile levels. On the other hand, very few Phase II test units were placed within Areas 2 and 3, and since most of these areas were excavated during Phase III after removing apprximately 1 m of topsoil—as well as any cultural material contained within—they did not provide a complete record of the cultural sequence at Harney Flats.

Ceramic Period Occupation

The excavations yielded seven aboriginal sherds, all of which were found in test pits just east of the block excavation in Area 1 (Table 4). Most of the sherds are an unidentified sand-tempered plain ware. One badly eroded St. Johns sherd, a limestone tempered Pasco plain body sherd, and a small punctated sand-tempered rim sherd were included. Most of these sherds are probably related to the Weeden Island (Manasota?) occupations of the Tampa Bay area. The one exception may be the punctated rim sherd which could represent a later Safety Harbor period occupation. These probably represent an ephemeral occupation of the site by late prehistoric groups.

Table 4. Prehistoric Ceramic Artifact Proveniences

Provenience	Comments	Provenience	Comments
133S/06E L-4	sand tempered plain	100S/15E L-4	St. Johns plain
125S/05E L-4	sand tempered plain	100S/15E L-4	sand tempered plain
133S/06E L-6	Pasco plain (?)	100S/15E L-4	sand tempered plain
90S/30W L-7 (disturbed)	sand tempered punctated rim (Safety Harbor?)		

With the exception of two sherds, all the ceramic pieces were recovered from level 4, 60-80 cm below surface. The single rim sherd recovered from level 7, 120-140 cm below surface, was definitely associated with a root disturbance, accounting for its unusual depth. No noticeable disturbance was observed in the recovery of the sherd from level 6, but it too is probably from a disturbed context. These artifacts were recovered from units that lacked a definable hardpan zone, which could have facilitated their vertical movement.

Newnan Occupation

A Middle Archaic component (dated to 7,000-5,000 BP (Milanich and Fairbanks, 1980)) which diagnostic Newnan points proved to be the youngest significant occupation at the site. Bullen (1975:31) describes the Newnan point as a medium to large sized projectile point with straight, but downward and outward sloping blade edges and a straight stem base. One hundred and seventy-five of these points were recovered at the type site of Newnan's Lake in Alachua County near Gainesville (Clausen, 1964). At Tick Island on the St. Johns River, Newnan projectile points were found in association with burials which were radiocarbon dated at 5,400 B.P. (Bullen, 1962a). Selected examples of the stemmed points recovered from Harney Flats are shown in Figure 11.

Seven Newnan points were found and plotted in Area 1 from depths ranging from 70-93 cm below surface (the lower half of level 4 and the upper half of level 5), although most were recovered from 70-85 cm below surface. The Newnan points occurred in, or just below, the organic hardpan of Leon fine sands. Levels 4 and 5 apparently also contained many more pieces of thermally altered debitage and silicified coral flakes. The prevalence of silicified coral and the marked increase in thermally altered lithic materials are indicative of a Middle Archaic period occupation (see discussions of Middle Archaic components at other sites excavated in the I-75 right-of-way, e.g., Daniel and Wisenbaker, 1981).

Suwannee/Bolen Occupation

The next component at Harney Flats is marked by side-notched Bolen points. Although Milanich and Fairbanks (1980) and Purdy (1981a) place these in what they term the Late Paleo-Indian or Transitional period, most investigators in the Southeast assign them to the Early Archaic (Goodyear, 1982a; Tuck, 1974). Tuck (1974) considers Bolen to be a variety of the side-notched Big Sandy I which he dates at 9,500-8,000 B.P. Bullen (1976:33) suggested that these early side-notched points were one of two discrete lithic traditions of the Florida Dalton period (10,000-8,000 B.P.).

Whatever their chronological placement and cultural association, the five Bolen projectile points recovered from Area 1 were found below the deepest Newnan point, at depths ranging from 108-155 cm below surface in levels 6, 7, and 8 (Table 5). Suwannee/Simpson points were found in the same 60 cm vertical band as the Bolen points. The Suwannee points appeared in the bottom half of level 6 and throughout

Figure 11. A-D: Archaic stemmed points; E-F: Kirk serrated points.

levels 7 and 8 (ranging from 114-151 cm below surface), although most occurred between 114 and 130 cm below surface.

Although Bullen (1975) postulated an age difference of about 2,000 years between Bolen and Suwannee tool forms, we were unable to separate them stratigraphically. We had intended our investigations at Harney Flats to provide new insights regarding the temporal relationship between these two tool forms (Daniel and

Table 5. Depths of Diagnostic Points from Area 1 (cm below surface)

Newnans	Bolens	Suwannees
70	108	114
75	124	115
79	130	119
82	130	123
85[a]	150[a]	124
85	155	130
93		151

[a] These depths are approximate (within 10 cm or less).

Wisenbaker, 1983:78), but there was no statistically significant difference (at 95% level of confidence) in the depth of the two projectile point types.

Suwannee points were found significantly lower than Newnan points (a t-score of 3.308 with 12 degrees of freedom $[n-2, n=14]$). This t-score indicated that the probability that the mean depths of the Suwannee and Newnan points were the same was between .01 and .001. A comparison of the mean depths of Bolen points and Newnan points also yielded a relatively high t-score of 2.24 (10 degrees of freedom), indicating a probability that the means were equal of .05, again indicating a statistically significant difference in the vertical placement of Bolen points and Newnan points in Area 1.

DISCUSSION

The stratigraphic sequence indicated by the diagnostic projectile points is summarized in Table 5. Although not shown, two Kirk projectile points were also recovered from Area 1. One appears to be a corner notched variety while the other is a stemmed form. Both were refitted from broken pieces; one was from pieces that had exact elevation depths (a tip recovered at 93 cm below surface and a base recovered from an apparently disturbed context at 114 cm below surface) while the second one was refitted from fragments with only general level provenience. The second specimen was refitted from a tip recovered from level 6 and a base recovered from level 7.

Although Kirk points have not been securely dated in Florida, Bullen (1976:34) argues that the Kirk Serrated (i.e., stemmed variety) probably represents the earliest stemmed point in Florida. Stratigraphic information from elsewhere in the southeast suggests that the Kirk forms would lie intermediate between Bolen (and other notched and ground stem forms) and Newnan points (including other Archaic stemmed varieties) in Florida (see Coe, 1964, Tuck, 1974; Goodyear et al., 1979).

The stratigraphic placement of the refitted corner-notched Kirk from Area 1 (93 and 114 cm below surface) conforms to this expectation. The tip and base from the stemmed Kirk are more difficult to place, since they have only general level provenience (levels 6 and 7). Based on the larger number of Bolen/Suwannee points recovered from these levels, we suggest that these refitted pieces have been displaced downward, and that the proper stratigraphic position for the Kirk points is roughly between 90 and 100 cm below the surface.

The relative depths of the diagnostic points and sherds recovered from Area 1 cluster in a manner consistent with the generally recognized Florida sequence (Figure 12). The sequence was generated from the above elevation data for the projectile points and the data on the piece plotted tools from the lower levels of Area 1. Although the site was occupied repeatedly and intensively at times, it should be emphasized that the Kirk and ceramic period occupations were ephemeral. The Bolen/Suwannee and the Newnan components represent the main site occupations. Finally, although the early component includes evidence for both Bolen and Suwannee period occupations, the component is primarily a Suwannee one. Although this is difficult to demonstrate stratigraphically, the general tool forms discussed in the following chapters are more representative of the Paleo-Indian time period.

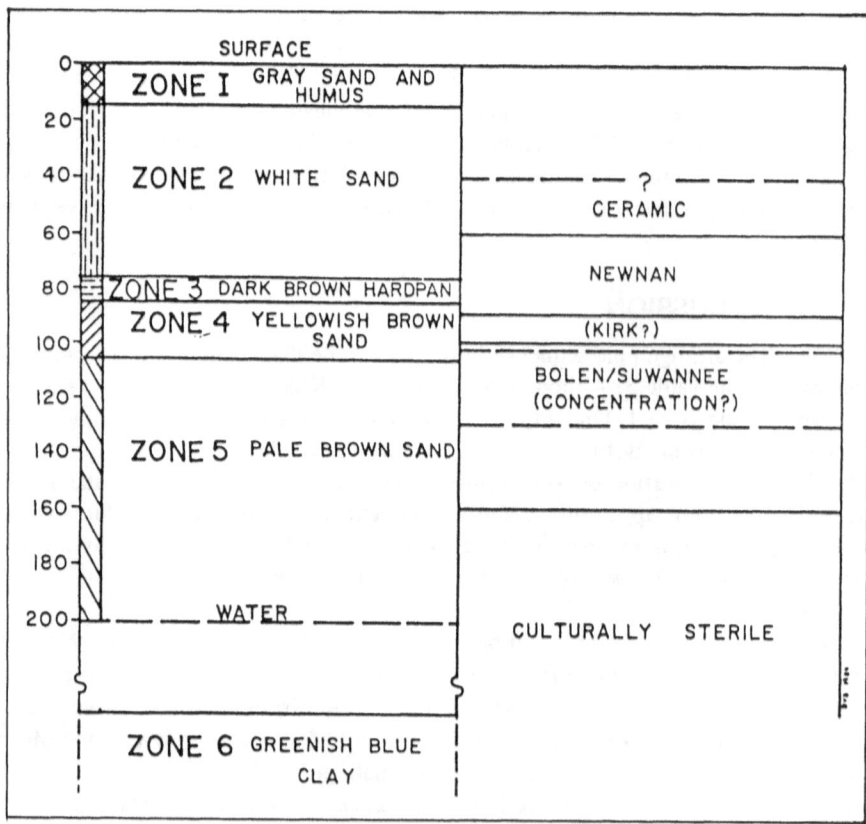

Figure 12. Schematic stratigraphic sequence at Harney Flats (depths in cm below surface).

Isolated pieces of charcoal were periodically uncovered during the excavations, and some were collected for dating. Although most were very small and none could be confidently associated with any cultural contexts, two samples were arbitrarily selected. Unfortunately, the resulting dates are much too recent to pertain to the early occupation and probably reflect the dating of burnt roots. The first date was 1390 ± 280 years B.P., 560 A.D. (Beta 5097), while the second sample was dated 3850 ± 120 years B.P., 1900 B.C. (Beta 5098). The large statistical errors are due to the nature of the small sample size.

VERTICAL AND HORIZONTAL DISPLACEMENT

Four projectile points in the Harney Flats assemblage were refitted, clearly indicating that some vertical movement of artifacts has occurred, although we cannot determine the specific factors responsible for the displacement. The conjoinable points included 1) the tip and base of a Suwannee preform in Area 1 separated by 5.5 m horizontally and 16 cm vertically; 2) the proximal and distal ends of a Simpson preform from Area 2 separated by 14 m horizontally and 30 cm vertically; 3) two halves of a Kirk projectile point in Area 1 separated by 13 m horizontally and 24 cm vertically; and 4) two halves of a second Kirk projectile point from Area 1 separated by 11 m horizontally and an excavation level vertically. These four bifaces suggest that vertical and horizontal movement of artifacts has occurred, although few signs of disturbance were visible in the profile walls of excavated units of the site.

Our impression in the field was that the early (i.e., Bolen and Suwannee) component at Harney Flats was isolated in a 40-60 cm band located approximately 100-160 cm below the surface. Our analysis of the elevations of projectile points from Area 1 indicates no significant stratigraphic separation between Bolen and Suwannee bifaces (there was, however, a stratigraphic separation between the early component and the overlying Middle Archaic component). We were also unable to separate the remaining Bolen and Suwannee artifacts on technological grounds, although technical similarities in the stone tools of Paleo-Indian and later Dalton and Early Archaic assemblages have been noted elsewhere (e.g., Goodyear, 1982a; Tuck, 1974).

Binford (1982:16) has noted that "there is no necessary relationship between depositional episodes and occupational episodes" and generally speaking, the burial of archaeological remains can be seen as the result of geological processes that for the most part operate independently of occupational episodes. "Rates of depositions are much slower than the rapid sequencing of events which characterizes the daily lives of living peoples; even under the best circumstances, the archaeological record represents a massive palimpsest of derivatives from many separate episodes" (Binford, 1981:197). This is particularly applicable to the formation of deep sand sites in Hillsborough county in general and Harney Flats in particular.

The lack of separation within the early component at Harney Flats can be best accounted for by postulating that the different occupations represented by the

Suwannee and Bolen points occurred on essentially one stabilized surface, somewhere between 100 and 160 cm below the present-day land surface. Apparently, there was not enough geological deposition between discrete occupations to stratigraphically separate materials. The main soil deposition likely occurred sometime after this, probably during the Middle Archaic period. Following deposition, the artifacts have been subjected to various processes that could have resulted, in various degrees, to some vertical displacement.

As a partial test of this postulate, elevations of plotted tools from levels 6, 7, and 8 were graphed in 10 cm intervals (Figure 13). This figure shows a concentration of artifacts in a 30 cm band within the three levels. A total of 56 percent of the plotted artifacts occur between 2.70 and 3.00 m below datum (i.e., about 1.00-1.30 m below surface). The figure also indicates two separate peaks of occurrences (i.e., from 2.71-2.90 m bd and from 2.91-3.00 m bd). To suggest that the two concentrations represent chronologically distinct occupations, we would have to assume that the artifacts have remained at the elevation at which they were deposited, an assumption we know to be suspect.

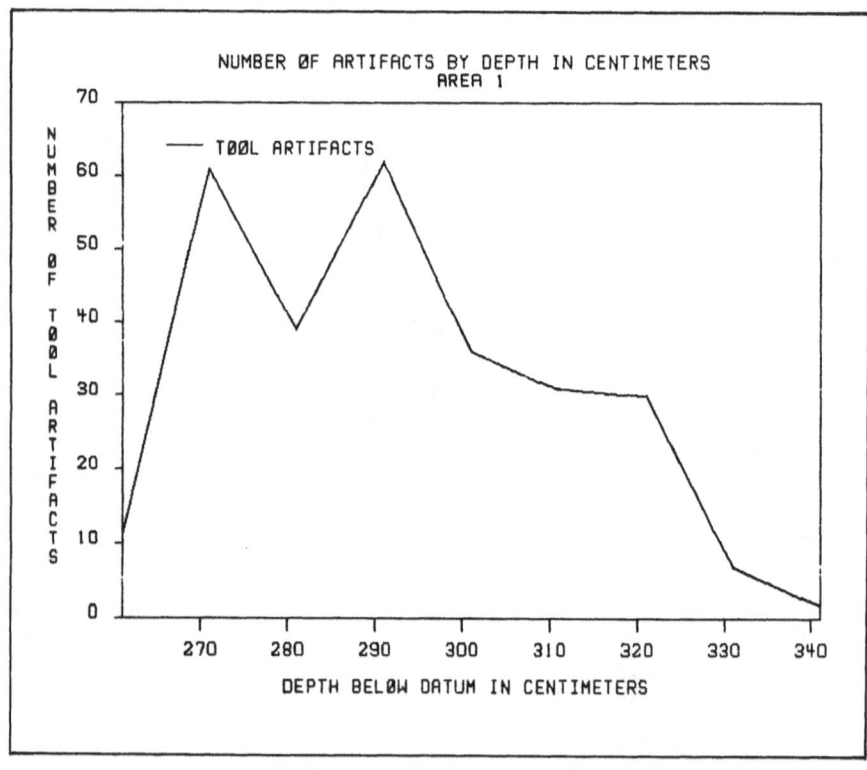

Figure 13. Elevations of plotted artifacts in 10 cm levels from Area 1 (2.70 mbd = approximately 100 cm bs).

The data are best interpreted as representing one former land surface between 1.00 and 1.30 m below the present surface on which the artifacts of the early component were deposited. The diagnostic (Bolen/Suwannee) bifaces occur at this depth, and the spread of artifacts within the sandy zone below the hardpan is seen as a result of post depositional processes. The compact hardpan zone above the early component apparently "sealed" it and helped prevent vertical artifact mixing with subsequent occupations at the site.

Satisfactory interpretations of buried sites require an understanding of the natural *and* the cultural processes that have affected the deposition of cultural remains (Schiffer, 1972; 1976). Of particular concern to us are those processes that result in the vertical displacement of artifacts. Because some refitted points recovered from Area 1 were vertically separated by several centimeters, it is apparent that not all artifacts were found at the elevation at which they were originally deposited. This, of course, affects the construction of the chronological sequence within the early component.

After artifacts are deposited in their original context, they can be disturbed through postdepositional events precipitated by such natural agents as wind, water, floral and faunal activities, and chemical action. Furthermore, we know that considerable vertical displacement (both upward and downward) of artifacts can occur even when the soil matrix has not been visibly disturbed or displaced (e.g., Villa, 1982:278-279).

> Soil is not a static body; it is a dynamic, open system in which a variety of processes may act to move not only soil matter, but objects (including artifacts) from one position to another. It must therefore be included as one of the major natural features we must contend with in interpreting the archaeological record (Wood and Johnson, 1978:317).

In a recent review of site formation processes, Schiffer (1983:685, 688) noted some problems regarding vertical displacement of artifacts and its relationship to stratigraphic interpretation. Trampling of artifacts by the early inhabitants is one such event that may have disturbed the integrity of the site. Although we have no proof that this happened at Harney Flats, experiments have demonstrated that trampling can mix materials that belong to two separate occupations. These findings indicate that mixing of this sort occurred in a 10-16 cm thick zone (Villa and Courtin, 1983). Observations by Stockton (1973) go even further by suggesting that trampled material will sort itself out according to size, with "larger" pieces remaining on or near the original surface, while smaller objects are pushed down to a depth of about 10 cm. Some researchers speculate that this type of sorting simply results from curation and reuse of large, older artifacts by later inhabitants at the same site (Baker, 1978), but Villa and Courtin (1983) note that pieces heavier than 50 g tended to stay on or near the surface on which they were first deposited, whereas pieces lighter than 50 g move more frequently both above and below the living floor.

Alternate wetting and drying of sediments, caused by a fluctuating water table or from percolating rainwater, sometimes results in vertical (downward) movement of artifacts into the soil (Villa, 1982:279). Over the past several millenia, many intervening rainy and dry periods have affected water table levels and the vertical disposition of artifacts at Harney Flats.

Biogenic activities (e.g., those of earthworms, termites, burrowing vertebrates, and tree roots) are other common causes of the upward and downward movement of artifacts. This was believed to be the mechanism of displacement at the Meer II site (an Epipaleolithic site in Belgium), where conjoined artifacts were separated by vertical distances of as much as 40 cm (Cahen *et al.*, 1979:662).

Plant roots, which we know can displace artifacts, were found (both as actual roots and as root stains) in practically all excavated levels at the site, especially those closest to the surface. In addition, traces of animal burrows, which also must have had an effect on the arrangement of cultural materials, were visible in many areas of the site. In fact, a gopher tortoise was caught tunneling through Area 1 during the Phase III excavations.

This discussion of post depositional artifact movement has emphasized vertical rather than horizontal displacement of artifacts, as does most relevant literature on the subject. We assume that postdepositional horizontal movement of artifacts within the site has been minimal and that the horizontal separation of refitted artifacts is primarily due to cultural (i.e., behavioral) and not natural processes.

CHAPTER 4

Artifact Analysis

TYPOLOGY

The concept of the type and the implications that its definitions have for archaeological research have generated much debate over the years (Rouse, 1960; Brew, 1946; Spaulding, 1953; Ford, 1954). The controversy has centered around the question of whether types are inherent, awaiting discovery (Spaulding), or are generated by the archaeologist (Ford) for his own ends. Simply put, are types "real" or are they "invented" by the archaeologist? This report will not belabor the question any further, although the artifact classification here leans in the direction of Ford. As Dunnell (1978:197) remarked, "in the end, most archaeologists working with types cite Spaulding but follow Ford." Any given typology may or may not correlate with the mental template of the prehistoric manufacturer, but it will always be a function of the archaeologist, generated from the data.

Today the debate has been restated in terms of empiricist and positivist positions (Hill and Evans, 1972). The empiricist (or traditionalist) views all phenomena as having meaning or significance inherent within themselves. Therefore, there is a single meaning, or at most very few meanings, inherent in artifacts; the archaeologist's task is to discover them.

Inherent meanings are usually ideas, customs, mental templates, functional meanings, or some historical index assigned to types (Hill and Evans, 1972:234). Inherent meanings are determined by intuitively judging similarities or differences over a wide range of observed but usually undefined characteristics. The archaeologist looks for the best, or at least, the most obvious, classification. This, of course, has worked for archaeologists in the past. The main problem with the empiricist viewpoint is its implicit assumption that these all purpose types are the only valid ones.

The positivist, on the other hand, holds that there is no single or best typology, nor are there any inherent meanings (e.g., norms, templates) to be discovered. An archaeologist begins work with problems, tentative inferences, and hypotheses about the material, then selects the kinds of attributes he feels will lead to the typology that will be useful in a particular analysis. Materials can, therefore, be typed in numerous ways.

Following the positivist argument, we believe that the potential exists for a myriad of types in the Harney Flats material, and that there are no inherent meanings to be discovered. As Hill and Evans note (1972:269):

> It is true, of course, that the prehistoric peoples who made our artifacts were consciously aware, and striving to make the things they made; but it is

insufficient to regard their 'templates' as explanations of these things. They would be descriptions that would themselves be in need of explanation—assuming that such description of templates could be made at all.

The Harney Flats typology is designed to measure certain cultural variables and is based on the assumption that there is a correlation between certain observable physical attributes of artifacts and specific kinds of behavior.

LITHIC TOOL CLASSIFICATION

Morphological Analysis

Traditionally, investigators have assumed that most if not all variations in tool morphology reflect specific differences in functions (e.g., projectile points, scrapers, gravers) (see Schiffer, 1979:19-20). Traditional classification criteria appear based on a mixture of both form (sometimes equated with "style") and function, and most classifications have used morphological characteristics to distinguish temporal and spatial clusters that are relevant to culture historical reconstruction (Jelinek, 1976; Sackett, 1973).

As Odell (1981) points out, morphological (formal) typologies are limited. Such typologies have been used less to address "behavioral" questions than to classify cultures on stylistic grounds. Archaeologists are now interested in using artifactual remains to answer questions relating to adaptation, activity areas, and spatial structure; it therefore becomes necessary to know the particular use of an artifact.

There are other problems with traditional classifications when they are used to address functional questions. Sheets (1975:369-370) notes that some tools break in manufacture and are used for other purposes, some are utilized for different tasks than anticipated, while others are simply used fortuitously. Finally, the problem of distinguishing function is compounded by the presence of multifunctional tools.

> The evidence for the manufacture of a multi-purpose functional tool group is itself somewhat revolutionary because it suggests that among certain tool types there is no possible one-to-one morpho-functional correlation, since more than one function is involved, and further shaping of tool margins and further utilization depend on factors such as edge sharpness and general suitability for specific tasks, independent of the general morphology of the piece (Odell, 1981:324).

Use-Wear Analysis

Perhaps the most telling criticisms of the morphological-functional typology have come from proponents of "use-wear" analysis. Semenov (1964), Tringham *et al.* (1974), Keeley (1974) and others have shown that the apparent gross morphology of a tool does not necessarily correlate with its use-wear patterns. The function of a stone tool is sometimes independent of its form.

Ethnoarchaeological studies have also demonstrated a lack of correspondence between form and function (e.g., Gould, Koster, and Sonty, 1971; Hayden, 1977).

Such work has demonstrated that almost any flake with an appropriate edge could be utilized for a task, and that shape played a minor role in the decision about use. Hayden (1977:179), working with Australian aborigines of the Western Desert, made these observations of tool use:

> There was no indication of any overall morphological type, "classic" form, or "perfect" specimen, as collectors are wont to say, and as archaeologists often tacitly accept in conversation. Rather, the traditional attributes of importance in the Western Desert were: effective edges (which were surprisingly variable in morphological expression), and a suitable size for holding in the hand and exerting pressure.

Some ethnographic studies have shown correlations between form and function, but these are not universal (Odell, 1981). When such correspondence does occur, the functional edge is often more important than the overall pattern of the tool. Odell (1981:323) suggests that stone tools can be placed on a continuum with function-specific tool shapes at one end and tool shapes where morphology has no relation to function. He also argues that such a range of variation probably existed in prehistory and we cannot know, *a priori*, where to place a specific tool. Finally, he emphasizes that even though form may coincide with function at some sites, the correlation is so variable that morphological categories alone should not be postulated without good supporting evidence to provide a functional interpretation. An extensive replication and use-wear experimental study was performed on Florida cherts as part of this project and formed the basis of our use-wear analysis.

Summary

There is no single best or correct stone tool typology. As Hill and Evans (1972) note, a typology should be based on the questions asked of the data. Consequently, the Harney Flats analysis and classification systems have been designed to incorporate information primarily on tool function, tool manufacture, and technological organization.

Our analysis of tool function was to delineate, within reasonable limits, the particular tasks or activities for which the tools were used. This is primarily accomplished by edge wear and edge angle analysis. Tool manufacture is viewed from examination of manufacture failures, rejects, and exhausted forms. Replication is a primary procedure in both these analyses. In analyzing the technological organization of the Harney Flats assemblage, we also consider how it resembles the postulated curated technology of a logistically organized group. Raw material selection, manufacture techniques, edge angles, haft elements, tool repair/rejuvenation, and discard patterns are all taken into consideration.

TOOL ANALYSIS

As is traditional in studies of Paleo-Indian tools (MacDonald, 1968), we make a distinction between two main groups of lithic artifacts—bifaces and unifaces. These groups are further divided into classes. A series of attributes (Appendix A) were examined to define each class visually, metrically, technologically and, to a certain extent, functionally.

At this point, it is important to remember that lithic reduction is a subtractive process (Deetz, 1967:48) and that a stone tool usually undergoes certain morphological changes during its use-life. Therefore, "types" are often a point in a dynamic process of transformation, and perhaps could be better viewed as steps along a continuum:

> That is, while some specimens may fit the ideal type descriptions, many will lack all of the defining criteria. The result is that not all morphological variability is accommodated, much less explained. The source of the difficulty lies in the classification of formerly dynamic tools into categories which are a reaction by the classifier to modal forms in the specimens, rather than as understanding of the processes which lead to formal patterns ("types") and gradations between. Once the sources of variation are understood, then the selection of attributes and construction of types becomes more meaningful behaviorally. Ideally, classification becomes more successful in that variation is accounted for rather than ignored or qualified by generating subtypes (Goodyear et al., 1983:47).

Bifaces

Forty-nine preforms, the majority of which were broken, were recovered. They vary in the extent to which they appear to have been finished, and enough specimens exist to suggest a manufacturing sequence (Figure 14, (A-H)). Some of the diagnostic specimens will be discussed in terms of this postulated manufacturing trajectory. Because of the limited sample and the fragmentary condition of many of the specimens, the following is only meant as a subjective outline, presented as a possibility that needs to be tested from better samples. All recorded measurements are listed in Table 6.

The Suwannee Point

Bullen originally defined the Suwannee point as (1975:55):

> An unusually large and fairly heavy, lanceolate shaped, slightly waisted point with concave base, basal ears, and basal grinding of bottom and waisted parts of sides. Basal thinning and suggestions of fluting are but rarely present. Workmanship varies from good to poor.

All of the Harney Flats specimens display shaping and thinning to some degree, so the blank type is difficult to determine. One large flake, however, appears to be a possible blank form very similar to the "blade-flake" used to replicate Clovis points that Callahan describes (1979:55, Figure 11):

> I have found the optimum spalls for Clovis point reduction to be fairly regular, wide flakes that would not be mistaken for prismatic blades, though they commonly bear longitudinal ridges and prepared platforms, are near parallel-sided, and often are nearly twice as long as wide. I call such specimens "blade-flakes" as the form is intermediate between a blade and a flake.

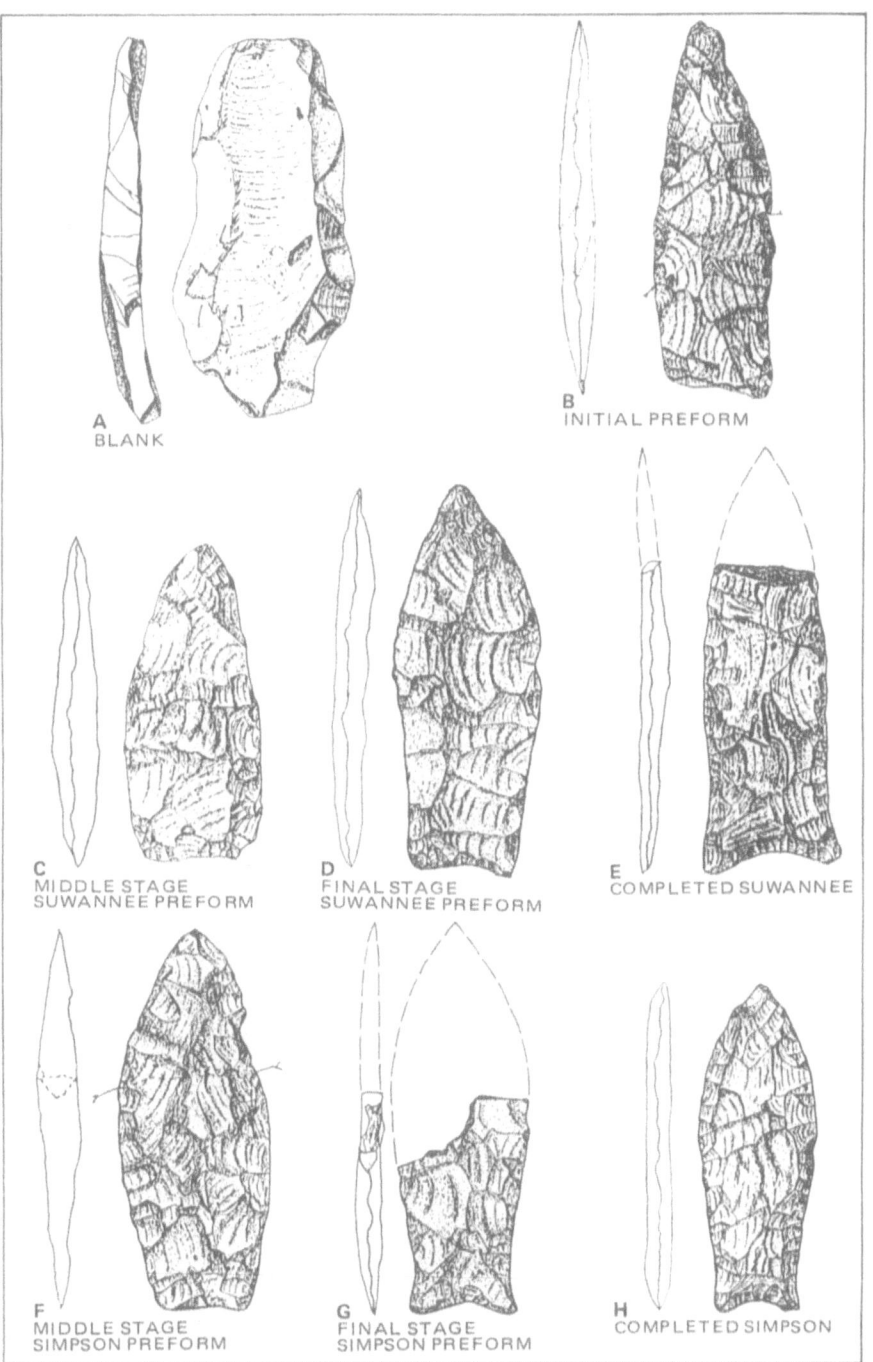

Figure 14. Suwannee/Simpson point continuum.

Table 6. Measurements of Bifaces

	Maximum Length	Maximum Blade Width	Maximum Width Ears	Maximum Stem Thickness	Maximum Stem Width	Basal Grinding	Comments	Figure No.
Completed Lanceolates								
81-163- 364-01	—	—	23.8	5.8	24.4	P	Base	19D
81-163-1379-02	—	—	31*	5.8	28.8	A	Base	19B
81-158- 229-01	—	—	22.7	6.1	21.5	A	Serrated Blade Hafted Knife?	19C
81-163-1814-01	40.3	25.5	26.1	5.4	24.2	P	Base reworked into endscraper?	19A
81-163- 650-01	92.8	—	36*	7.4	29.0	P	Suwannee Base	19H
81-163- 855-01	92.8	34.6	21.0*	6.5	24.1	P	Simpson	12F
81-163- 646-01	67.0	29.1	30.8	5.0	28.6	P	Suwannee (exhausted?)	20E
81-163-1026-01	—	—	33.8	5.0	33.2	P	Suwannee Base	19E
81-163- 83-01	—	34.5	—	—	—	—	Simpson (?) Tip	20A
81-163- 84-01	—	29.7	—	—	—	—	Tip	20B
81-163- 793-01	—	—	35*	7.5	33*	P	Suwannee Base	19F
81-163-4193-01	—	—	33*	6.3	35.5	A	Suwannee Base	19G
81-163- 17-01	—	—	39.2	9.0	35.3	P	Suwannee Base	
81-163- 802-01	68.9	31.1	28.4	7.5	29.9	A	Suwannee (exhausted?)	20C
81-163- 854-01	62.3	23.4	29.0	5.9	24.0	P	Suwannee (exhausted?)	20D
81-158- 233-01	110.2	42.0	30.5	8.3	33.0	—		
81-158- 177-01	—	34.7	40.2	6.6	34.7	P	Suwannee	
Preforms								
81-163- 985-01	—	39.4	—	—	—	—	Tip	
81-163- 653-01	—	32	—	—	—	—	Tip	
81-163-1002-01	—		(See -369)	—	—	—	Tip refits 369	16C
81-163- 249-01	—	42.2	—	—	—	—	Tip	

Catalog #							Description	Plate
81-163- 648-01	—	—	28.9	8.8	31.7	A	Base	
81-163- 511-01	—	—	33.4	9.2	37.4	A	Base	
81-163- 369-01 (refitted with 1002)	109.4	43.6	28.5	10.5	37.2	A	Base refits 1002	16C
81-163-1076-01	—	43.4	—	—	—	—	Blade?/body	
81-163- 491-01	—	—	—	—	—	—	Body fragment	
81-163- 880-01	—	—	—	—	—	—	Body fragment	
81-163- 463-01	—	—	42.7	9.3	48.1	—	Base	
81-163- 712-01	—	—	27.5	5.8	32.3	—	Base	
81-163- 452-01	—	—	46.0	12.9	52.0	—	Base	
81-163- 811-01	—	—	56	13.0	66.8	—	Base	
81-163- 592-01	—	38*	—	—	—	—	Tip	
81-163- 751-01	—	29*	—	—	—	—	Tip	
81-163- 530-01	—	31*	—	—	—	—	Tip	
81-163- 469-01	—	32	—	—	—	—	Tip	
81-163- 885-01	—	—	—	—	—	—	Tip	
81-163- 883-01	—	29.9	—	—	—	—	Tip	
81-163- 450-01	—	50.1	—	—	—	—	Tip	
81-163- 882-01	—	39.1	—	—	—	—	Tip	
81-163- 682-01	—	37*	—	—	—	—	Tip	
81-163- 563-01	—	33.4	—	—	—	—	Tip	
81-163- 541-01	—	23.1	—	—	—	—	Tip	
81-163- 86-01	89.6	36.5	32.4	11.2	41.0	—	Whole	15G
81-158- 756-01	89.9	39.2	29.7	11.0	43.0	—	Whole	16A
81-163- 377-01	—	—	36.9	9.7	46.1	A	Base	
81-163- 372-01	—	—	42.7	17.7	50.9	A	Base	
81-163- 376-01	—	—	31.0	7.4	28.3	A	Simpson preform base	16E
81-163- 358-01	—	—	39.4	10.7	43.4	A	Base	15E
81-163- 88-01	150.0	50.9	46.7	9.5	48.4	A	Base refits 3965	15B
81-163- 357-01	—	—	39.3	8.5	44.6	A	Base	
81-163-3965-01			(see 88-01)					15B
81-163- 78-01	—	—	48.9	18.4	56.3	A	Base	
81-163- 370-01	—	—	33.9	12.1	41.1	A	Base	15D
81-163-1876-01	—	—	—	—	—	—	Tip	

47

Table 6. (Cont'd)

	Maximum Length	Maximum Blade Width	Maximum Width Ears	Maximum Stem Thickness	Maximum Stem Width	Basal Grinding	Comments	Figure No.
Preforms (Cont d)								
81-163- 317-01	—	—	—	—	—	—	Tip	
81-163-3315-03	—	—	—	—	—	—	Tip	
81-163-4191-01	—	27.6	—	—	—	—	Tip	
81-163- 354-01	—	30.0	—	—	—	—	Tip	
81-163- 355-01	—	37.8	—	—	—	—	Tip	
81-163- 127-01	—	26.5	—	—	—	—	Tip	
81-163- 330-01	—	—	—	—	—	—	Tip	
81-163- 368-01	—	39.4	—	—	—	—	Tip	
81-163-3969-05	—	—	33.6	6.3	38.5	A	Base	16D
81-158- 176-01	90.7	41.0	23.0	10.6	37.7	A	Whole	16B
81-158- 436-01	—	—	42.2	9.2	48.3	A	Base	
81-163- 211-01	—	—	32.5	8.6	36.4	A	Base	15F
81-163- 309-01	—	—	—	—	—	—	Body fragment	
81-163- 166-01	—	—	—	—	—	—	Body fragment	
81-163- 06-01	—	15.6	—	—	—	—	Serrated blade	
81-163- 970-01	—	—	—	—	—	—	Body fragment	
81-163- 911-01	—	—	—	—	—	—	Body fragment	
Other Bifaces								
81-163- 342-01	—	—	—	10.0	32.5	—		
81-163- 111-01	—	—	—	10.4	39.1	—		
81-163- 263-01	—	—	—	14.2	43.0	—		
81-163- 108-01	—	—	—	11.9	52.5	—		
81-163- 298-01	—	—	—	11.7	33.2	—		
81-163- 430-01	—	31.6	—	—	—	—		
81-163- 49-01	—	32.5	—	—	—	—		

ID							Type	Fig
81-163-2988-01	—	—	—	—	—	—	Tip	
81-163- 149-01	—	24.7	—	—	—	—	Tip	
81-163- 115-01	—	44.0	—	—	—	—	Tip	
81-163- 361-01	—	—	—	—	—	—		
81-163- 385-01	—	47.5	—	—	—	—		
81-163- 365-01	—	39.6	—	—	—	—		
81-163- 68-01	—	—	—	—	—	—	Body fragment	
81-163- 363-01	—	—	—	—	—	—	Body fragment	
81-163- 850-01	—	—	—	19.9	71.4	—	Base (early blank?)	
81-163- 759-01	—	—	44.0	11.6	45.9	—	Base	
81-163- 692-01	—	50*	—	—	—	—	Tip	
81-163- 85-01	—	48.0	—	—	—	—	Tip	
81-163- 476-01	—	34.2	—	—	—	—	Tip	
81-163- 860-01	—	48.3	—	—	14.0	A	Body fragment	
81-163- 982-01	—	—	—	—	32.1	—	Body fragment	
81-163-3873-01	—	—	27*	6.3	65.2	A	Base	
81-163- 374-01	—	34.1	—	18.5	—	A	Early blank?	
81-163- 478-01	—	—	—	—	10.0	A	Tip	
81-163-3948-01	—	33.5	—	—	—	—	Body fragment	
81-163- 522-01	—	—	—	—	—	—	Tip fragment	
81-163- 777-01	—	—	—	—	—	—	Tip fragment	
81-163- 488-01	—	—	—	—	—	—		

Lozenge Bifaces

ID							Type	Fig
81-163- 879-01	70.6	29.6	31.0	7.4	32.3	A	Whole	18A
81-163- 658-01	62.0	23.1	24.3	7.7	25.5	A	Whole	18G
81-163-1009-01	62.0	29.2	31.3	10.0	31.4	A	Whole	18I
81-163- 451-01	63.0	18.9	19.5	5.2	19.2	A	Whole	18C
81-158- 740-01	55.9	26.4	30.7	9.9	31.7	A	Whole	
81-163- 942-01	—	—	—	9.4	33.5	A	Base	
81-163- 696-01	—	—	38.3	14.2	38.8	A	Base	
81-163- 989-01	—	—	24.6	7.7	27.2	A	Base	18N
81-163- 170-01	—	—	19.5	4.3	21.0	A	Base	18B

49

Table 6. (Cont'd)

	Maximum Length	Maximum Blade Width	Maximum Width Ears	Maximum Stem Thickness	Maximum Stem Width	Basal Grinding	Comments	Figure No.
Lozenge Bifaces (Cont'd)								
81-163- 693-01	—	—	20.7	5.0	21.0	A	Base	18F
81-163- 801-01	—	—	31.7	8.4	33.3	A	One side notch	18J
81-163- 761-01	68.8	30.0	32.0	10.1	32.1	A	Whole	
81-163-1066-01	50.0	25.2	23.5	5.0	24.9	A	Whole	
81-163- 697-01	73.6	23.5	23.0	9.4	27.9	A	Whole	
81-163- 810-01	—	11.8	25.0	6.8	25.0	A	Tip missing	
81-163- 589-01	—	—	33.1	9.1	35.9	A	Base	
81-163- 708-01	—	—	—	7.7	—	A	Base	
81-163- 212-01	—	—	32.0	13.0	31.6	A	Base	
81-163- 926-01	—	—	35.7	14.4	34.6	A	Base	
81-163- 94-01	—	—	—	8.7	33.7	A	Base	
81-163- 159-01	—	—	—	6.7	27.8	A	Base	18D
81-163- 239-01	—	—	36.1	12.0	37*	A	Base	
81-158- 234-01	—	19.7	—	4.7	19.7	A	Blade and mid-section	
Notched Points								
81-163- 367-01	41.1	20.7	6.9	18.9	25.6	A	Exhausted?	17D
81-163- 450-01	—	21.2	7.2	12.4	15.1	A	Exhausted?	17J
81-163-3960-01	34.0	18.8	7.2	15.2	17.2	A	Exhausted?	17E
81-158- 232-01	47.4	27.9	5.5	20.9	25.2	A	Exhausted?	17F
81-163- 375-01	—	—	8.6	—	—	A	Broken	17M
81-163-2744-01	—	—	—	15.5	25.6	A	Haft element	17K
81-163- 09-01	46.1	26.1	7.6	12.5	—	A		17H
81-163-1027-01	—	—	—	—	—			17B
81-163- 461-01	29.8	—	7.4	11.7	21.2		Exhausted?	17G
81-163- 371-01	49.6	25.1	9.6	19.8	24.3		Exhausted?	17C
81-163- 804-01	—	31.2	8.2	11.5	24.8		Tip broken	17I
81-163- 685-01	—	—	7.2	—	—		Broken	

A = Absent
P = Present
* = Estimated
— = Unmeasurable

This description fits the specimen in Figure 15(A) quite nicely. This blank is approximately 15.5 cm long and 7.8 cm at its widest point and about 1 cm thick, although a longitudinal ridge along one side is as much as 1.4 cm thick. Two longitudinal scars along its dorsal ridge suggest the removal of previous blanks, and consequently it appears somewhat trapezoidal in cross-section.

Further evidence supporting this interpretation can be seen in one broken preform which retains much of the ventral surface of the flake blank from which it came. Only a few subsequent flakes were removed from the lateral margins. The reverse side exhibits larger flake scars taken from the margin extending to the midline of the piece. This piece probably broke because it was from an unusually thin blank.

If such "blade-flakes" were being used as blanks, it is likely that special cores were being prepared to produce them. No such cores, however, were uncovered during the excavations. Small polyhedral cores (the source of blade-like flakes) were found; however, none were large enough to have produced a flake like that discussed above. Possibly no such cores were present at the site, but rather blanks or blade-flakes were brought there for finishing.

The next manufacturing stage is the preform. The refitted example is roughly shaped to a lanceolate form (Figure 15(B, C)) and appears to represent the initial shaping of a preform stage. Both are relatively thick, and still have a plano-convex cross section (suggesting a blade-flake blank), although both examples exhibit large flake scars on both faces. Most of these flake scars appear to have originated from the lateral margins. These two characteristics, broad flake scars and lateral thinning of the base, are noted by Goodyear as diagnostic characteristics of Suwannee and Simpson points:

> It is worthwhile to note here, along with the lateral thinning of the base..., that the broad, expanding flake scars usually surviving on the central portion of a Suwannee can be described as a technological hallmark of this point. This method of manufacture not only helped thin and shape the preform, but created a remarkably flat bifacial tool when viewed in cross section. Judging from the size of these scars, they were struck from much larger preforms. Their frequent presence on smaller finished points indicates such scars were left there intentionally. Subsequent pressure flaking is restricted to the biface margin for purposes of final shaping and for sharpening the tip and blade margins (Goodyear *et al.*, 1983:48).

Although the basic lanceolate form is present in the refitted specimen (Figure 15(B)), the edges are somewhat irregular, and the lateral and basal margins are definitely not ground. Moreover, the ears are unformed in both examples, although specimen (Figure 15(C)) exhibits a slight concavity at the base.

The refitted specimen (Figure 15(B)) is broken by a perverse fracture. "These are usually caused by an irregularity in the platform at the point of applied force that produces a fracture on two planes, thereby removing a flake and splitting the biface at the same time" (Frison and Bradley, 1980:42). Such fractures are almost invariably associated with manufacture.

Figure 15. Suwannee point: blade flake (Suwannee blank) (A); refitted initial stage preform (B); initial preform stage preform (C); middle stage preform (Suwannee base) (D-F); middle stage Suwannee preform (G); final stage Suwannee/Simpson preform (H); broken Suwannee point (I); and Suwannee base (J).

The remaining preforms are smaller and display considerably more flaking on their surfaces. The one distinguishing feature in the group is the shape of the lateral margins of the base. Two forms appear to be present: One is straight sided, while the other is more contracting or tapering. This may reflect the difference in the haft areas of the Suwannee and Simpson points (Bullen, 1975:54-57). The specimens with more parallel, straight sided bases are suggested to represent Suwannee preforms (Figure 14(C, D)) while the specimens with contracting or tapering bases are thought to represent Simpson preforms (Figure 14(F, G)). The Simpson point has a noticeably indented or waisted haft area compared to the blade, as opposed to the Suwannee which is only slightly waisted. Moreover, the ears are not as well formed as in the Suwannee.

The specimens in Figure 15(D-F) represent a middle stage preform for a Suwannee point. Note that the lateral margins and the base are straight sided. Lateral thinning is present along the midsection and base of both pieces. The artifact in Figure 15(G)) displays some pressure flaking restricted to the margins for shaping on one face. Some basal thinning is also present, although this appears to be associated with straightening the base in the preform stage and shaping the concavity and the ears in the final stages.

The specimen in Figure 15(H) represents a completed, thinned and shaped, Suwannee/Simpson preform. Lateral thinning scars are prominent on one side, while the other side displays smaller pressure flaking at the lateral margins that obscures the larger thinning scars. Most of the pressure flaking is restricted to the base, which is slightly waisted. A hint of the eared base is present; however, the ears need to be developed further and the haft area needs to be ground. Finally, the blade needs to be sharpened. The final step would result in a finished Suwannee like those pictured in Figure 15(I, J).

The Simpson Point

Examples of probable middle stage Simpson preforms (Figure 16(A-C)) exhibit lateral thinning flake scars from larger preforms. The stronger tapering of the base in these preforms is needed to finish the final waisting (tapering base) that is one of the primary distinguishing characteristics of the Simpson. Such tapering apparently is not necessary for the parallel sided Suwannee.

Two later stage preforms (Figure 16(D, E)) are thinner than the previous three and display shorter flake removals along the lateral margins. Specimen 16(D) shows bifacial flaking on the margins and a straightened base. The final stage of shaping the ears by indenting along the margins and at the base remains to be done. The subsequent form would look like Figure 16(E), which is a final stage preform. The basal concavity is well formed and indented, but lacks basal and lateral grinding, and appears to have been broken in manufacture due to the presence of inclusions. Figure 16(F) shows a completed Simpson, although a portion of one ear is broken and a flaw is present at the tip of the blade along one side.

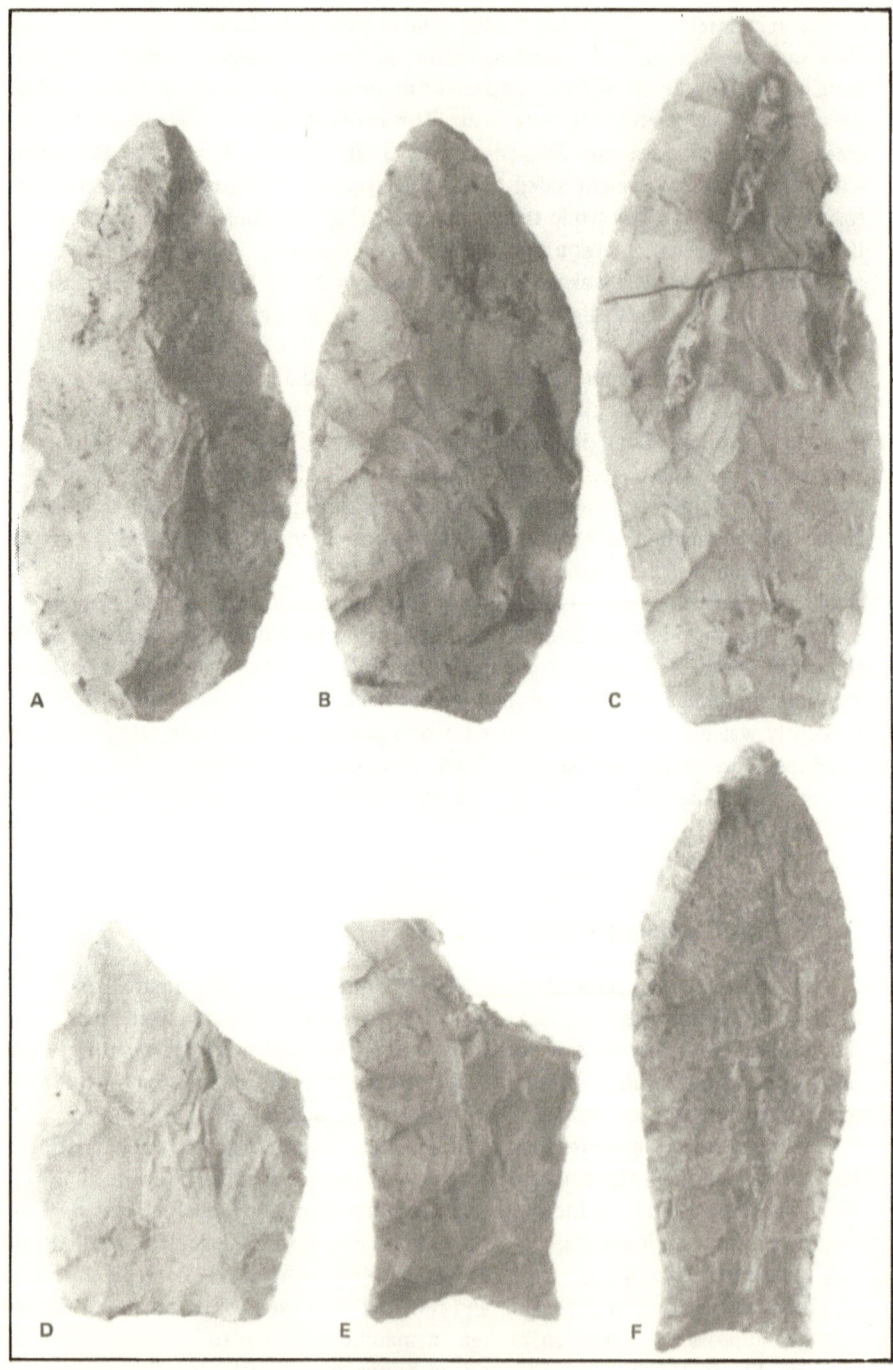

Figure 16. Simpson point: middle stage preforms (A-C); middle/late stage preform (D); final stage preform base (E); and finished point (F).

Bolen Points

Thirteen notched points would probably be identified as Bolen points. Bullen (1975:51-52) originally defined two basic types of this notched series: Bolen Plain and Bolen Beveled. Each type contained five subtypes based on the shape of the base or placement of the notch: concave based, side notched, high notched, corner notched, and expanded notched. The beveled series often appeared with serrated edges.

Beveling does not represent a different type of tool, but rather a strategy that conserves the length of the blade during tool resharpening (Sollberger, 1971). Furthermore, serrating may improve the cutting quality of blades that otherwise might experience a decrease in cutting efficiency with increased use-life (Morse, 1971; Goodyear, 1974). Beveling and serrations on Bolen points may not signify a distinct functional specialization, but may instead indicate later stage resharpening. The notches in the haft element may reflect the same practice. Resharpening can transform a corner notched base into a side notched variety once blade width becomes less than the basal width.

Although the haft element may be subject to change, it would not be as predictable as blade changes. Haft changes are typically the result of breakage and repair, while blade changes are primarily the result of use and resharpening (Claggett and Cable, 1982:408). These random occurrences of haft breakage and repair, since they can happen at any stage in the life history of a tool, are not as predictable as the patterns resulting from use and resharpening of the blade. Therefore, a diversity of forms and structure in the tang elements is not unexpected.

Consequently, the two types of Bolen points are not considered here as functional types, but rather as gradations in a dynamic process of tool transformation. The specimens (Figure 17) can be viewed from the perspective of stages in point transition. Artifacts initially resembling those in Figure 17(A, B) could have been transformed into those pictured in Figure 17(D, F, G). Those in Figure 17(A, B) are large side notched forms (Bullen's Subtype 2) and fairly straight edges and without beveling. Those in Figure 17(C-G) exhibit side notching and straight or slightly concave bases (Subtypes 1 and 2) are viewed as exhausted stages in the life history of a point. The suggestion of bifacial beveling along the blade edges of the specimens in Figure 17(C-F) is reminiscent of the double bevel present on Greenbriar points, which these resemble (Bullen, 1975:53). Figure 17(G) definitely exhibits the alternate bevel characteristic of Bolen points and is also exhausted. The specimen in Figure 17(H) is more corner notched (Subtype 4), exhibits straight sides, is not beveled, and appears to be exhausted. Figure 17(J) is similar to the expanded notch subtype (Subtype 5) and has a broken tip. The remaining four are broken bases (Figure 17(I-M)).

Although the preforms discussed earlier were generally assigned to either Suwannee or Simpson types, such lanceolate forms possibly could also be preforms for the Bolen point. The nature of our sample, however, did not permit further distinction (if there is any) between the two point type preforms.

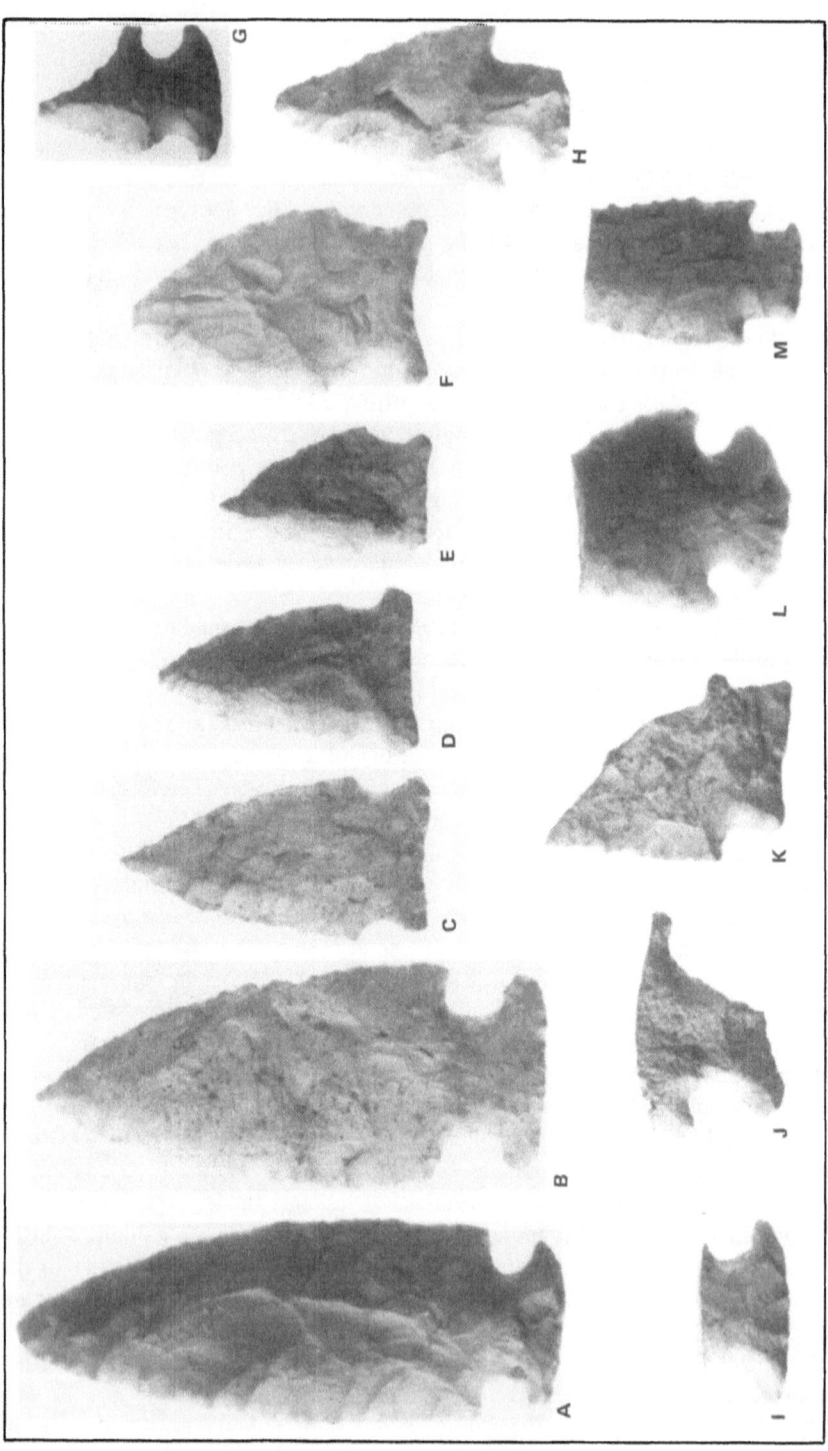

Figure 17. Bolen points: (A–H); Bolen points bases (I–M).

Lozenge-Shaped Bifaces

A group of twenty-three small lanceolates recovered during the excavations are similar to what Goodyear et al. (1983:51, Figure 4) describe as "narrow lozenge-shaped forms." These are small, sometimes delicately made, and should date to the Paleo-Indian period based on their technological attributes.

Those specimens in Figure 18 appear to be completed, or at least they appear more nearly complete than the remaining examples. The first four are thin and have square bases. Lateral thinning is common although some specimens exhibit small basal flake scars that originate from their bases. No lateral grinding as is usually present on Suwannees is exhibited on the edges. The other tools (Figure 18(G, H)) are different in that the bases are more rounded. Both appear complete and are very well made. They exhibit lateral thinning, but no lateral grinding is present. The specimen in Figure 18 (E), although broken, is unique in that it has a distinct notch on one edge very near the base. No other notches were observed in any of the other lozenge forms. The remaining specimens in Figure 18 are similar, but appear incomplete and are probably in a preform stage. They display larger flake scars and are relatively thicker than those just discussed. These forms could be preforms for the smaller Suwannee points but some appear to be finished rather than in a stage of transition. Moreover, they are rather small to be preforms.

Other than those mentioned by Goodyear, these bifaces have not been emphasized in the literature as dating to the Paleo-Indian period. This is not difficult to understand, however. Although they do have certain technological similarities, as a group they lack the general basal distinctiveness that characterizes a Suwannee or Simpson point. Nevertheless, this biface form can now be confidently assigned to this early period on the basis of contextual as well as technological association.

Remaining lanceolates, with one exception, appear to be broken or exhausted forms. The four bases in Figure 19(A-D) are similar to the smaller variety Suwannee or Simpson described by Goodyear et al. (1983). One of these exhibits reworking of the distal end into a steep edge similar to the Suwannee endscrapers that have been described elsewhere (e.g., Goodyear, Thompson and Warren, 1968:91; Purdy, 1981a:11-12, Figure 3b). Multiple use and recycling is a pattern typical of Eastern North American Paleo-Indian lithic technologies (Goodyear, 1979).

The four remaining bases in Figure 19(E-H) are also Suwannee or Simpson bases, while those specimens in Figure 20(A, B) are broken tips from finished lanceolates. Three points (Figure 20(C-E)) are all Suwannee-like, but exhibit less well developed ears than the typical Suwannee point. The specimen in Figure20(E) appears more like Bullen's (1975:47) Beaver Lake point: small, lanceolate shaped, and well made with basal grinding and waisted edges. The base is straight and displays only a suggestion of basal ears. The specimen in Figure 20(C) may represent an unfinished lanceolate rather than a resharpened one.

Finally, the lanceolate biface in Figure 20(F) is a variety that does not appear to have been formally described in the Florida literature. It is very well made, exhibits lateral and basal grinding, and is basally thinned. One corner of the base is

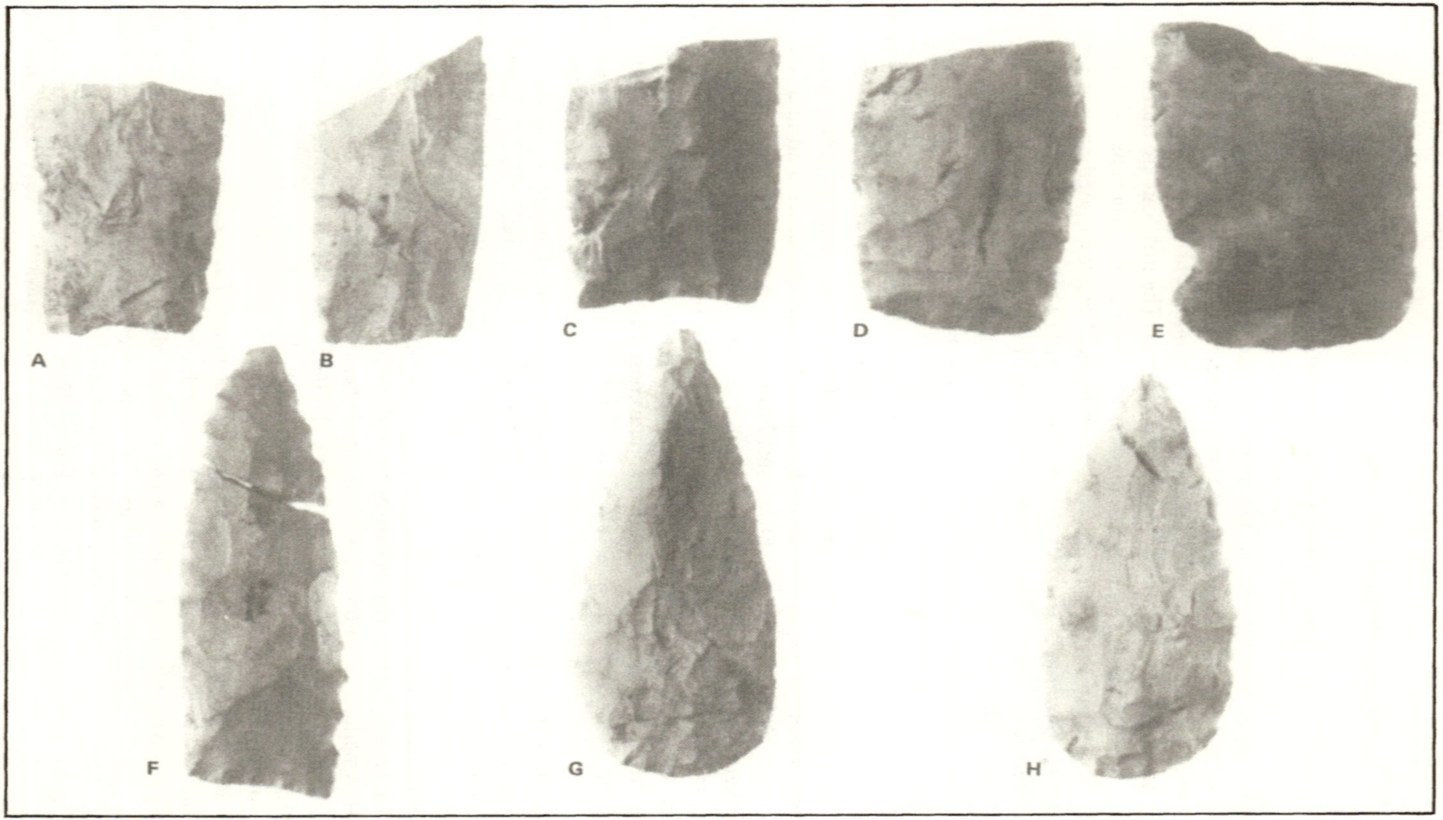

Figure 18. Lozenge-shaped bifaces: Biface bases (A-E); Lozenge shaped biface (F-H).

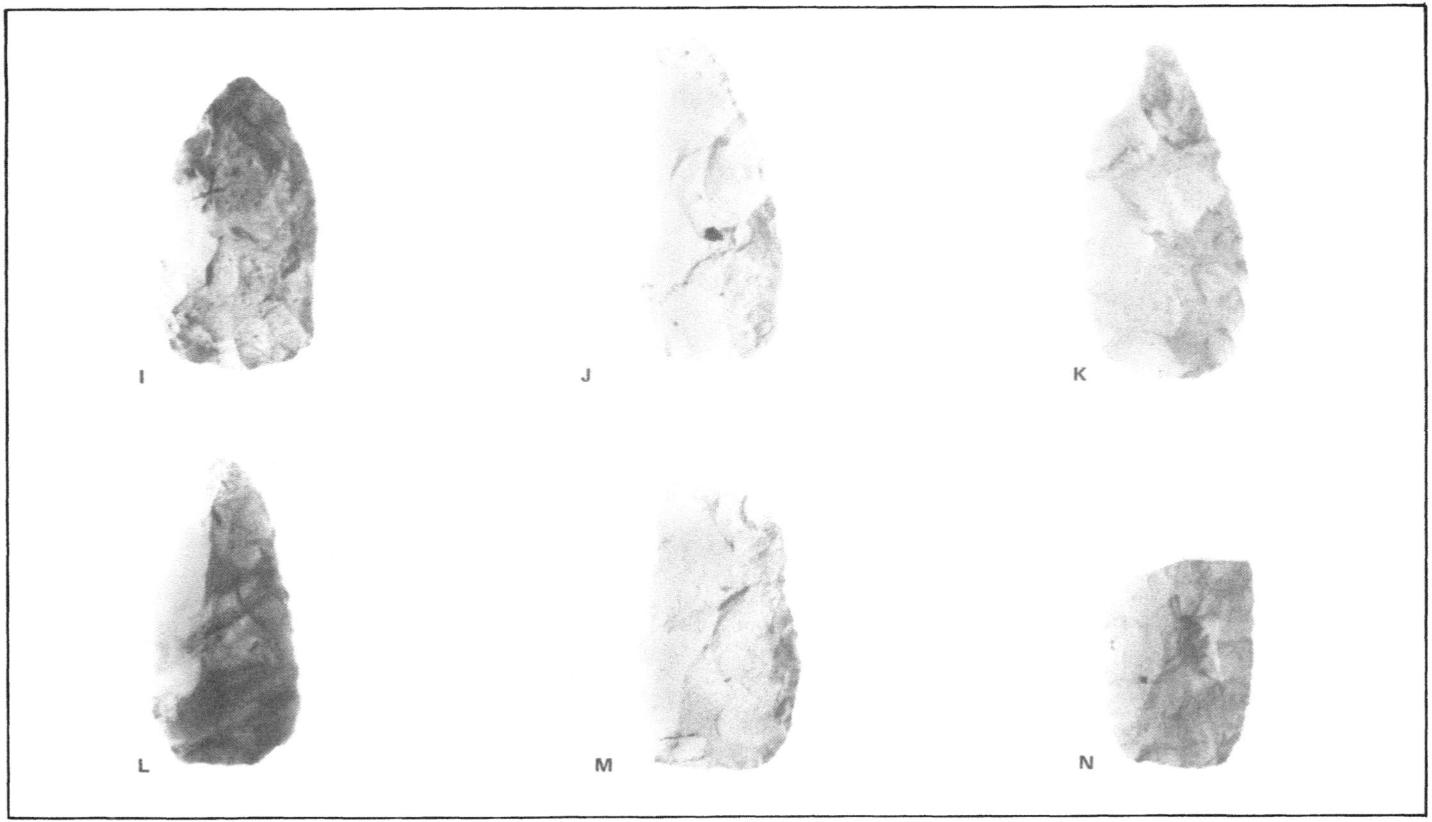

Figure 18 Continued. Lozenge-shaped biface preforms: (I-N).

60 / HARNEY FLATS

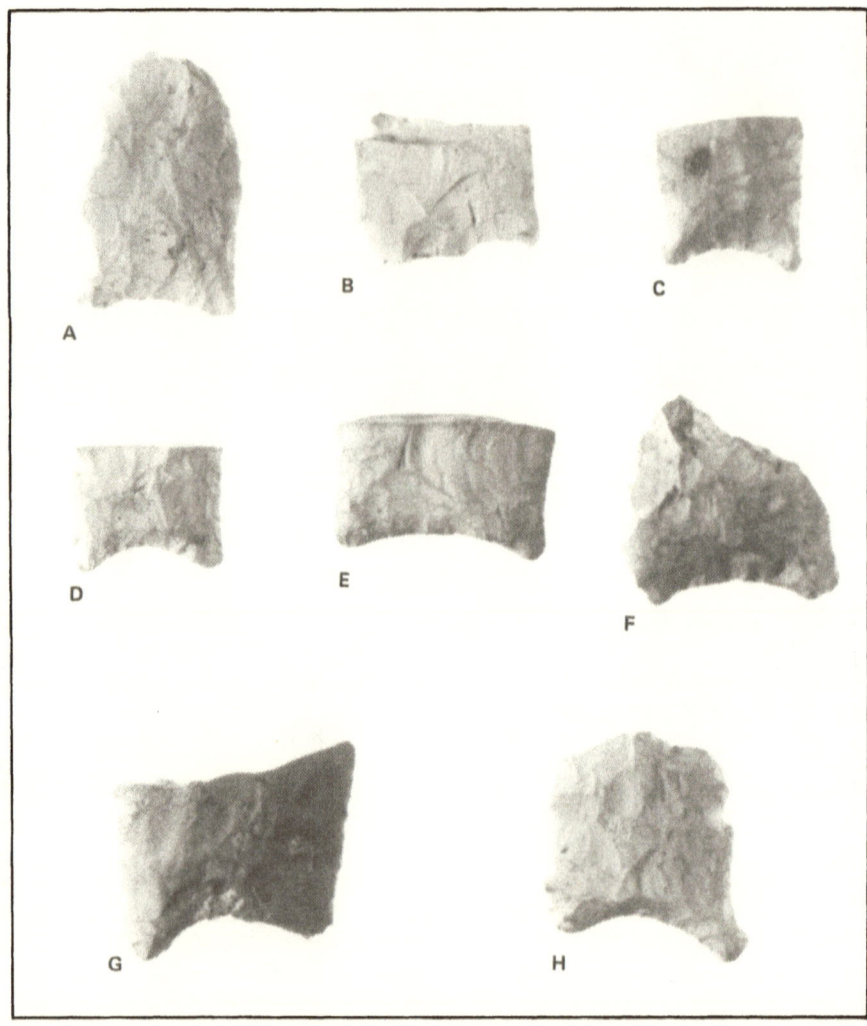

Figure 19. Other lanceolate bases (A-H).

broken, but the other is slightly rounded. The biface has a straight base and appears not to have had basal ears. Light serrations extend from the ground lateral edges to the tip of the blade. These serrations, along with the use-wear examination, suggest a cutting function. A similar specimen is pictured in Milanich and Fairbanks (1980:41, Figure 4a) and labeled a bifacial knife.

Other Bifaces

A number of other bifaces (34), all of which are broken, cannot be confidently placed in any of the above categories because of their incomplete nature. They all probably represent rejects from early stages of point manufacture.

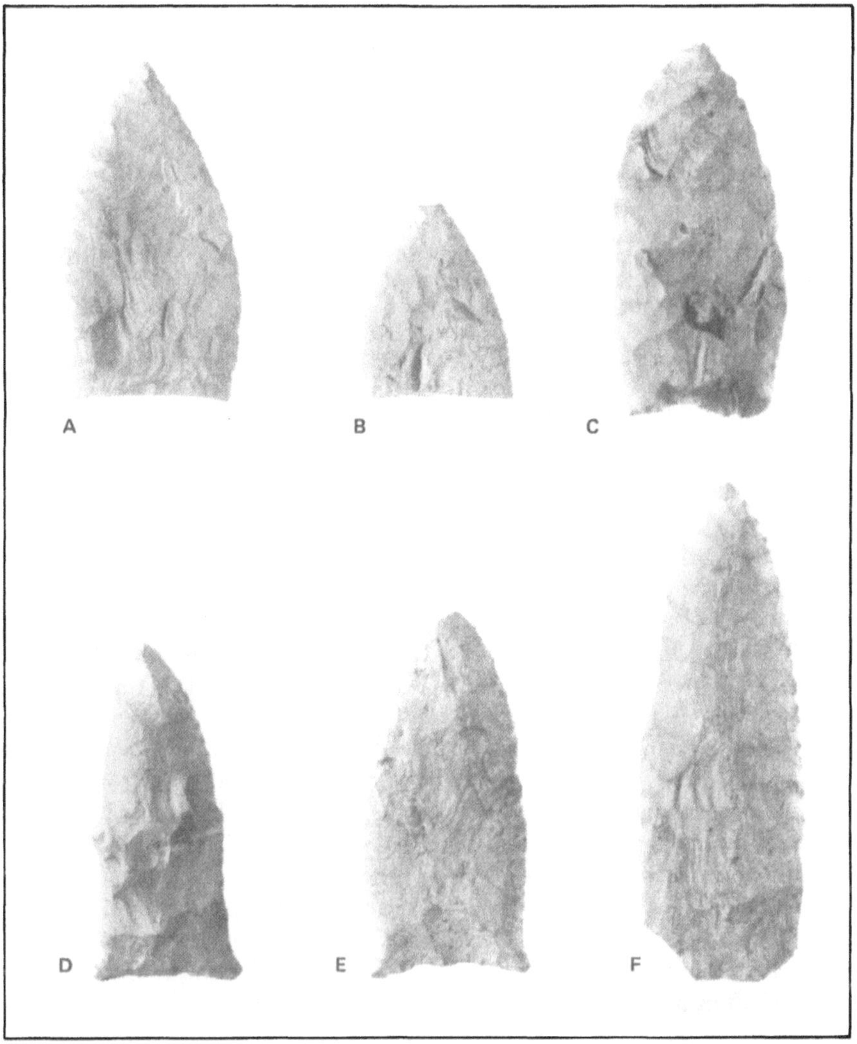

Figure 20. Broken tips from finished lanceolates (A, B); Suwannee-like bifaces (C-E); and hafted Suwannee knife (F).

Functional Implications of Bifaces

Recently Goodyear *et al.* (1983:52-55) offered some observations on the function of the Paleo-Indian lanceolate bifaces that are relevant to our study.

The Suwannee, especially the larger ones, give the impression of being used as heavy cutting tools. The relatively large width of their blades and stems would not seem conducive to penetration required for spearing and thrusting.

Smaller Suwannees with identical forms occur at the lower and middle ranges of the size spectrum, and would not be eliminated as projectile points based on size. The smaller sizes of the Simpson and more slender lanceolate forms such as Beaver Lake and Sante Fe and the lozenge-shaped specimens, suggest that projectile functions would be possible (1983:54-55).

They also note a possible relationship of the width of the stem to the size of the haft itself.

The variability in the size of the stem width of the Suwannees versus the Simpson and smaller lanceolates ... could perhaps be a function of the hafting mechanisms of each. The high variation in Suwannees might reflect a wooden haft since wood is easy to shape and can be worked to any size. The small widths of the other forms as well as their tighter statistical range might reflect hafts based on bone, antler or ivory where it is easier to chip stone to match natural diameters of more intractable materials (1983:55).

Our use-wear analysis of the bifaces is not conclusive, but some interesting comments can be made. The sample consisted of all of the completed lanceolates, notched points, and lozenge bifaces discussed ($N = 36$) and a 20 percent random sample ($N = 26$) of the remaining broken bifaces studied for a total of approximately 45 percent of the recovered bifaces (Ballo, 1985).

As would be expected, none of the completed bases displayed traces of wear. Consistent with the interpretation that they represent manufacturing failures, none of the sample of broken bifaces exhibited any use on their blade edges. Possible use-wear suggestive of their use as gravers was detected on the broken edges of two specimens. The completed Suwannees and Bolens are generally resharpened, making any confident determination of use difficult. A light rounding, suggestive of use on less resistant materials, can be observed on some specimens, however. Certainly, no crushing indicative of use on harder materials was seen. The completed lozenge-shaped bifaces pictured in Figure 18 were particularly troublesome to analyze since no detectable wear is present. Rather, a rounding more suggestive of grinding than use is seen on the lateral margins. This grinding might be associated with platform preparation for reworking or resharpening. Evidence of reworking and/or resharpening and hafting places these bifaces into the curated gear category.

Unifaces

The unifaces that appear to meet the criteria for curated or personal gear include endscrapers, discoidal scrapers, and oblong scrapers. All have a consistency in tool form seen in stone tools described from other Paleo-Indian sites in the Eastern United States. They also display considerable effort in manufacture, suggesting a longer intended use life (Goodyear, 1974; House, 1975). These tools also exhibit evidence of maintenance (i.e., resharpening), portability (i.e., hafting or small size), and flexibility (i.e., designs that can be transformed from one tool form to another).

The remaining unifaces (i.e., thick and thin unifaces and perhaps the large unifacial adzes) are classed as expedient or situational gear. The primary distinction between thick and thin unifaces is an arbitrary one—the thickness of the working edge. If the edge of the tool was consistently over 10 mm in thickness, it was considered to be thick. If it was 10 mm or less, it was classed as a thin uniface. Both classes appear to have been made from flakes of various sizes that tend to be larger than the formal tools described above.

Formal tools are ones having a great consistency of overall tool morphology—relative size, shape, thickness, and nature of retouch—rather than sharing only functional or use-wear attributes. Nonformal tools are expedient edge-damaged or marginally retouched flakes.

Based on their large size and variable form, we assume that the thick unifaces were predominantly hand held tools (Keeley, 1982:801). When an item is hafted, its margins tend to be regular. Since hand held tools can conceivably have any or all of the edges modified or resharpened, they can display greater morphological variability. Almost all of the retouch on these tools is restricted to the flake margins, and is apparently just enough to shape the working edge, although a few of the specimens exhibit the more extensive flaking characteristics of formal tools. Based on Gould's ethnoarchaeological work (1980:118-119; 127-129) such marginally retouched, hand held tools would tend to be used expediently and discarded rather than be curated.

Endscrapers

One hundred and thirty-four endscrapers are present in the assemblage, ninety-five of which are whole (Figure 21). The remainder are mostly proximal and distal fragments. These tools are similar to the "trianguloid endscrapers" found on many early sites in the Southeast, including the Hardaway site (Coe, 1964), the Brand site (Goodyear, 1974), Russell Cave (Griffin, 1974), and the Stanfield-Worley Bluff Shelter (DeJarnette, Kurjack, and Cambron, 1962). Similar endscrapers are also described in Cambron and Hulse (1967:4, 5).

A prominent tool in early assembalges, the endscraper has been traditionally described as a roughly triangular or tear-drop shaped flake with a rounded working edge outline usually opposite the platform end "characterized by a tapering stem, by extensive retouch often tending to diminish the lateral margins, and by a steeply chipped working edge" (MacDonald, 1968:90).

Over 47 percent of the endscrapers recovered from Harney Flats are ovoid or oval, with most of the remainder being more rectangular in plan view. The cross sections are primarily plano-convex (35%), trapezoidal (31%), and triangular (22%). The basic flake form is evident, as approximately 51 percent still retained the striking platform or bulb of percussion. Moreover, the majority of them have a flat ventral surface as opposed to the more arched ventral face noted elsewhere (MacDonald, 1968:91; Cambron and Hulse, 1967:3; Goodyear, 1974:44). The preform flake for this tool could have come from either a bifacial or nonbifacial core. Almost all the flakes are non-decortication, and thicker at the scraping end. A list of the tabulated attributes is given in Table 7.

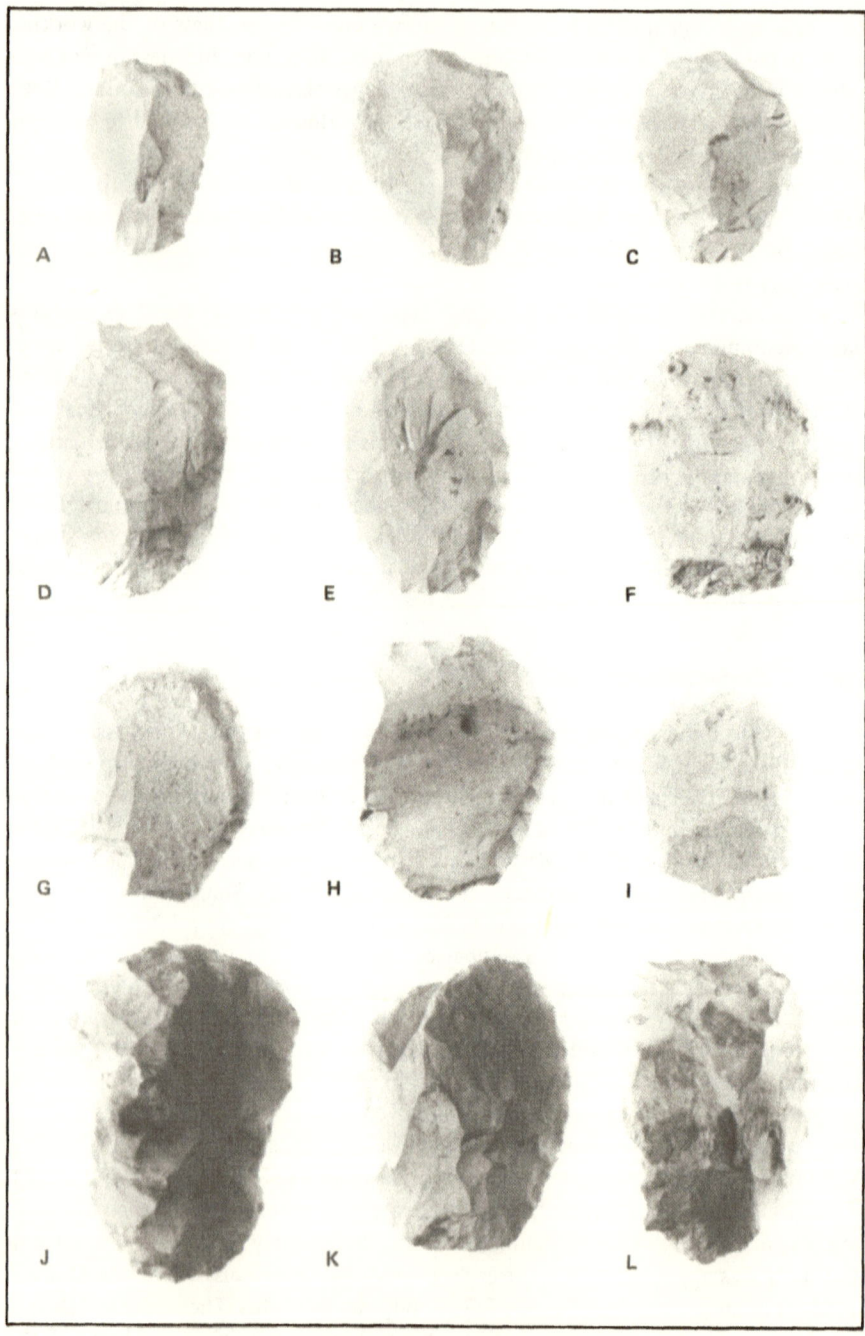

Figure 21. Endscrapers (A-L) and oblong scrapers reworked into endscrapers (A-C).

Table 7. Unifaces

Unifaces	Provenience					Material			Condition					Cortex				Dimension			
	Area 1	Area 2	Area 3	Test Pits Miscellaneous	Total	Silicified Limestone	Silicified Coral	Total	Whole	Proximal Fragments	Distal Fragments	Miscellaneous Broken	Total	Primary	Secondary	None	Total	Mean Length (mm)	Mean Width (mm)	Mean Thickness (mm)	Mean Weight (gm)
Scrapers																					
End	46	41	37	10	134	129	5	134	84	14	22	14	134	0	14	120	134	44.9 N=98	35.3 N=103	10.3 N=106	21.4 N=94
Percent	34	31	28	7	100	96	4	100	63	10	17	10	100	—	10	90	100				
Discoidal	21	22	18	7	68	67	1	68	66	—	—	2	68	0	16	52	68	46.1 N=66	42.8 N=67	13.1 N=67	34.3 N=66
Percent	31	32	26	10	99	99	1	100	97	—	—	3	100	—	24	76	100				
Oblong	8	30	28	14	80	73	7	80	67	—	—	13	80	0	12	68	80	75.9 N=69	39.8 N=74	17.4 N=79	57.9 N=68
Percent	10	37	35	17	99	91	9	100	84	—	—	16	100	—	15	85	100				
Thick	74	77	69	20	240	236	4	240	150	—	—	90	240	0	80	160	240	69.3 N=160	52.4 N=170	18.2 N=240	95 N=153
Percent	34	32	29	8	100	98	2	100	62	—	—	37	99	—	33	67	100				
Thin	26	63	45	8	142	138	4	142	79	—	—	63	142	0	40	102	142	53.2 N=85	39.4 N=99	7.0 N=126	23.8 N=79
Percent	18	44	32	6	100	97	3	100	56	—	—	44	100	—	28	72	100				
Blade-like flakes	9	15	8	2	34	34	—	—	19	—	—	15	34	0	2	32	34	61.7 N=20	29.9 N=31	6.1 N=32	13.2 N=21
Percent	26	44	23	6	99	100	—	100	56	—	—	44	100	—	6	94	100				

Table 7. (Cont'd)

Unifaces	Striking Platform Bulb of Percussion				Location of Retouch												Percentage of Dorsal Surface Retouch						
	Present	Absent	Indeterminate	Total	Right Lateral	Left Lateral	Bilateral	Distal	Proximal	Right Lateral Distal	Left Lateral Distal	Bilateral Distal	Circumferential	Other	Indeterminate	Total	1-25%	26-50%	51-75%	76-100%	Marginal	Indeterminate	Total
Scrapers																							
End	68	66[a]	—	134	0	0	0	12	0	8	12	45	21	—	18	116	7	8	6	29	47	—	97
Percent	51	49	—	100	—	—	—	10	—	7	10	39	18	—	16	100	7	8	6	30	48	—	99
Discoidal	26	42	—	68	—	1	4	—	—	4	4	15	40	—	—	68	3	8	11	23	22	1	68
Percent	38	62	—	100	—	1	6	—	—	6	6	22	59	—	—	100	4	12	16	34	32	1	99
Oblong	14	64	2	80	1	3	55	—	—	1	—	7	2	—	11	80	0	7	18	41	4	10	80
Percent	17	80	3	100	1	4	69	—	—	1	—	9	2	—	14	100	—	9	22	51	5	12	99
Thick	68	172	—	240	14	11	35	13	1	14	17	25	29	—	82	240	15	21	18	44	60	81	239
Percent	28	72	—	100	6	4	14	5	1	6	7	10	12	—	35	99	6	9	7	18	25	34	99
Thin	49	93	—	142	8	16	22	7	—	5	14	9	3	—	57	142	3	2	7	9	65	55	142
Percent	34	65	—	99	6	11	15	5	—	3	10	6	2	—	41	99	2	1	5	6	46	39	99
Blade-like flakes	34	—	—	34	1	7	4	1	—	—	2	3	—	16	—	34	—	—	—	—	—	—	—
Percent	100	—	—	100	3	20	12	3	—	—	6	9	—	47	—	100	—	—	—	—	—	—	—

[a] Includes 20 distal fragments.

Table 7. (Cont'd)

Unifaces	Plan View												Cross Section											
	Lanceolate	Crescentric	Triangular	Irregular	Circular	Oval	Ovoid	Square	Rectangular	Trapezoidal	Other	Total	Irregular	Triangular	Trapezoidal	Crescentric	Biconvex	Plano-Convex	Rectangular	Square	Parallelogram	Indeterminate	Other	Total
Scrapers																								
End	—	—	—	3	4	27	46	2	10	3	2	97	3	21	30	3	1	34	—	—	—	—	5	97
Percent	—	—	—	3	4	28	47	2	10	3	2	99	3	22	31	3	1	35	—	—	—	—	5	100
Discoidal	—	—	1	2	43	17	4	—	—	—	1	68	4	12	16	2	1	31	1	—	—	1	—	68
Percent	—	—	1	3	63	25	6	—	—	—	1	99	6	18	23	3	1	46	1	—	—	1	—	99
Oblong	9	4	5	2	—	33	14	—	2	1	10	80	1	16	6	—	—	45	—	1	1	10	—	80
Percent	11	5	6	3	—	41	17	—	3	1	12	99	1	20	8	—	—	56	—	1	1	12	—	99
Thick	3	—	20	41	13	37	28	3	5	3	87	240	18	33	33	1	7	60	1	1	3	78	5	240
Percent	1	—	8	17	5	15	12	1	2	1	37	99	7	14	14	.5	3	25	.5	.5	.5	33	2	100
Thin	1	—	4	29	2	19	26	1	1	2	57	142	17	21	14	2	3	27	2	—	5	50	1	142
Percent	1	—	3	20	1	13	18	1	1	1	40	99	12	15	10	1	2	19	1	—	3	35	1	99
Blade-like flakes	—	—	—	—	—	—	—	—	—	—	—	—	—	—	—	—	—	—	—	—	—	—	—	—
Percent	—	—	—	—	—	—	—	—	—	—	—	—	—	—	—	—	—	—	—	—	—	—	—	—

Lateral marginal chipping, resulting in a tapering effect, has traditionally been interpreted as an attempt to shape the stem for hafting. This feature was noted on almost all of the Harney Flats endscrapers. Roughly equal frequencies were chipped on the right (8%) or left stem (10%), while about 10 percent evidenced no lateral modifications. About 18 percent, however, had retouch around the entire circumference of the tool, while 39 percent exhibited retouch on both lateral edges and the distal end. This shaping of the margins allows the artifact to be easily hafted without binding by inserting it within a hollowed out antler handle (Morse, 1973: 27). This is not to say, of course, that this was the only means by which the scraper could have been hafted. Keeley (1982:799) describes two other types of haft arrangements besides the "jam" or wedge haft just mentioned. These are the "wrapped" or tied haft where the tool is simply lashed to a handle or shaft and a mastic haft where the implement is secured by means of a glue, resin, or tar. Moreover, many tools could be hafted by combinations of these basic methods.

Two other lines of evidence suggest that the endscrapers were hafted. The first is the removal of one or two flakes from the ventral surface at the proximal or stem end of the tool. This deliberate removal of a few flakes from an otherwise unchipped surface is viewed as thinning the stem (particularly the bulb of percussion) for better securing the handle. Second, evidence is also present in the broken portions of the scrapers. Most of these pieces are either proximal (stem) or distal (scraping) ends. Breakage is frequently caused by lateral snaps where the stem joins the scraping end, suggesting strong force applied through the stem. This same breakage pattern has been observed at the Brand site where Goodyear (1974:44) considered it unlikely that using the tool in the hand could provide enough force to snap such a thick part of the tool. Apparently, only hafted tools would exhibit such breakage patterns. Finally, no grinding was observed on the lateral margins and so-called "haft-notches" (Coe, 1964:75) were absent on all of the endscrapers.

Marginal retouch can be seen on 48 percent of the endscrapers and retouch over the entire dorsal surface can be seen on 30 percent. However, this may be a function of the resharpening process. Most of the scrapers that exhibited over all dorsal flaking were smaller specimens thought to be near exhaustion. An endscraper could start with only marginal retouch, but as it was used and resharpened it could ultimately end with most of the dorsal surface being flaked. Resharpening probably also affected the shape of the working edge, the majority of which are either convex (39%), subconvex (19%), or straight (11%). This would also account for the variable lengths of the tools.

Although this class of tool varies little from the specimens described from other early sites, there appears to be a morphological heterogeneity at Harney Flats perhaps related to a greater availability of raw material (Hayden, 1977; Binford, 1979). As a whole, they are probably more like Coe's (1964:75) variety of Class I endscrapers that are made on trimmed, flat prismatic flakes than they are like the teardrop variety with flaking covering the dorsal surface. A few of the endscrapers are larger and shaped differently than those described above (Figure 21). They are triangular in shape, much thicker, and are probably recycled from the broken oblong unifaces described below.

ARTIFACT ANALYSIS / 69

Approximately half of the sample displayed evidence of use on medium to hard materials, suggestive of woodworking, although a few exhibited very light damage on the working edge. One endscraper showed both cutting and scraping wear on two different margins of the tool edge. Another endscraper displayed predominately cutting wear along its working edge. The remaining endscrapers exhibited either no detectable wear or could not be assessed because they were broken, excessively patinated, or too grainy (Ballo, 1985).

A possible small graver spur was found on one specimen. The significance of the overall absence of graver spurs on the bit ends of the endscrapers is not known. These were present in the assemblages from Bull Brook (Byers 1954, Figure 92A), Debert (MacDonald, 1968:91) and the Brand site (Goodyear, 1974:45).

Discoidal Scrapers

These unifaces are similar to the trianguloid endscrapers described above except they are more circular in outline (Figure 22), and may actually be a hand held version of the hafted tool (Morse, 1973:27). Sixty-seven are present in the

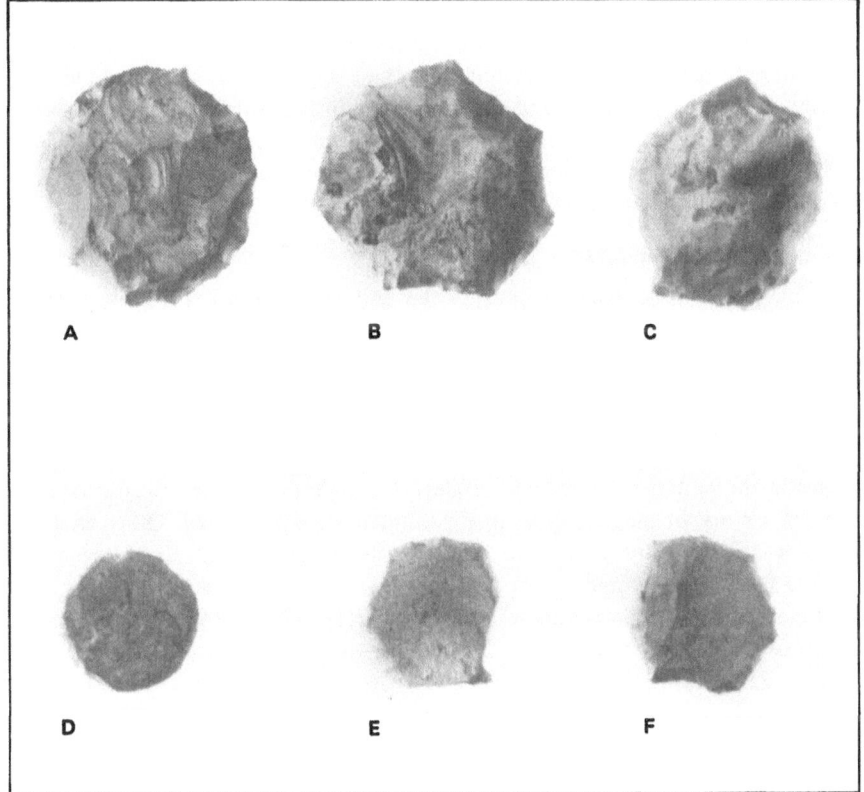

Figure 22. Discoidal scrapers (A-F).

assemblage, of which sixty-five are whole. Approximately 62 percent lack a striking platform; about 59 percent exhibit retouch around their entire circumference, and many have their entire dorsal surface retouched. The next highest percentage (22%) are bilaterally and distally retouched with unworked proximal or platform edges. These tools could have been hand held and the working edge used and rotated as needed. Three of these specimens have opposite marginal beveling.

Most of these unifaces (46%) are plano-convex in cross section, although many are trapezoidal (23%) or triangular (18%). They are circular (63%) or oval (25%) in outline. A summary of the measured attributes is given in Table 7. These unifaces appear to be similar in form to Coe's oval scrapers (1964:78), one variety of which he describes as being made from broad thin flakes. Coe's specimens retain their platform end, but the remaining edges of the tool are laterally retouched. The discoidal endscrapers pictured from the Brand site (Goodyear, 1974:46 Figure 15, o-p) are also similar to some of the small thin discoidal unifaces included in this group, but the Brand site specimens had graver spurs, which were absent on those from Harney Flats. The group with retouch around their entire circumference appears similar to those pictured in Cambron and Hulse (1967:7) and from the Nalcrest site (Bullen and Beilman, 1973:7) in central Florida.

Use-wear analysis indicates that these tools were used predominately for scraping on materials in the light to medium range. One appeared to have functioned primarily as a cutting tool. Two of the sample are of indeterminate function due to the nature of the raw material from which they were manufactured. One uniface is noteworthy for the presence of pronounced rounding, suggestive of hide-working, around its circumference (Ballo, 1985).

Oblong Scrapers

The final formal tool type in the uniface category is the oblong scraper (Figure 23). Eighty (sixty-six unbroken) were recovered during the excavations. About 51 percent of the collection are chipped over their entire dorsal surface. This tool tends to be somewhat oval (41%) or ovoid (17%) in plan view although other shapes such as triangular (6%), crescentric (5%), and lanceolate (11%) are also present. These shapes are not seen as different types of tools, but rather different stages in the resharpening and use process. A simple three stage transformation in the life history of an oblong scraper is illustrated in Figure 24. Other examples showing the flexibility of this tool form are shown in Figure 25. Early stage manufacture forms are pictured in Figure 25(A, B), which by use and resharpening could be transformed into the examples in Figure 25(C, D). Ultimately the oblong scraper can appear as any of the exhausted forms in Figure 25: an elongated diamond shape (Figure 25(A, B)), a slender straight or crescentric shape (Figure 25(C, D)), or a pointed oblong form designed for graving (Figure 25(E, F)).

Most (56%) of the oblong unifaces are plano-convex in cross-section, with the remaining specimens tending to be either triangular (20%) or trapezoidal (8%). Approximately 82 percent of these unifaces display no evidence of a striking platform, which when present, is located parallel to the long axis of the tool suggesting they

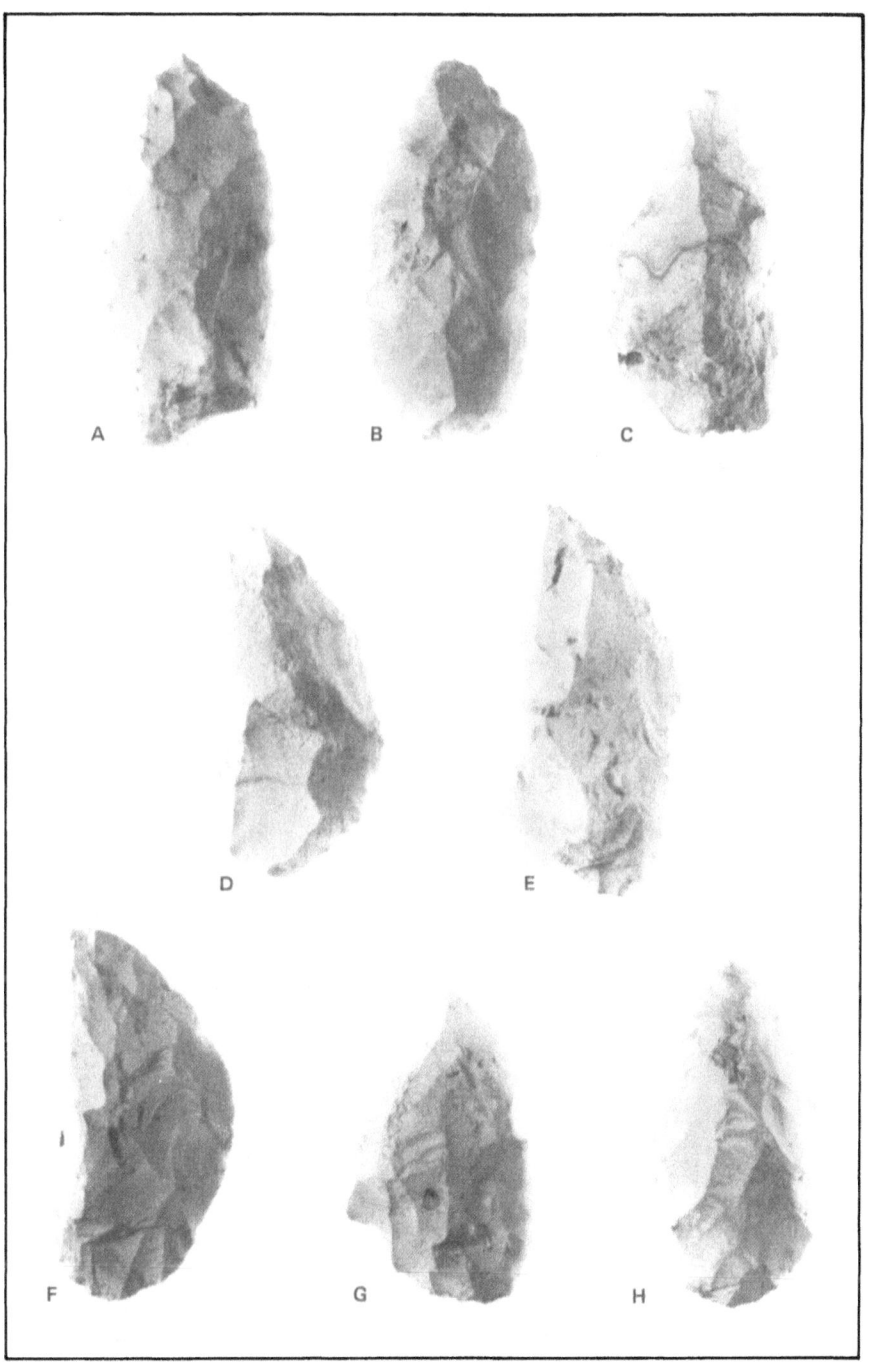

Figure 23. Oblong scrapers (A-H).

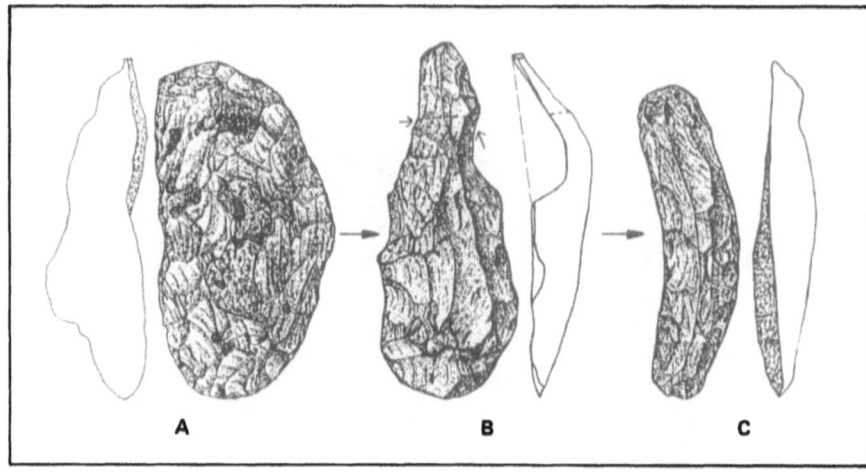

Figure 24. Oblong scraper continuum.

were made from a thick flake rather than a blade. The vast majority of these unifaces exhibited retouch along both lateral edges, although a few have retouch on only one side. Some of these are shaped to a point at one end. Although all these tools are considered unifacial, a few show some flake removal on the ventral side, apparently to flatten the surface. A summary of attributes is given in Table 7.

Similar forms have been recovered from various contexts in Florida. Warren (1973:119-120) describes a single specimen recovered from a bulldozed area in St. Petersburg: a "well made tool," with a longitudinal crest, ridge, or keel running almost its full length. In cross-section this object is reminiscent of the modern wood worker's parting tool (1973:119) and would have the outline of a nearly equilateral triangle. Purdy (1981a:18-19) describes a collection of thirty-three specimens which she refers to as "Hendrix scrapers" and identifies as being part of a Paleo-Indian "tool kit." She pictures seven tools (1981a:19, Figure 7-8) which are nearly identical to those recovered at Harney Flats. Moreover, she notes a difference in the size range of this type that we would view as a result of use and resharpening. She also notes that all specimens were used as scrapers, but five had been used for cutting or piercing, and many exhibited a tapering or pointed end. This last characteristic is also observed on some of the Harney Flats specimens. Purdy also describes a "snub-nosed scraper (oblong)" as being part of the Paleo-Indian tool kit, but sees it as a different type than the Hendrix scraper. Again, we would not view the Hendrix scraper and the snub-nosed scraper as different types, but as variations of one type. She also notes that these implements are not very common in Florida. Her one illustrated example came from the Container Corporation of America site in Marion County (Purdy, 1981b:98) where it was found in deep sand at the contact between sand and clay deposits. A somewhat discrete Paleo-Indian component may be present at the site (1981b:104).

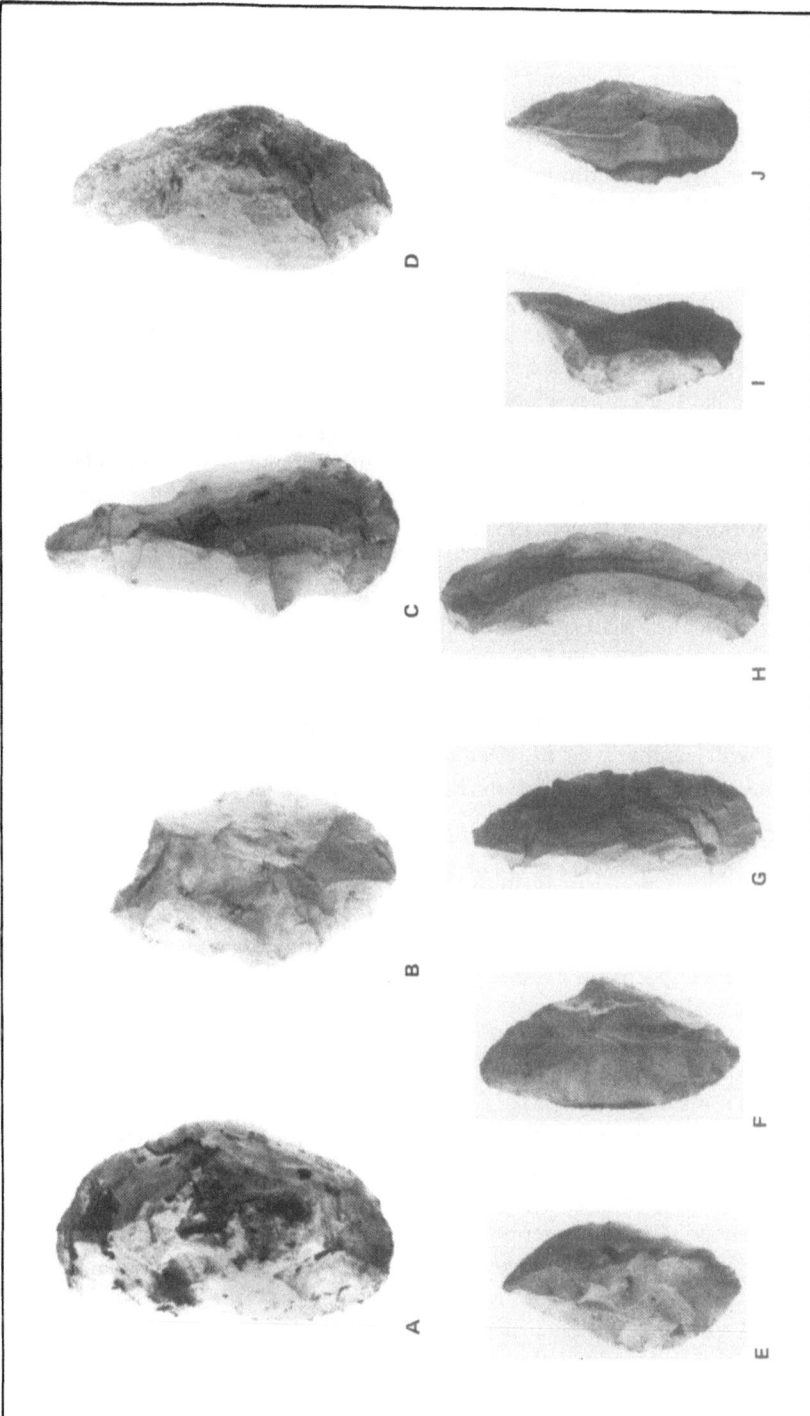

Figure 25. Oblong scrapers: Initial stage (A, B); completed (C, D); and exhausted (E–J).

Another similar specimen (called a pointed side scraper) was excavated from Camp Ranch at Bolen Bluff (Bullen, 1958: Plate VIII G) in the lower levels identified by him as being Early Preceramic. A Bolen point was also excavated from the same lower level. In addition, a number of both Bolen and Suwannee points had been collected from Bolen Bluff.

It is uncertain if this form of uniface is present in other Paleo-Indian assemblages; however, some morphologically similar specimens may be present at the Shoop and Bull Brook sites (Witthoft, 1952; Byers, 1954). Witthoft (1952:478) has described the Enterline side scraper as an unifacial, unhafted pointed tool, 2.5-8 cm long and made of a flat or curved flake steeply retouched on the two long edges and also at the tip. Unlike the Harney Flats specimens, the remnants of the bulb of percussion are generally at the pointed end rather than along the long axis. Edge-retouching is extensive, and the tool is relatively thick and either trapezoidal or triangular in cross-section. Witthoft states that these were scraping and gouging rather than cutting tools. Similar forms, which Byers (1954:349; Figure 92(i)) calls "typical Enterline side scrapers," appear at Bull Brook and resemble oblong unifaces from Harney Flats.

Use-wear is difficult to characterize on these unifaces. The majority appear to have been used, as a light smoothing is common on all lateral margins of the sample; however, some of this could be confused with weathering of the tool edge. Nevertheless, a somewhat more distinct and heavier damage is present nearer the tips of the more pointed oblong forms. Overall the sample suggests lighter scraping and gouging with emphasis on use near the pointed ends. One tool displays some evidence indicating a cutting function (Ballo, 1985).

Thick Unifaces

Two hundred and forty thick unifaces were found at Harney Flats. One hundred and forty-six of these are whole (Figure 26). This class includes flakes that are unifacially retouched along their margins with working edges greater than 10 mm in thickness. Five specimens exhibit opposite marginal beveling. A general flake morphology is evident as 28 percent still retain a striking platform with a wide variety of plan view shapes (see Table 7). The predominant forms are irregular (17%), oval (15%), ovoid (12%), and triangular (8%). Form could not be determined for broken specimens (34% of the sample).

A variety of cross sectional shapes are also present. While the predominant form is plano-convex (25%), equal percentages (14%) of trapezoidal and triangular shapes are also present. The next highest percentage (7%) is irregular in cross section, but approximately 34% are indeterminate. Twenty-five percent of the specimens exhibit only marginal retouch. The next highest amount (18%) exhibits characteristics of form tools displaying retouch over 75-100 percent of the dorsal surface (Figure 26(E)). Approximately equal percentages (6-9%) are distributed throughout the remaining categories of dorsal surface retouch (Figure 26(F-H)).

The retouched working edge is typically found on the lateral edges—either bilaterally (14%), or on a single lateral edge (6% right lateral; 4% left lateral). This attribute is also present in some combination of lateral and distal edges: bilateral

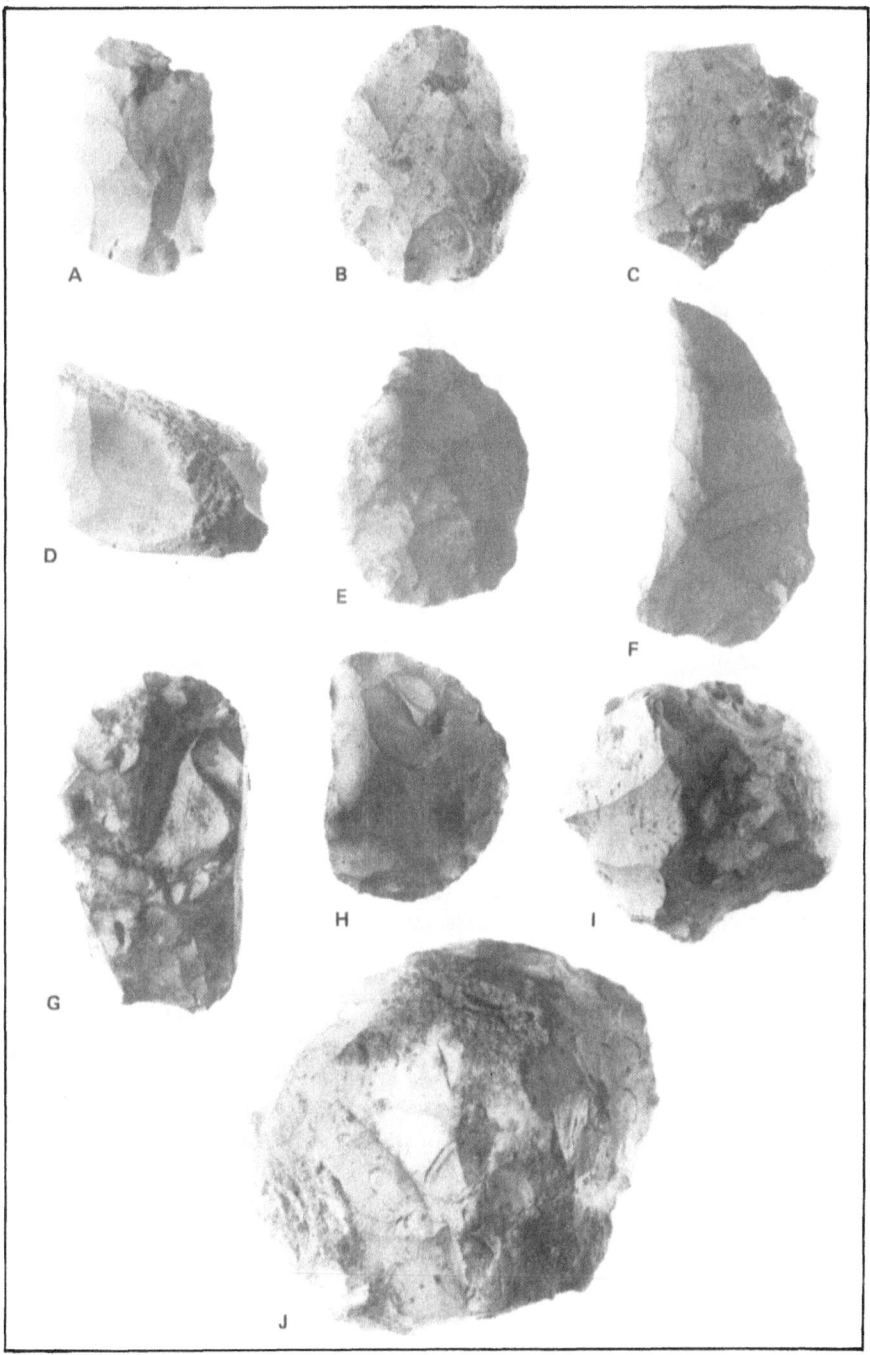

Figure 26. Thick unifaces (A-J).

distal (10%), right lateral distal (6%), and left lateral distal (7%). It also occurs alone (distally) on 5 percent of the specimens.

The working edges are mostly convex, subconvex or straight; a few, irregular or concavo-convex. The shapes of the working edges are thought to be primarily the result of two factors. Since these tools were made from flakes with minimal retouch, the shapes of the edges generally conform to the outline of the flake. The other possibility is that use and resharpening influenced the shape of the edge to a certain degree. Consequently, the convex, subconvex, and straight edges could actually be a continuum of use and resharpening. This latter possibility is not likely, since the majority of the specimens were simply expedient tools with little shaping along the edge beyond the initial retouching. Consequently, they were probably manufactured for a specific task and discarded upon its completion with little chance for further reuse or resharpening.

Some of these specimens appear equivalent to Coe's (1964:77-78) sidescraper I or II types. Type I is described as:

> ... made from large, wedge shaped flakes that were struck from a flat or prepared striking platform. Most of these specimens retained a considerable portion of this platform, as well as the bulb of percussion, in their finished form. The working edge of this type was rounded or crescent shaped and either one or both ends were rounded and curved back. The working edge remained sharp and irregular.

Type II is described as:

> ... made from a large irregular flake, and unlike the type I side scraper, there was no attempt to shape the working edge into any other form than what existed. These large flakes were simply picked up, sharpened, and used. Occasionally, more than one edge on the same flake would be used.

Dragoo (1973:27) describes a large flake side scraper found at the Wells Creek site that resembles the thick unifaces; he notes they are of variable form, as a result of the shape of the primary flake utilized.

This category also includes a type of uniface sometimes referred to as humpedback or turtleback scrapers (Figure 26(I, J)). Harney Flats examples are generally round, plano-convex in cross-section and exhibit steep edges. Many appear to have originally been polyhedral cores that were slightly reshaped for use in scraping. Similar tool forms have been recovered from other excavations in Hillsborough County (Daniel, 1982:117). Cambron and Hulse identify similar specimens as oval core scrapers that appear to be associated with Paleo-Indian and Early Archaic sites in Alabama (1967:7).

The use-wear analysis reveals that scraping medium to hard materials appears to have been the predominant function of these tools with a much lesser degree of scraping light to medium material. Cutting/sawing wear is also represented in the sample. A tool that appears to have served as a chopper, a large uniface that possibly functioned as a spokeshave, and a specimen exhibiting use in much lighter work (possibly hide scraping) is also present. Approximately half the sample exhibited no wear. These specimens represent both broken unifaces and possibly early production pieces that are likely to be manufacture rejects. In sum, we suggest that the tools displaying wear were manufactured and used as needed for a particular task. These tasks generally include scraping or cutting/sawing functions, most likely on materials like wood (Ballo, 1985).

Thin Unifaces

This class includes a vast array of unifacially retouched flakes with working edges 10 mm or less in thickness including some unifacially retouched flakes that are usually placed in a modified flake or flake tool category (Figure 27). One hundred and forty-two thin unifaces of which 79 are whole (Table 7) were found at the site. A basic flake morphology is evident in these tools. Approximately 34 percent of the tools retain a striking platform and about 72 percent exhibit no cortex. The general concern was only for retouch of the working edge, although some examples did exhibit more formal attributes or shape with more extensive retouch extending over the dorsal surface. Eight of the tools evidenced opposite marginal beveling.

Retouch predominates on the lateral edges and occurs most often bilaterally (15%), although retouch on single lateral edges, either left lateral (11%) or right lateral (6%), is also found. Just as often, however, lateral retouch occurred in combination with distal retouch, occurring as left lateral distal (10%), right lateral distal (3%), and bilateral distal (6%). The shape of the retouched edges are mostly convex, subconvex, or straight and was probably most influenced by the original shape of the flake.

The overall plan view of this class is variable; with irregular (20%), ovoid (18%), or oval (13%) outlines being most common. This is seen as a function of a general flake morphology as is the cross-section views, which are most frequently planoconvex (19%), triangular (15%), trapezoidal (10%), or irregular (12%).

Many of these unifaces may approximate Coe's Sidescraper Type III made from "thin narrow flakes" (Coe, 1964; 79, Figure 66c), although they are not restricted to this. Similarly, the steeply chipped side scraper at the Brand site (Goodyear, 1974:47-50) also appears to be similar.

Dragoo (1973:27) describes a small flake side scraper from the Wells Creek site.

> These flake scrapers consisted of primary flakes modified by chipping the dorsal surface along one or more points of the perimeter. The general outline or cross-section of the flake was not modified to any marked degree by this chipping which was less extensive than that of the side scrapers described above. The actual cutting edges were usually less than 20 mm and variable in shape with some being straight while others were convex or slightly concave. Many of these flakes had more than one—usually two or three—cutting edges at various points around the flake. In contrast to the side scrapers with long, straight cutting edges that were usually made from an end flake, in this group flakes of any shape were used. The 663 scrapers assigned to this category ranged from 10 mm to 72 mm in maximum dimension.

Use-wear is particularly difficult to detect on these unifaces. Over half of the sample exhibits evidence of light rounding on the retouched edges that could be

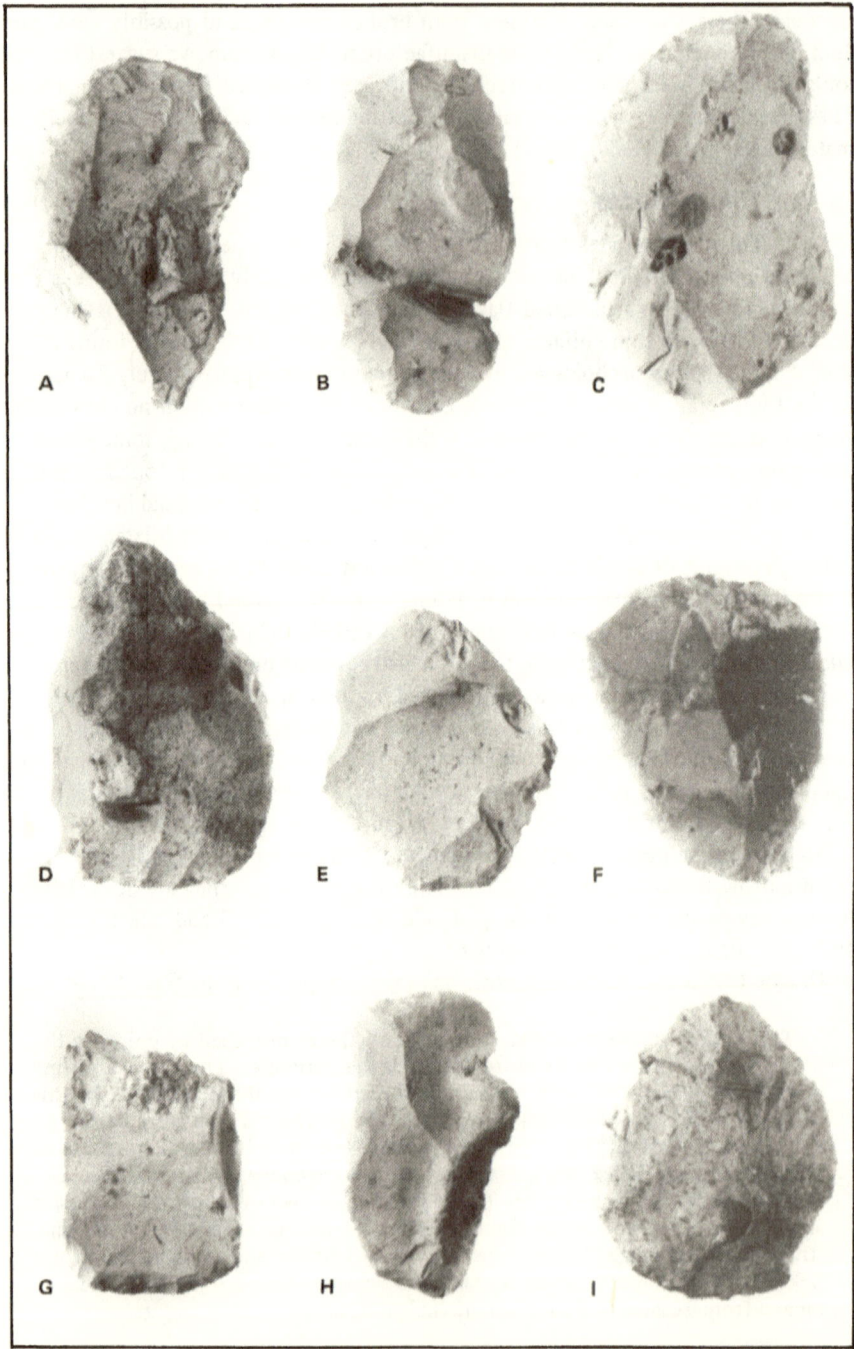

Figure 27. Thin unifaces (A-I).

attributed to light scraping or severe weathering. The small size of these tools, along with their minimal retouch, makes proper distinction difficult. Traces of a cutting use, however, could be detected on one specimen while possible graving wear was seen on another. The remaining third of the sample is indeterminate or exhibits no detectable wear due to their fragmented nature or the character of the raw material from which they were manufactured (Ballo, 1985).

Adzes

Five of the following six specimens might be included in the thick uniface class; however, they appear to be hafted, heavy duty tools and will be described separately (Table 8). Five are unifacial and one is bifacial. Three of these unifacial tools are ovoid in shape and plano-convex to trapezoidal in cross section. To a certain extent they resemble polyhedral cores recycled for use as unifaces. An important difference is the evidence for hafting.

Two of these exhibit a tapering or constriction at one end that suggests they were socketed or bound. One specimen is extremely tapered as a result of steep unifacial chipping and blunting along its lateral edges. Some grinding is also present on the lateral edges. Also at the constricted end, but on the very top of the dorsal surface, is evidence of some battering (linear slit-like depressions) and slight grinding (Figure 28(A)). This is assumed to result from attempts at thinning and smoothing the surface for better binding. The working edge is steeply chipped and convex in shape and was probably resharpened. A few flakes have been removed from the ventral surface, perhaps as a result of use.

The second specimen (Figure 28(B)) is also ovoid in shape and trapezoidal in cross section. There is a slight tapering about halfway down the lateral margins, but no grinding or blunting was observed. In addition, a suggestion of shallow, unground notching is present along both lateral margins. The working edge of this specimen is convex in shape. Use-wear examination of this artifact reveals no detectable traces of use and it is thought to represent a tool in production.

The next specimen (Figure 28(C)) is, with one exception, similar to the previous two in morphology. Evidence for hafting appears in the middle of the tool. These notches were formed by flake removals and thinning on the dorsal and ventral face

Table 8. Adze Dimensions

Illustration	Maximum Length (mm)	Maximum Width (mm)	Maximum Thickness (mm)	Weight (gm)
Figure 28(A)	76	51	30	126
Figure 28(B)	93	64	29	175
Figure 28(C)	89	68	37	231
Figure 28(D)	59	44	23	60
Figure 28(E)	38	28	20	23
Figure 28(F)	120	90	38	426

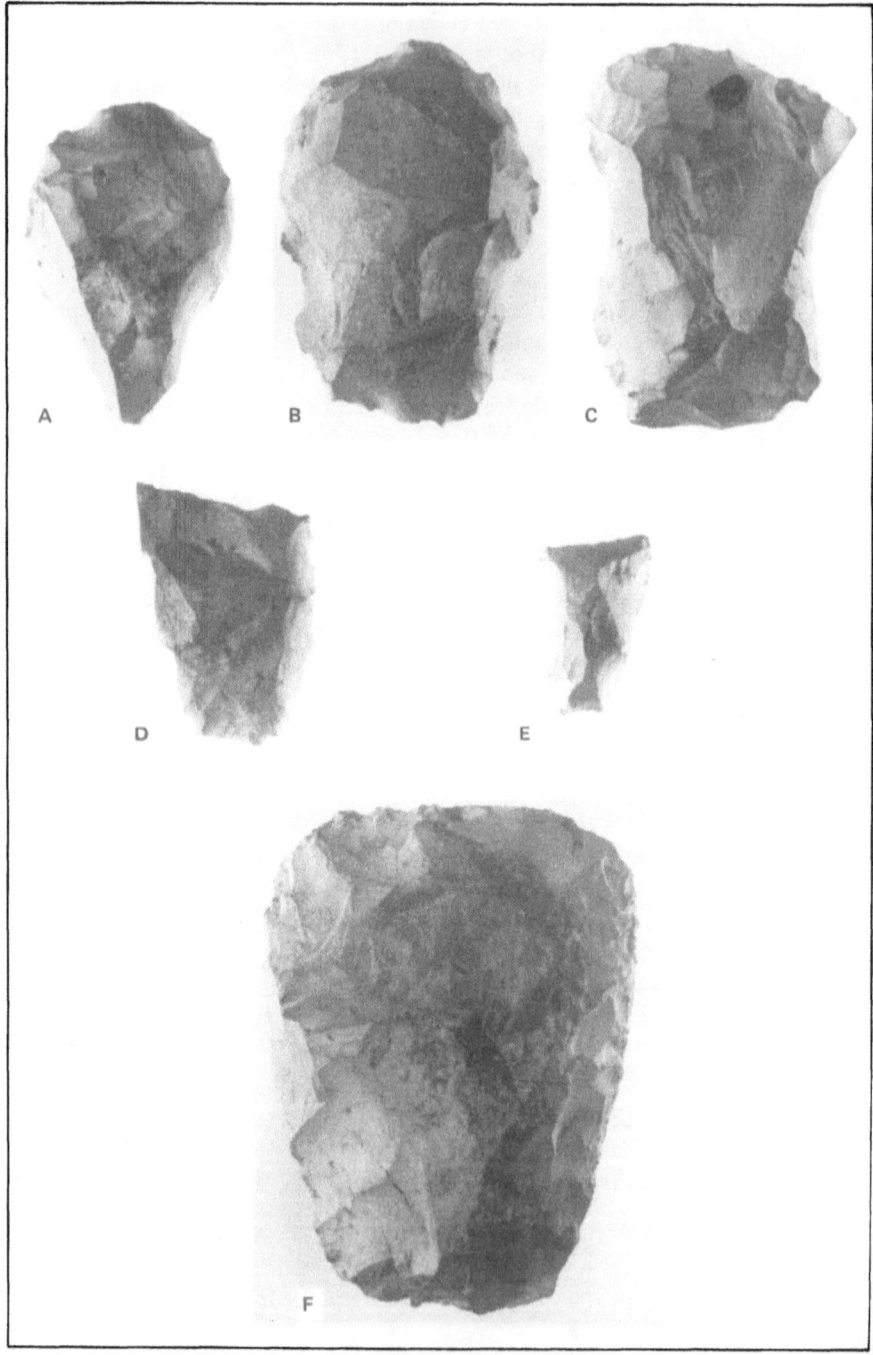

Figure 28. Adzes (A-F). (Note: F is bifacial).

of one lateral side and by ventral flake removal on the other. Both notches are noticeably ground. They are 29 and 33 mm in length and indented 4-5 mm from the side. As with the first specimen, there is blunting and grinding along the top of the dorsal ridge at a point even with the notching. The working edge is subconvex and evidences more careful retouch and shaping than the opposite end. Moreover, use-wear analysis indicates chopping or adzing use on medium to hard materials such as wood.

The next two specimens (Figures 28(D, E)) are much smaller and more triangular in shape—resembling large hafted spokeshaves. They have straight, retouched working edges and laterally retouched margins that taper, again presumably for hafting. Grinding, however, is absent. Both were apparently used for scraping wood.

The final piece (Figure 28(F)) differs in that it is bifacially retouched and trapezoidal. The lateral edges taper and, while one edge appears blunted, blunting is absent on the opposite edge. Flakes have been removed at the butt end making the tool narrower or thinner for easier hafting. Our use-wear analysis, however, indicates no use along what should be the working edge. Rather, use damage occurs along one lateral edge suggesting a function as a hand-axe.

Miscellaneous Uniface

A unique uniface made from a flake or perhaps even blade-like flake (Figure 29) is large (135 X 71 mm), relatively thin (8-13 mm) for its size (156 gm), and could conceivably be placed in the thick uniface class except it displays a greater degree of effort in manufacture than do the members of that class. The uniface's dorsal surface is flaked in a manner similar to that described for Suwannee manufacture: evidence of large flake scars originating from lateral edges crossing the midline of the dorsal surface with shorter, more numerous secondary flake scars present around its entire circumference. The larger flake removals are seen to thin the specimen, while the smaller flake removals shape and sharpen the edges of the tool. No evidence of hafting is seen and, since it is a relatively large tool, it could easily have been used unhafted. Both lateral margins are lightly smoothed, suggesting this tool was used for scraping on less resistant materials such as hide.

Cores

There are four main types of cores in the Harney Flats assemblage: bifacial, unidirectional (polyhedral), multidirectional, and possible micro-cores. Numerous core fragments were also present. Virtually all are of chert.

Bifacial

Of sixteen bifacial cores and fragments recovered from the main excavation areas, two complete chert cores are noteworthy. The first is a large oval piece resembling a "handaxe" (Figure 30), weighing 654 gm and measuring approximately 155 mm X 103 mm, which exhibits large flake scars, presumably from hard percussion flake removals, and appears to be in an early state of preparation. The second specimen, also of chert, recovered during the bulldozer work just outside of Area 2

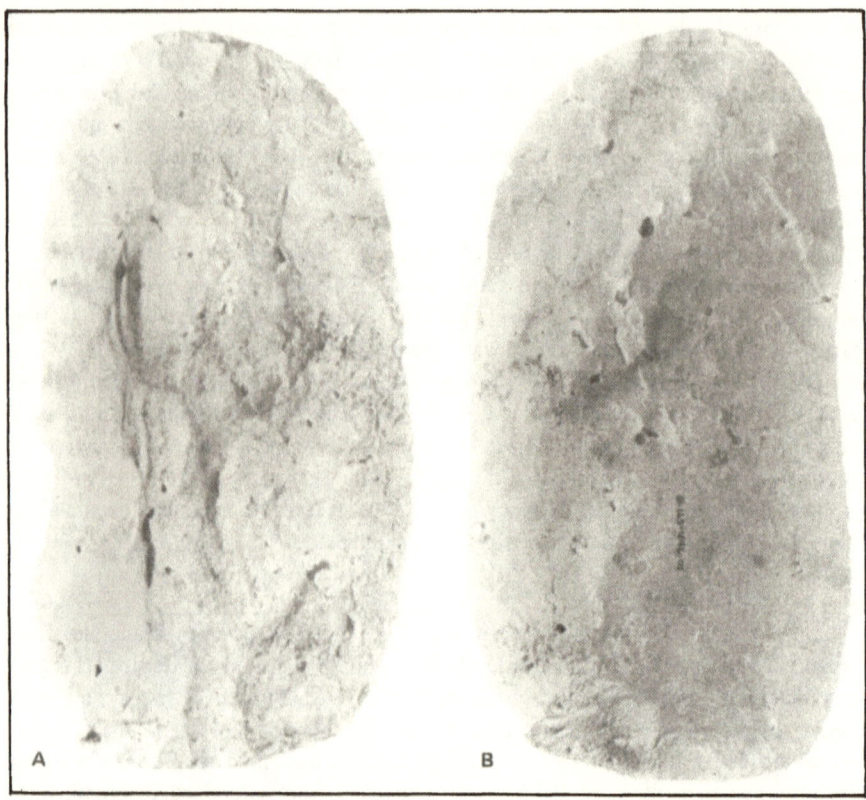

Figure 29. Miscellaneous uniface A–(obverse), miscellaneous uniface B–(reverse).

is more circular in outline (131 mm × 121 mm), weights 766 gm (Figure 30(B)), and also exhibits large flake removals, presumably from early stage reduction. The bifacial core can be used to manufacture flakes for subsequent use, or it can be modified and used as a tool, such as a "handaxe" itself as noted in the bifacial cores recovered from Wells Creek (Dragoo 1973:20).

Unidirectional (Polyhedral)

Most of the eighteen cores of this type exhibited a prepared, flat top (the striking platform) and are cone-shaped from the removal of unidirectional blade-like flakes. Others are wider and more dome-shaped, and resemble large unifaces (and many probably functioned as such). Many of the thick unifaces appeared to have been from reshaped cores. Polyhedral cores, many of which were used as scrapers, were also recovered from Wells Creek (Dragoo 1973:39-42). Selected examples are illustrated in Figure 31.

Multidirectional

Of the thirty-two multidirectional cores most are large, amorphous pieces, some of which weigh several hundred grams. They all exhibit flake removal from

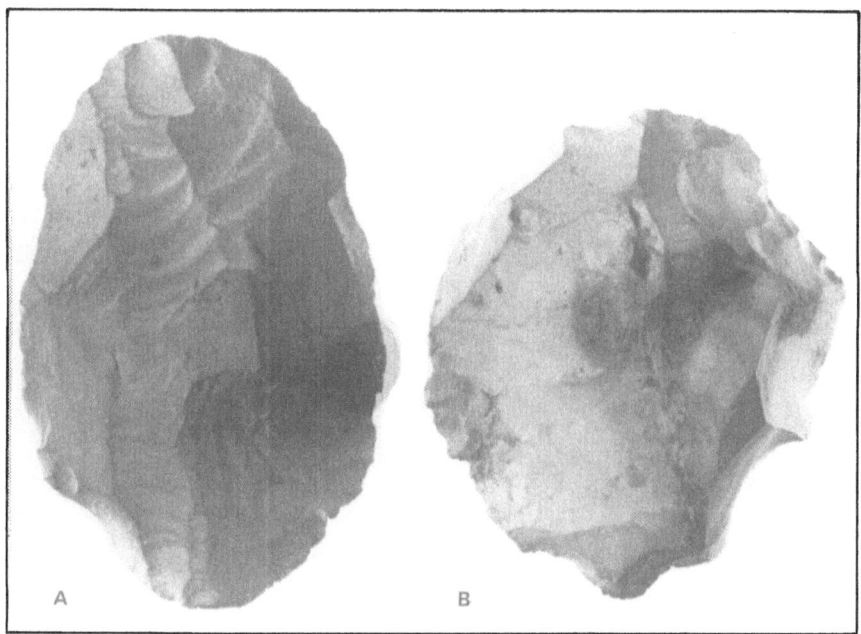

Figure 30. Bifacial cores (A, B).

several different directions; however, almost all the larger specimens contain bands of impurities or inclusions which probably discouraged further reduction. Although they are classified as cores, some of the larger specimens may also have functioned as anvils, as they display small round pits and linear cut-like depressions. These pits appear on the smoother portions of the specimen which are not generally conducive to proper flake removal.

Micro

The final class of cores consists of seven specimens that may be described as micro-cores (Figure 31). They are small, roughly 20-25 mm on a side, range in weight from 6 to 37 gm, and exhibit flake removals from at least two directions, but none would be considered bipolar. Similar specimens have been removed from (mostly) Archaic contexts at other sites in Hillsborough County (e.g., Gagel, 1981: 282; Welsh, 1983:79).

The exact function of these cores is uncertain. They could be used for the production of microliths; however, no microliths were recovered from the site. If microliths were intentionally manufactured, it is possible that, due to their small size and fragility, they could have broken or been missed in the screening process. Alternatively, these specimens could simply represent exhausted cores. Given the proximity of available resources, this seems improbable unless these specimens were used elsewhere, where raw material was not available, and were brought to the site and expended.

Figure 31. Cores and unidirectional cores (A-D), micro-cores (E, F).

ARTIFACT ANALYSIS / 85

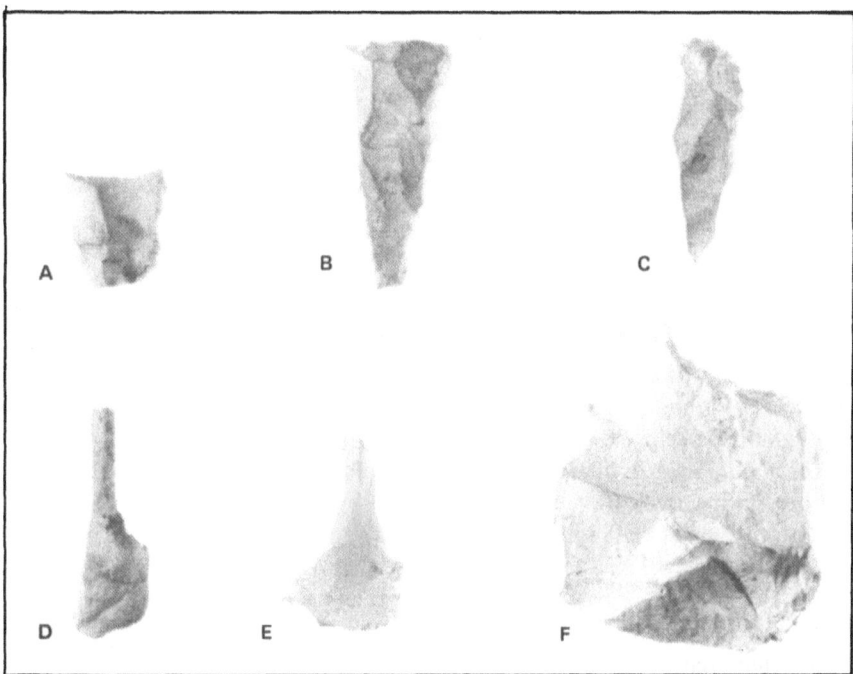

Figure 32. Hafted spokeshaves, A-C and flakes with projections D-F.

Hafted Spokeshaves

Three hafted spokeshaves were recovered from Harney Flats (Figure 32 (A-C)). This tool type was originally defined by Goodyear (1973, 1974), who noted striking similarities between types collected from the Brand site and the central coast region of Florida.

> The hafted spokeshave can be described as having a roughly ovoid-triangular shape from the obverse view with one end tapered by predominant unifacial retouch to give a stemmed effect. The working edge is slightly to deeply concave, formed by steep unifacial retouch, and the variation in the amount of concavity is probably attributable to repeated resharpenings. There are usually two graver spurs on either side of the working concavity but one spur is usually more pronounced. The sides of the stem were heavily ground on all four Brand site specimens indicating the tool was prepared for hafting. Hafting is also suggested by the small size of the tools as it would be difficult to use the implements with much force unless they were hafted to permit greater mechanical leverage (1973:40).

The three Harney Flats specimens are very similar. The first is made of a simple thin flake with a slightly concave working end opposite the striking platform. The lateral edges have been lightly retouched, resulting in a slight tapering towards the striking platform (Figure 32(A)). Slight traces of wear are present on the working

Table 9. Hafted Spokeshave Dimensions

Illustration	Maximum Length (mm)	Maximum Width (mm)	Maximum Thickness (mm)	Weight (gm)
Figure 29(A)	20	18	4	2
Figure 29(B)	41	20	6	6
Figure 29(C)	38	14	4	3

edge. The second is thicker, triangular in shape, and deliberately retouched over its entire dorsal surface (Figure 32(B)). The working edge is straight and the presence of a graver spur is not noted. The lateral margins of the stem are steeply retouched producing a strong tapering effect. The striking platform is absent. The working edge exhibits scraping wear, suggestive of woodworking.

The final specimen differs somewhat from the previous two and from the general description given by Goodyear. Although about the same size as the others, this hafted spokeshave has what appears to be a rounded or convex working end at the proximal end of the flake. Although the striking platform is mostly obscured by retouch, the bulb of percussion is prominent on the ventral surface. Furthermore, lateral retouch extends approximately halfway down the margin where the tapering of the stem appears to have been completed by burin-like blows. Consequently, this tapering results in the stem converging to a point (Figure 32(C). No evidence of use is observed on the rounded "working" edge. The burin-like tip might have been meant to be the working edge, while the opposite end was hafted. Unfortunately, damage at the burin tip prevents determination of this. Dimensions of the three specimens are given in Table 9.

By conducting a simple experiment, Goodyear showed that a socketed tool could quite effectively be used on wood (Goodyear, 1974:52). He thought that bone might also be a material on which this tool was used. He considered this tool to be a probable cultural marker for late Paleo-Indian or Early Archaic contexts in the Southeast. The excavations at Harney Flats corroborate this observation. A large number of these tools (described as small concave endscrapers) were recovered from the Nalcrest site in central Florida (Bullen and Beilman, 1973:6-7), and a number of other specimens from around the state are in the Florida State Museum collections.

Retouched Flakes

Flakes with Projections

Spurred or beaked tools are common in early assemblages (Irwin and Wormington, 1970:29-30; Wilmsen and Roberts, 1978:85). Sometimes they occur as projections such as a graver spur located on an endscraper, or as simple tips or projections on flakes. MacDonald (1968:100) states that the delicate spurs on the flake graver recovered from the Debert site would be suitable for etching designs on bone and antler, while Goodyear (1974:55) claims that gravers could possibly be applied to bone antler, or even wood for perforating or for incising designs.

Table 10. Flakes with Projection Dimensions

Illustration	Maximum Length (mm)	Maximum Width (mm)	Maximum Thickness (mm)	Weight (gm)
Figure 29(A)	37	12	3	1
Figure 29(B)	32	22	6	3
Figure 29(C)	55	52	14	46

Only three flakes with projections were identifed at Harney Flats (Figure 32 (D-F)), but these are not the spurs with small tips typically described (Goodyear, 1974:55). They exhibit an elongated projection made by steep unifacial retouch. The projection is about 19 mm long on the first specimen (Figure 32(D)), and 17 mm on the second (Figure 32(E)), although both are missing their tips and were originally longer. No detectable wear is exhibited on these pieces, although they were probably used as perforators. They look very similar to a specimen from the Vail site (Gramly, 1982:29, Plate 20e). Although the Vail specimen is lumped into a broad category with flakes containing spurs, Gramly described it as an "awl."

The final specimen has a 12 mm long projection near the distal end of a chunky flake of silicified coral. The overall flake morphology of the specimen is evident, as the striking platform is present. The flake is broken at the distal end (Figure 32(F)) and the tip evidences use on medium to harder materials. Dimensions of these tools are given in Table 10.

Blade-like Flakes

True blades are considered to be part of the Paleo-Indian assemblage in general (Irwin and Wormington, 1970), and have been found at early sites in the east (Byers, 1954; Witthoft, 1952). The criteria generally used to identify true blades are a length to width ratio of 2:1 and blade margins that are roughly parallel. In addition there should be flake scars on the dorsal surface evidencing the previous removal of blades in the same direction (Bordes and Crabtree, 1969:1).

Although some of the flakes recovered from Harney Flats may not exactly conform to the above definition, thirty-four were similar enough to be classified as blade-like flakes (Figure 33). Of these, nineteen are complete. Approximately 80 percent of the flakes exhibit some unifacial retouch on their lateral margins. The remaining appears utilized, but exhibit no other modification (Table 7).

These flakes were apparently removed from two core types. Several polyhedral cores, from which these flakes are typically produced, were found at Harney Flats, and most of the recovered blade-like flakes were apparently produced from these cores. In addition, some of the flakes were probably produced from bifacial cores, as they evidenced more of a curved or arched ventral surface longitudinally. This is in contrast to the flatter ventral face generally associated with flakes removed from a polyhedral core.

Figure 33. Blade-like flakes: whole (A-D); broken (E-G).

Hammerstones

Fifty-five hammerstones and twenty-eight hammerstone fragments including several cores recycled as hammerstones were recovered. Three general shapes are present in the group, although there is overlap. The first group is roughly spherical and varies in size from approximately 31-80 mm in diameter. This group included six smaller hammerstones that weighed 20-80 gm (Figure 34(C)). Due to their small size and weight, it is tempting to speculate that these hammerstones were "personal gear" although this, of course, cannot be proven. Regardless, this group certainly contrasts with the larger round hammerstones that ranged in weight to over 500 gm (Figure 34(D, E)).

The second group includes oblong hammerstones that tend to be about one and a half times longer than they are wide (e.g., 119 × 65 mm, 70 × 100 mm, 109 × 63 mm) (Figure 34 (F, G)). They varied in weight from approximately 80 to 560 gm.

ARTIFACT ANALYSIS / 89

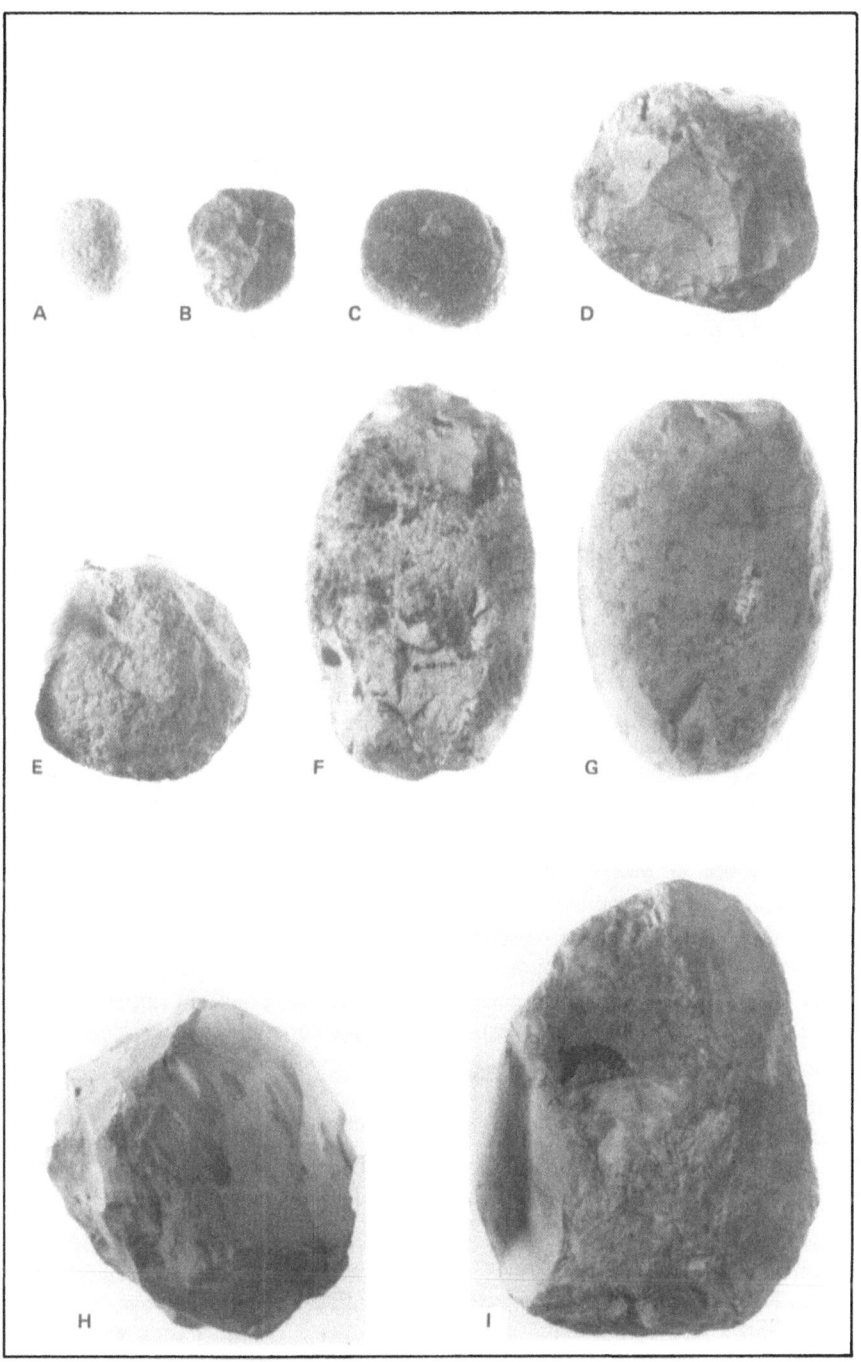

Figure 34. Hammerstones: spherical (A-E); oblong (F, G) and core (H, I).

The final group is more irregularly shaped and consists largely of hammerstones recycled from cores (Figure 34(H)). Their irregular shape is seen as a function of the original core form. They display battering and pitting primarily on former edges or striking platforms and weigh several hundred grams. Of the whole hammerstones, five are silicified coral, one of the small round ones is quartzite, and the remainder are chert. On at least three occasions, two or three hammerstones were found together in the excavations and appeared to have been "cached" for future use.

Abraders

Six pieces of sandstone, three of which definitely functioned as abraders, are also part of the assemblage (Table 11). The first two, found together in an apparent cache in Area 2, are made of foraminiferal packstone, a form of limestone composed of quartz, sand, and phosphate pellets, with abrasive qualities. Outcrops of this sandstone are common in the area; the nearest known source being along Cowhouse Creek just north of the site (Sam Upchurch, personal communication). The first is a blocky piece weighing 501 gm and exhibits two grooves on opposite sides (Figure 35(A)). The first groove running across one flat face for about 75 mm is about 2-5 mm deep, approximately 4-6 mm wide, and appears somewhat U-shaped in cross section. The groove on the opposite flat face is 62 mm long, distinctly more V-shaped in cross section, and is 2-5 mm deep and 4-8 mm wide.

Its companion piece is also blocky, but it is heavier (675 gm) and exhibits no grooves (Figure 35(B)). It is characterized by smooth flat working faces on four sides of the block suggesting that the flat face of the stone was being placed against the material worked. These faces are smooth to the touch in contrast to the rougher, grainy natural surface. Under microscopic examination the grains in the matrix appear worn quite smooth. This piece also exhibits an apparently natural oval depression on one unworked face that could have served as a thumb hold for a better grip on the stone.

Another sandstone piece was also recovered in Area 2, less than 1 m away from the pair described above. It contains larger quartz particles, is smaller (132 gm), and more amorphous in form (Figure 35(E). At least eleven grooves at various locations and angles on the piece vary in length and depth and sometimes cross cut each other.

Table 11. Abrader Dimensions

Illustration	Length (mm)	Width (mm)	Thickness (mm)	Weight (gm)	Comments
Figure 35(A)	95	84	63	502	2 grooves on opposite faces
Figure 35(B)	81	71	71	676	4 flat working faces
Figure 35(E)	73	53	43	132	multiple grooves
Figure 35(F)	39	33	27	38	no apparent use
Figure 35(G)	66	44	25	92	no apparent use
Figure 35(H)	119	64	43	248	no apparent use

ARTIFACT ANALYSIS / 91

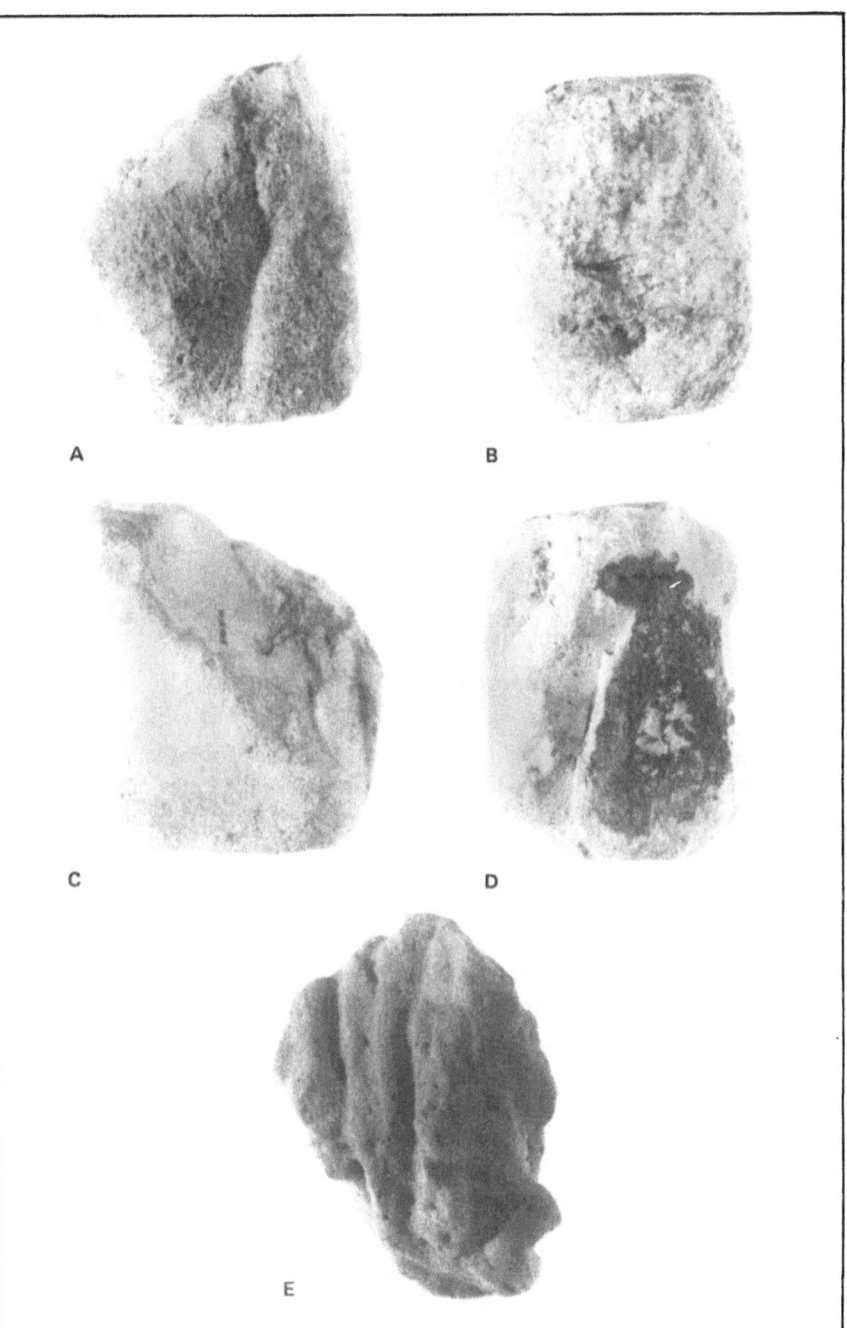

Figure 35. Abraders: Sandstone (obverse) (A, B); sandstone (reverse) (C, D); sandstone (E).

Figure 35. Other abrabers (F, G, H). (Continued)

The longest (56 mm) is also the deepest (5-6 mm), and is somewhat V-shaped in cross section and about 6 mm wide. An adjacent groove is 37 mm long, 5 mm deep and U-shaped in cross section. One short groove or notch at one end of the piece is wider than the group as a whole, being 10-11 mm in width.

The grooved abraders were probably used either for grinding and smoothing the hafted edges of points or for the production of bone implements such as points, pins, and perforators. Bone tools are believed to be an important part of the Paleo-Indian assemblage (Frison and Zeimens, 1980), while bone pins in particular are alleged to be important in Florida for this time period (Waller, 1983). The presence of varied types of bone artifacts can be traced to at least Archaic times in central Florida as evidenced by their recovery from two Archaic cemeteries (Jones, 1981a; Wharton, Ballo, and Hope, 1981). The flat abrader may have been used for bone working.

The three remaining pieces of sandstone were recovered from Area 3. Unlike the specimens described above, they exhibit no grooves or apparent utilization and may be fragments of larger pieces (Figure 35(F-H)).

Exotics

The artifacts in this category are grouped on the basis of their unique material rather than any particular form or function. Evidence of use on these specimens is difficult to determine, and the following descriptions of their function are speculative at best. All appear to be of metamorphic rock not indigenous to the Tampa Bay area (Upchurch, 1984).

ARTIFACT ANALYSIS / 93

The first two specimens (Figure 36(A, B)) were recovered as an apparent cache from a test pit in Area 1. The first (Figure 36(A)) is roughly semi-circular in shape, weighs 464 gm, and may exhibit some attempts at flaking along its convex edge; however, this material obviously does not lend itself to predictable knapping as does the local cryptocrystalline material. Based upon its shape and size, it could have functioned as a handaxe. Its companion piece (Figure 36(B)) is approximately the same size (509 gm), but more rectangular. No attempts at flaking are seen; however, one surface is concave and appears smoothed or polished, suggesting its function as a possible plane or abrader.

Another specimen (Figure 36(C)) is smaller (342 gm) than the previous two and is roughly wedge-shaped. One flat surface is smoothed and could have been utilized for abrading. It was recovered from Area 2 near three sandstone abraders.

The final metamorphic rock is a large amorphous piece that weighs 4536 gm. Due to its extreme size and location in a test pit in Area 3, it probably functioned as an anvil.

The presence of "exotic" (i.e., non-local) stone in Paleo-Indian assemblages is not uncommon. Most "exotic" raw material in early sites is thought to be the result of group mobility (Goodyear, 1979). Different lithic raw materials are gathered as a group travels through different regions. Since exotic materials usually consist of cryptocrystalline stone used in the manufacture of tools, the metamorphic rocks at Harney Flats do not fit the stone raw material needs generally exhibited in Paleo-Indian collections. It cannot be knapped in as predictable a fashion as the stone

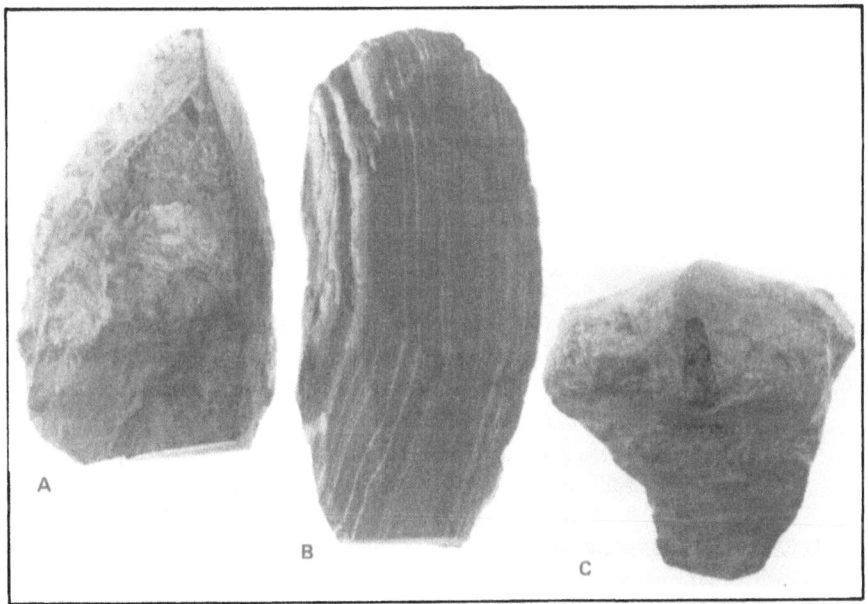

Figure 36. Exotics (A-C).

they typically used for tools. Since all of the proposed functions of these specimens are apparently duplicated by tools made of native stone in the assemblage the presence of this material at the site is somewhat puzzling, especially if the nearest source is some 800 km to the north.

Two points, however, would appear to argue against accepting a group mobility explanation for the presence of the metamorphic rock at Harney Flats. First, only local cherts were found in the examination of the sampled tools from the site (Upchurch, 1984). If group movement included travel into the piedmont area of central Georgia (or elsewhere), it would seem likely that cryptocrystalline stone, as well as metamorphic rock, would be gathered and used from these areas. Why then, are no examples of cryptocrysalline stone from outside the immediate vicinity of the Tampa Bay area represented in the sample?

Secondly, the size of these specimens (particularly the possible anvil) would seem prohibitively large for normal group mobility. Evidence of exotic material in other Paleo-Indian sites is present in the form of broken and exhausted tools or debitage; rather than completed specimens, as is present at Harney Flats (Goodyear, 1979:9). Comparable examples are apparently unknown from reported Paleo-Indian sites.

Nevertheless, the stone did reach the site by some mechanism. Excluding procurement of stone as a function of mobility or a special procurement trip (Binford, 1979; Goodyear, 1979), one possible alternative exists. These specimens might be the result of trade or exchange between different bands. Along this line, it is tempting to view this stone as representing evidence for some type of interband exchange (e.g., Sahlins, 1972:281-282). This, of course, is speculative.

DEBITAGE ANALYSIS

The lithic debitage was analyzed in terms of a reduction trajectory to determine at what stage cores and tools arrived at and left the site. To this end, all flakes were sorted into the following categories:

1. *Primary decortication*—any flake or shatter fragment that had a dorsal face completely covered by cortex material. Not to be confused with inclusions.
2. *Secondary decortication*—any flake or shatter fragment that exhibited any other amount of cortex on the dorsal face.
3. *Non-decortication*—any flake that did not have any cortex on its dorsal face. This category was initially divided into the two subcategories described below; however, these have been combined for the purposes of our analysis.
    a. *Thinning flakes*—all diagnostic flakes with complete or partial striking platforms, including broken flakes with platforms.
    b. *Other flakes*—all other characteristic flat, thin flakes without striking platforms.
4. *Shatter*—all non-directional striking debitage. Usually angular, chunky fragments that do not exhibit the characteristic flat face of a true flake.
5. *Cortex fragments*—fragments of cortex without parent stone.
6. *Utilized flakes*—any flake that exhibited use-wear scars only; no manufacturing.

This classification categorizes the relative amounts of the early and late stages of tool manufacture or maintenance by measuring the amount of cortex present in the flake sample. Although not an ideal method, along with measurements of the relative weight of flakes, this technique can provide a fair assessment of position in a reduction trajectory.

This classification is similar to the Bifacial Thinning Flake Model used by House and Ballenger (1976:89-93) and House and Wogaman (1978:59-60). This model attempts to determine whether debitage represents the waste from tool manufacture or maintenance. Some reservations have been voiced about the model's assumptions (Goodyear et al., 1979:159) and its use at Harney Flats is obviously questionable, since a large number of unifacial tools were used and manufactured at the site. With few exceptions (see below), attempts to distinguish flakes removed from bifaces from flakes removed from unifaces are not likely to be successful. Preliminary experimental results indicate that distinctions between biface and uniface production flakes cannot be made with any degree of confidence (Austin and Jackson, 1983).

Some pieces of debitage, however, could be placed in a biface or uniface category. The uniface fragment category includes small tool fragments that were found among the debitage, which appear to have been broken in use or manufacture. Often, inclusions or material flaws were present. Also included in this category are what have been described as uniface retouch flakes (Shafer, 1970) that possess remnants of the edges of unifacial tools that usually served as the striking platform (Figure 37(A-F)). Bulbs of percussion and ripple marks caused by the force of the blow are sometimes present. These flakes are believed to result from either manufacture or resharpening.

Most of the retouch flakes would fall into one of two categories described by Shafer. The first includes pieces formed by striking the ventral surface of the uniface, while the second includes pieces formed by striking the dorsal surface near the edge of the tool.

For flakes of the first category, the ventral surface of the tool is the striking platform (Figure 37(A-D)). This technique involves striking the ventral surface of the scraper near the edge to remove a section of the trimmed edge. This method created a sharp new edge with an angle suitable for scraping (varying from about 40°-70°) (Shafer, 1970:484).

The second category consists of flakes formed by striking the uniface at its retouched edge at an angle to remove a flake from the ventral surface (Figure 37(E, F)). Consequently, the striking platform is a portion of the working edge of the uniface. Technically, this creates a biface; however, the general plano-convex cross section of the tool is retained.

A third flake category (those removed by the burin technique) is also described by Shafer, but few of the Harney Flats flakes could be confidently assigned to this category. Flakes in this category are removed by blows to the working edge of the flake so that spalls are removed transversely, obliquely, or longitudinally, depending on the angle of the blow in relation to the edge. No attempt was made to quantify the different unifacial fragments beyond counts by provenience.

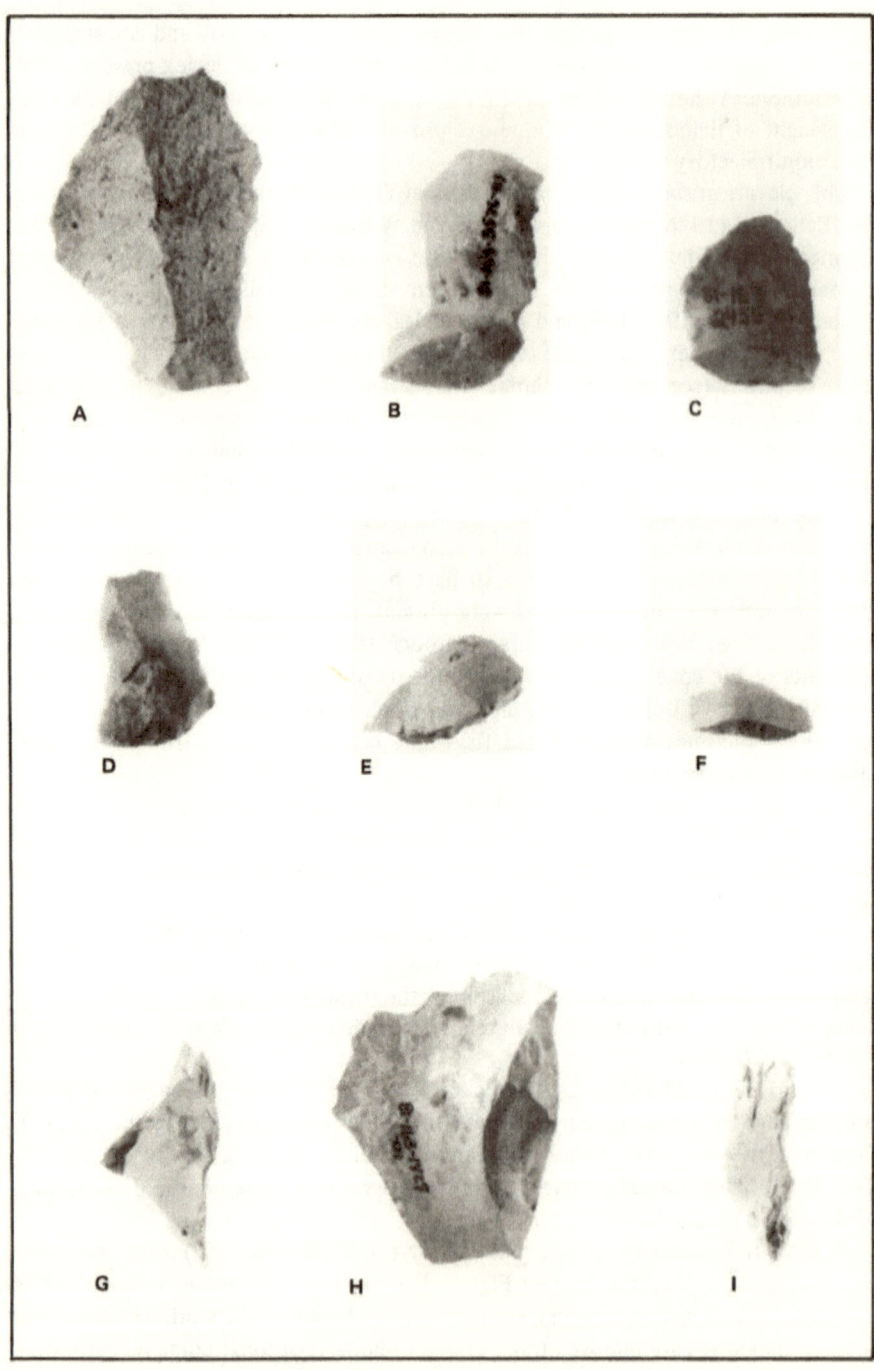

Figure 37. Uniface retouch flakes (A-F) and biface fragments (G-I).

Another flake category present in the debitage assemblage consists of biface fragments, which can be distinguished by a striking platform that is usually faceted, as it includes a small part of one side of the biface. Most of these pieces are small, and they appear to result from manufacture errors or unsuccessful attempts at bifacial thinning. An example of this would be an "overshot termination" flake (Callahan, 1979: 85-86). Some examples of biface fragments are shown in Figure 37(G-I)).

A final category consists of utilized flakes that exhibit some form of edge scarring produced by use rather than intentional modification. Since these flakes were not examined in as much detail as the intentionally modified tools, the counts should be viewed with some caution. Although the utilized flakes were not systematically studied, it is our impression that they were simply waste flakes from tool manufacture or core reduction, rather than blade-like flakes that were intentionally modified to a specific shape.

CHAPTER 5
Intra-Site Spatial Analysis

Elucidating the internal spatial structure of Harney Flats was a major factor in determining the excavation design. Test pits were placed to locate the early component and any significant areas of occupational concentrations within it. Subsequently, the large contiguous area excavations coupled with point provenience mapping of certain artifact classes was designed to reveal the assemblage composition within each area as well as any patterning in the association of tool classes or activity loci.

STATISTICAL TECHNIQUES

Spatial analysis of activity patterning has long been recognized as an important feature in the analysis of archaeological site remains. Important concepts related to spatial analysis include "toolkit," "activity," and "activity area." Recently, Binford proposed refined definitions of these important concepts (1983:147-148).

A toolkit is a set of tools used in the execution of a task. An activity is an integrated set of tasks, generally performed in a temporal sequence and in an uninterrupted fashion. Identical tasks may be integrated with different activities: for example, the task of cutting meat may be integrated with the activity of butchering or preparation of meat for cooking or eating. Activity areas are places, facilities, or surfaces where technological, social, or ritual activities occur. We can readily imagine individual activities which make use of a number of toolkits and, conversely, different activities which utilized one or more identical toolkits.

Many of these concepts came from a model of spatial patterning presented by Whallon (1973a:115-130), one of the first to investigate statistical techniques of spatial analysis. Whallon's models of the distribution of human activities across space is based on the idea:

> ... that at least some activities will result in the differential distribution of tool types over an occupation area as a consequence of their different uses in the various activities carried out at the site (1973a:116).

Whallon argued that there was a need for a certain separation in activities across space; however, he cautioned that:

> ... our arguments do not necessitate the constant spatial separation of all activities into mutually exclusive areas, only that some activities must, at least, some of the time, be spatially distinct (1973a:117).

He also recognized the important differences in the properties of a living cultural system and the archaeological context in which these properties might be observed. This distinction is particularly important in interpreting patterns observed in the archaeological record.

Schiffer's concept (1972, 1976) of site formational processes is a profitable perspective from which to examine these differences. The recognition of how site formation processes influence the archaeological record is important in drawing inferences from perceived artifact associations.

Whallon attempted to establish a methodological basis for the analysis of patterning among artifacts scattered over occupation surfaces (1973b:266-278; 1974a:16-34) following three steps: 1) determine if the distribution is uniform, random, or clustered; 2) delineate the nonrandom concentrations; and 3) measure the association of artifact concentrations on occupation floors. Most quantitative forms of spatial analysis have generally used this or a similar approach.

Archaeologists have encountered problems with early techniques of spatial analysis. While methods such as nearest neighbor analysis, and various forms of quadrat analysis have enabled archaeologists to become more rigorous in their spatial analysis, the results have often been inconsistent or difficult to interpret. Perhaps the most telling criticisms have been those addressing the applicability of the statistical techniques themselves, since they are borrowed from geography and plant ecology (Riley, 1974:489-490), and the set of assumptions may or may not always apply to archaeological examples.

As a result of further work, Whallon (1978:27-35) outlined a few problems that he had encountered, which occurred at all levels of spatial analysis: a typology problem (using morphological types to form functional areas), the problem of determining at what scale the "patterning" can be observed, and the problem of multiple scales of patterning or clustering. Moreover, statistical tests require the assumption that clusters will be uniform in size, shape and density. This, of course, will not always be true.

More recently, another drawback to these "traditional" quantitative techniques has been identified. This is one of the "context" of a given situation which has not been particularly tailored to archaeological needs and refers to information known in addition to the location of artifacts (Kintigh and Ammerman, 1982:32).

> For example, nearest neighbor analysis uses only point locations in space; however, in formulating an interpretation of a settlement map, human analysts employ the site locations displayed on a map along with general and specific knowledge of the environment, geography, and human behavior.

In short, as Whallon (1978:32) himself has noted, the traditional models and methods of spatial analysis have been for the most part over-simplified and misleading, but currently, there are few alternatives. Although some new techniques have been proposed, presumably in response to some of the problems mentioned above (e.g., Berry et al., 1983:547-553), they remain unevaluated.

In summary, methods of spatial analysis in archaeology are still under development. No one method has yet emerged as being appropriate to interpret site structure.

This should come as no surprise, as archaeological sites are often the result of complex interactions of many processes, both cultural and natural, that can exert considerable influence on the archaeological record.

CONTRIBUTIONS OF ETHNOARCHAEOLOGY

Archaeologists have turned to the study of modern hunter-gatherers to obtain models for the interpretation of archaeological remains. Of particular importance for our study is the work aimed at correlating site assemblage patterns and behavioral events. Although not an alternative to statistical methods of determining spatial patterning, ethnoarchaeology offers interesting potential for interpreting the results that statistical methods give us. Eventually it may prove to be one of the best methods for accurately interpreting observed patterns in the archaeological record.

Among the more important studies is Yellen's investigation of the Dobe Bushmen of the Kalahari desert in which he proposed a general model for Bushmen residential camps which he called the Ring Model (1977:125-131). In ideal form this would consist of huts composed of nuclear families grouped in a circle. The greater the number of huts, the more the camp conforms to a circular shape. Moreover, the huts are located around the circumference with entrances facing the center of the circle. The organization of space within the camp includes nuclear areas in and around the huts and family hearth (e.g., for eating and for manufacturing activities), a communal area in the center of the hut circle (e.g., for dancing and the first distribution of meat), and special activity areas (e.g., hide scraping and bread roasting) outside the hut circle (1977:85-97). This, of course, is an idealized model and is dependent upon such factors as the time of season, length of stay as well as the number of people, and as Yellen notes, may not always be useful to archaeologists (1977:130-131).

One of the more interesting results of Yellen's work is his questioning the traditional notion, which he attributed to both Whallon and Binford, of assuming a functional correlation between type of activity and distinct clusters of debris. The assumption of activity specific areas that underlies a number of analyses is overly simplistic. He concludes that:

> ... it is unfounded to assume that activities are spatially segregated or arranged by type within a single camp. Most tasks may be carried out in more than one place and in more than one social context; and, conversely, in any single area, one can find the remains of many activities all jumbled together (1977:134).

Binford responded, implying that Yellen misunderstood his model. Based on his own ethnoarchaeological work, Binford acknowledges that generalized work areas can occur; however, he maintains that such areas where many activities have taken place still have meaningful information for inferring past behavior. He is quick to point out that specialized activity areas do indeed exist on some sites, as even Yellen's work shows (Binford, 1978:355). The argument will not be pursued here except to note that Schiffer (1981:355) regards the differences between Binford and Yellen as more philosophical than empirical.

Recently, Binford (1983:144-192) presented a model of site structure based on his ethnoarchaeological work (primarily with the Nunamiut Eskimo). His inferences are important as they relate general spatial patterns to particular activities he observed. For example, a group of seated persons working around an outside hearth often results in a distinct pattern of semi-circular or doughnut shaped disposal zones referred to as drop or toss zones.

> The debris which was dropped produced a ring of small items centered around the hearth; the disposal of large items, however, was different, these objects being tossed behind the people away from the sitting area (1983:153).

The drop zone can be made up of small items such as tiny bone chips created by breaking open bones for marrow or lithic debitage from the reduction of cores. The distribution of larger items reflects preventive maintenance as they are tossed away from the seating area. This can take place in front of or behind the group. The presence of several individuals around a hearth, however, can contribute to variability in the content and distribution of debris.

Binford noted three different modes of disposal around a hearth.

> ... (1) dropping discrete items *in situ*, (2) tossing away discrete items, and (3) tossing away aggregated items *en masse*. In the case of dropping, the items tend to come to rest in the immediate area where they were processed or worked; larger items or aggregates of smaller items, in contrast, are tossed to the periphery of the work areas where they were used (1983:154).

Binford (1983:156-163) also demonstrated variability in patterning depending on whether activities take place inside or outside a house. Outside and inside hearths, for example, vary in their distribution of ash. Hearths used for cooking inside are usually stone-lined to prevent the spreading of ash inside the house. Outside hearths, on the other hand, are usually not contained and generally appear spread out and smeared. In addition, distinctive dump and toss zones generally do not occur inside a house because wastes are rarely thrown against the walls of a home. Inside spaces are more intensively used, cleaned, and maintained. "Door dumps" just outside entrances to huts have been associated with this activity.

Extensive activity areas have also been discussed by Binford (1983:165) who notes that since these activities are usually done from a standing position, they result in large scatters of debris. Examples in the form of debris from roasting pits, animal butchering, and hide working are given. An important realization from this work is the extensive amount of space used in these activities, when compared to the usually small amount of space that is excavated archaeologically. Another interesting observation in considering site structure is that such activities usually take place peripheral to the residential area. It is generally true, in fact, that activities like roasting and butchering, which monopolize considerable amounts of space, are located away from areas used intensively on a day to day basis (1983:170).

Binford has combined these elements and attempted to form a preliminary (general) model of site structure: Although a range of variability is seen ethnographically, some patterns can be detected; similar patterns are found among different hunter-gatherer groups in the spacing of houses, sleeping areas, and external hearths as a result of the size of the human body, which he feels is the primary conditioning factor in the camp structure.

> ... since these properites are the same for all humans, it is no wonder that there is a tremendous degree of repetitiveness in the spatial measurements of camps used by hunters and gatherers (Binford, 1983:173).

Finally, some additional factors influence the structure of archaeological sites especially the effect of long term use. Both Binford (1983:189-190) and Yellen (1977:75-77) demonstrate that the longer a camp is occupied the more diverse are the activities that are likely to be conducted there. Yellen stated that subsistence activities varied with the environmental zone exploited, but nevertheless occurred daily. The occurrence of maintenance tasks, however, was less certain and appeared to be a function of length of occupation, (i.e., the longer a particular camp was occupied, the greater the chances a particular maintenance task would be carried out). In addition, such work has suggested that the longer the occupation, the greater the number of the expected special purpose activity areas peripheral to the main living area. Similarly, a strong relationship between length of occupation of a site and the amount of effort expended in its maintenance can also be expected.

Along these lines, Schiffer (1972:156-165; 1976) has argued that archaeologists must distinguish between primary and secondary refuse in discussions of waste or debris as it relates to disposal. Primary refuse is material discarded in the general location of use. Deposits accumulated in toss zones or drop zones as described above would be examples of this type of refuse. Secondary refuse, on the other hand, consists of material discarded away from its location of use. Items accumulated as a result of use and discarded in the same area and items simply accumulated in a disposal area cause two different patterns of refuse disposal that need to be distinguished.

INTRA-AREA ANALYSIS

Our understanding of the site formation processes at Harney Flats suggests that although the archaeological materials were deposited during three distinct periods (corresponding to the Suwannee, Bolen, and Newnan components), the main geological deposition occurred subsequent to the Bolen and prior to or during the Newnan occupation. No significant stratigraphic separation could be found between the Suwannee and Bolen points, but a significant stratigraphic break was found between the earlier materials and the later Newnan points. While the early levels at Harney Flats are as "pure" an early component as is known from Florida (and perhaps the Southeast), they probably reflect a number of separate occupations on a stabilized land surface during the Suwannee-Bolen time period. These different occupational episodes were not separately buried and individually preserved, and our distribution maps of artifacts should not be interpreted as representing discrete living floors.

Given that some vertical displacement of artifacts occurred, the present analysis assumes that the horizontal depositional context of artifacts has not been badly disturbed, but we know of no way of measuring such a transformation. Most relevant literature on the subject emphasizes vertical as opposed to horizontal displacement of artifacts. Hence, we view any horizontal post depositional displacement as typically being non-cultural.

Work focused on block excavations in three separate areas thought to represent (possibly functionally) distinct areas of occupation within the site. Such areas have been identified in other Paleo-Indian sites and a preliminary model of living areas separate from special activity areas will be presented. We propose to apply this model at Harney Flats by emphasizing an inter-area analysis in much the same way that other early sites with broad-scale patterning were examined. If significant differences are found among the areas, these differences would constitute evidence for site structure—given that the areas are from widely separate parts of the site. An additional assumption, of course, is that the artifacts deposited in the areas reflect these presumed functional differences.

Each large area may be made up of smaller activity areas or loci of particular behavioral events. However, while particular patterns or clusters of items may exist on a fine grain level, our understanding of the site formation processes at Harney Flats makes determination of these particularly difficult.

Although attempts are being made to refine such patterning, the data are simply presented here with our preliminary interpretations. Each area will be discussed individually focusing first on the distribution of lithic debitage followed by the distribution of tools of each class.

Unlike tools, which may be manufactured, used, and discarded in different locations, lithic debitage is frequently found in primary refuse deposits. Consequently, its distribution might well reflect the distribution of activity areas across a site. This also appears to be the case for small fragments of broken tools, resharpening flakes or any general by-product of tool using activities (cf. Whallon, 1978:34; Cahen et al., 1979:682). These residues will most likely fall at the location of use and "barring extraordinarily careful cleanup or severe disturbance, that is where we will find them" (Cahen et al., 1979:682). Such areas are likely to correspond to Binford's "drop zones."

Our analysis of the debitage categories focuses on the study of SYMAPs. The recovered waste flakes were divided into categories that would permit us to observe the lithic reduction trajectory in stages. Distribution maps of piece-plotted specimens of each tool class were also generated and nearest-neighbor statistics were calculated. There are, of course, many problems associated with the use of this test and we do not mean to imply that this test yields behaviorally significant results; nor do we assume that each distribution represents a discrete living floor. We are merely using this method of analysis as a heuristic device to describe the nature of patterning.

This exercise has, if nothing else, illustrated some of the better known problems with the method. Virtually all tool classes were clustered. This proved somewhat difficult to interpret when each distribution was examined. For example, when a distance equal to 1.65 standard deviations above the mean nearest neighbor distance was employed as the cut-off (Whallon, 1974a:23), clusters of artifacts that almost covered an entire excavated area were obtained. Such results are, of course, unsatisfactory and unrealistic.

Area 1

Debitage Analysis

Figure 38 is a SYMAP representing the distribution (by count) of all debitage in Area 1. Total counts are not high, ranging from 13 to 112 per m^2. The flakes are generally very small with most units having a total weight of less than 167 gm. Several isolated high density areas are evident, and tend to be relatively small, on the order of 1-2 m in diameter. In addition, several larger areas of low density are also noticeable. This distribution is almost identical to that of non-decortication flakes.

Secondary decortication flakes are the second most numerous type; however, counts are also low, ranging from 0-34 m^2. As with the non-decortication flakes, isolated locations of medium to high density (between 1 and 34 m^2) are dispersed across Area 1. For the most part these locations do not overlap with the high density non-decortication flake clusters, with relatively low counts, significance is questionable.

The distributions of primary decortication flakes, shatter, and cortex fragments, generally exhibit a homogeneous distribution of counts across the area. Some small areas of relatively greater density are present, but these densities are still extremely low, making any meaningful distinctions difficult. Counts for primary decortication and shatter flakes vary from 0-4 per square meter. Most of the cortex fragment counts are under 11, but a few squares have counts between 11 and 17. A few of these flake types appear in many units evenly distributed across the area, although the higher counts generally occur away from the high density of non-decortication flakes.

Tool Distribution

The distribution of all artifacts in Area 1 is shown in Figure 39. The distribution of cores and core fragments is a clustered pattern. Three or four groups are observable: one in the northeast corner of the area; one in the center of the area; and one or two in the southwest corner. Some specimens are also present in the southeast excavation block, but not enough of the area is open to reveal any real patterning.

A somewhat clustered distribution is also suggested for the bifaces. One large, somewhat oval group of fifteen artifacts is present just west of the center of the area. The horizontal position of the Bolen points in relation to the Suwannee points is noteworthy. Three Bolens or portions thereof lie together in the large oval cluster with a Simpson preform base on one side and a Suwannee base and preform on the other. Two other notched points lie dispersed nearer the edges of the excavation. Although not conclusive, the small cluster of three Bolens at least suggests a deposition separate from the Suwannees and some chronological separation may be inferred.

Also of interest here are the pieces of a broken Suwannee preform. The base was recovered from the main excavation block (123S/32E-H) while the tip was recovered approximately 5.5 m to the southeast outside of the excavation area in a bulldozer trench. If the horizontal positions of the artifacts within the site are relatively unaltered, then the separation of these two pieces may possibly be accounted for by the

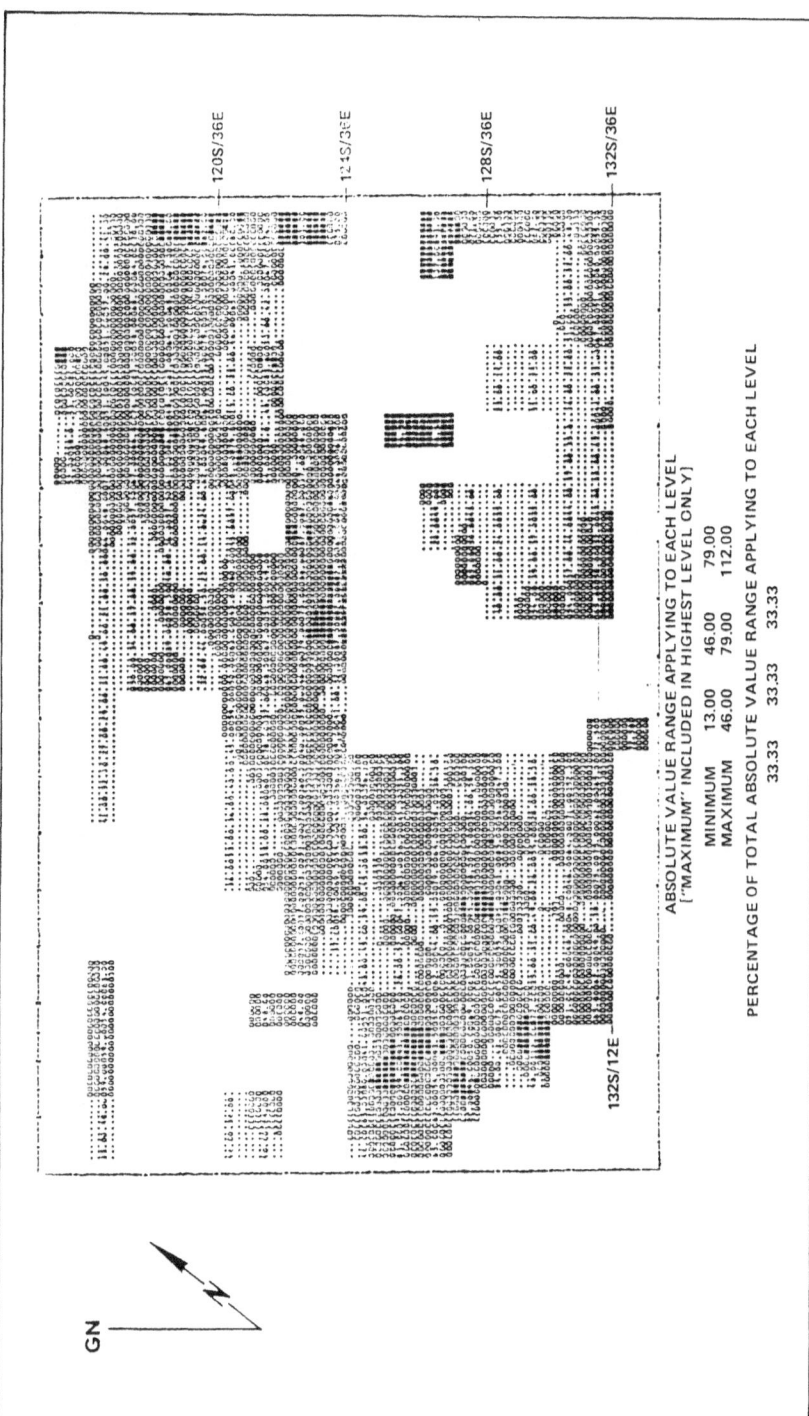

Figure 38. SYMAP distribution of total debitage counts for Area 1.

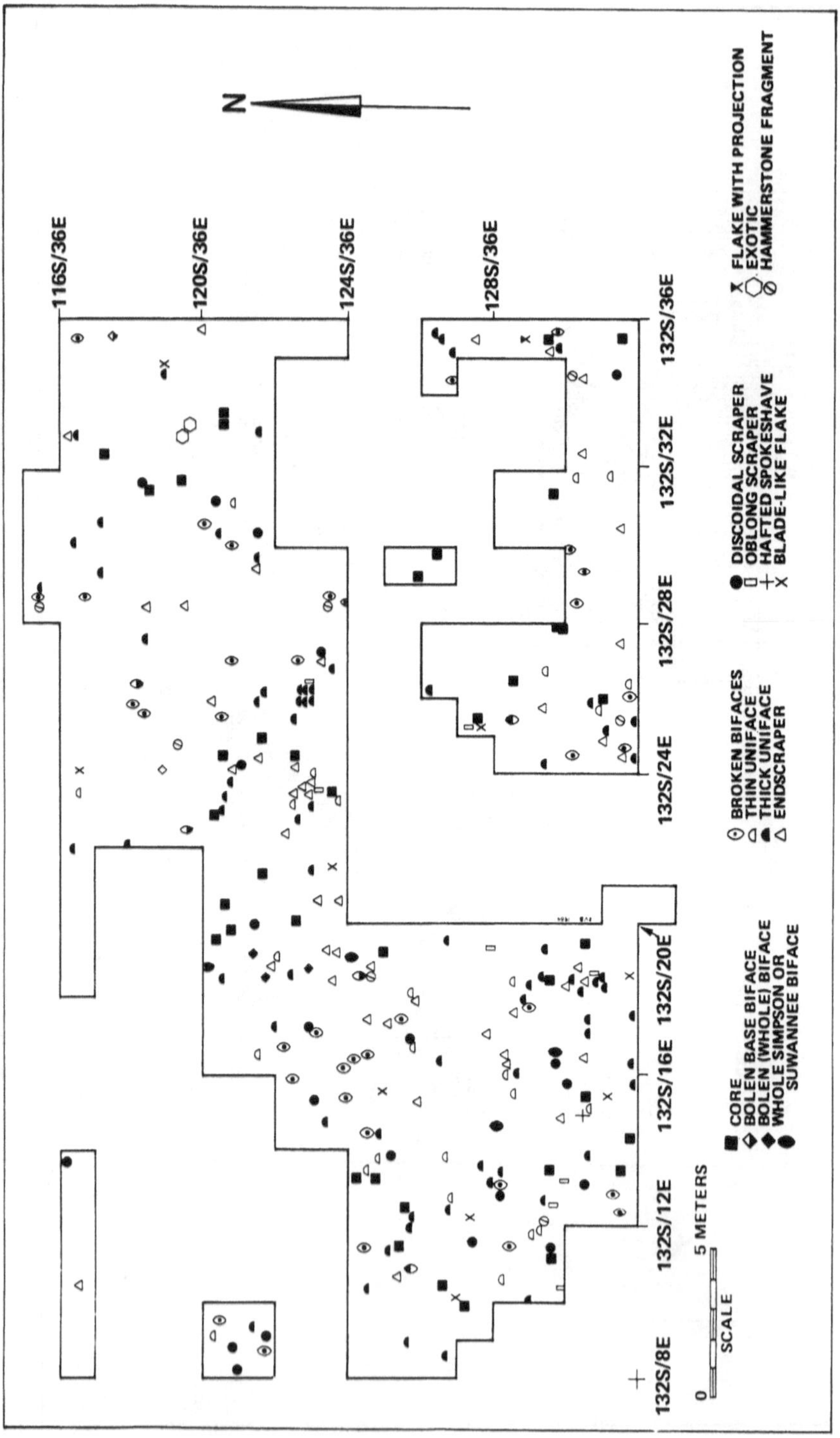

Figure 39. Area 1 artifact proveniences.

ethnoarchaeologically described tossing behavior. Moreover, this same phenomenon has been observed in other sites in the region.

Ruling out excessive bioturbation and extreme fracture displacement, we propose that this phenomenon may have been caused by what we term emotional displacement. It is possible that during the time immediately following the fracture of a nearly completed implement, the frustrated manufacturer displayed his anger by excessively discarding one or more of the remaining fragments (Austin and Ste. Claire, 1982:187).

The thick unifaces are well distributed across Area 1 as mostly isolated occurrences, making but two large clusters present. The first consists of ten artifacts and is located just east of the center of Area 1 near the southern edge of the excavation. The second consists of eleven artifacts and is located in the southwest corner. The distribution of the thin unifaces, on the other hand, is mostly confined to the southwest corner of the excavation area and occurs in clusters of two and three.

The highest percentage of endscrapers among the three areas was recovered from Area 1. They are found in small clusters grouped across the southern edge of the large excavation block in Area 1. The arc includes three main clusters that are 6-7 m^2 in size, and composed of eight to nine artifacts each including three or four proximal ends. The remaining specimens are mostly whole. Isolated occurrences are present, especially in the southeastern block, but not enough of the area was excavated to discern any patterning.

The remaining curated unifaces exhibit much less tendency to cluster. The distribution of discoidal scrapers shows no real clustering. The presence of so few oblong scrapers likewise makes any clustering difficult to determine. Almost all of the specimens are located near the edge of the excavation area.

The spread of hammerstones is not particularly revealing. Most are fragments, occurring near the edge of the exacavation. Also included are the isolated occurrences of a hafted spokeshave, a flake with a projection, and the two exotics, which likely represent a cache and are probably the best example of a behavioral event that can be currently identified in Area 1.

Area 2

Debitage Distribution

The distribution of all debitage in Area 2 has counts ranging from 10-232 pieces per square meter (Figure 40). Flake counts steadily increase toward the southern half of the area, with the highest density occurring in the southern portion. A similar distribution is reflected in the flake weight per square meter. The debitage weight per square ranges from 3-391 gm^2, but most of the occurrences are under 261 gm.

Non-decortication flakes are the major component of the assemblage in this area, their distribution is virtually identical to the total flake count distribution. Counts range from 3-186 per square meter with the highest density along the southern edge of the area.

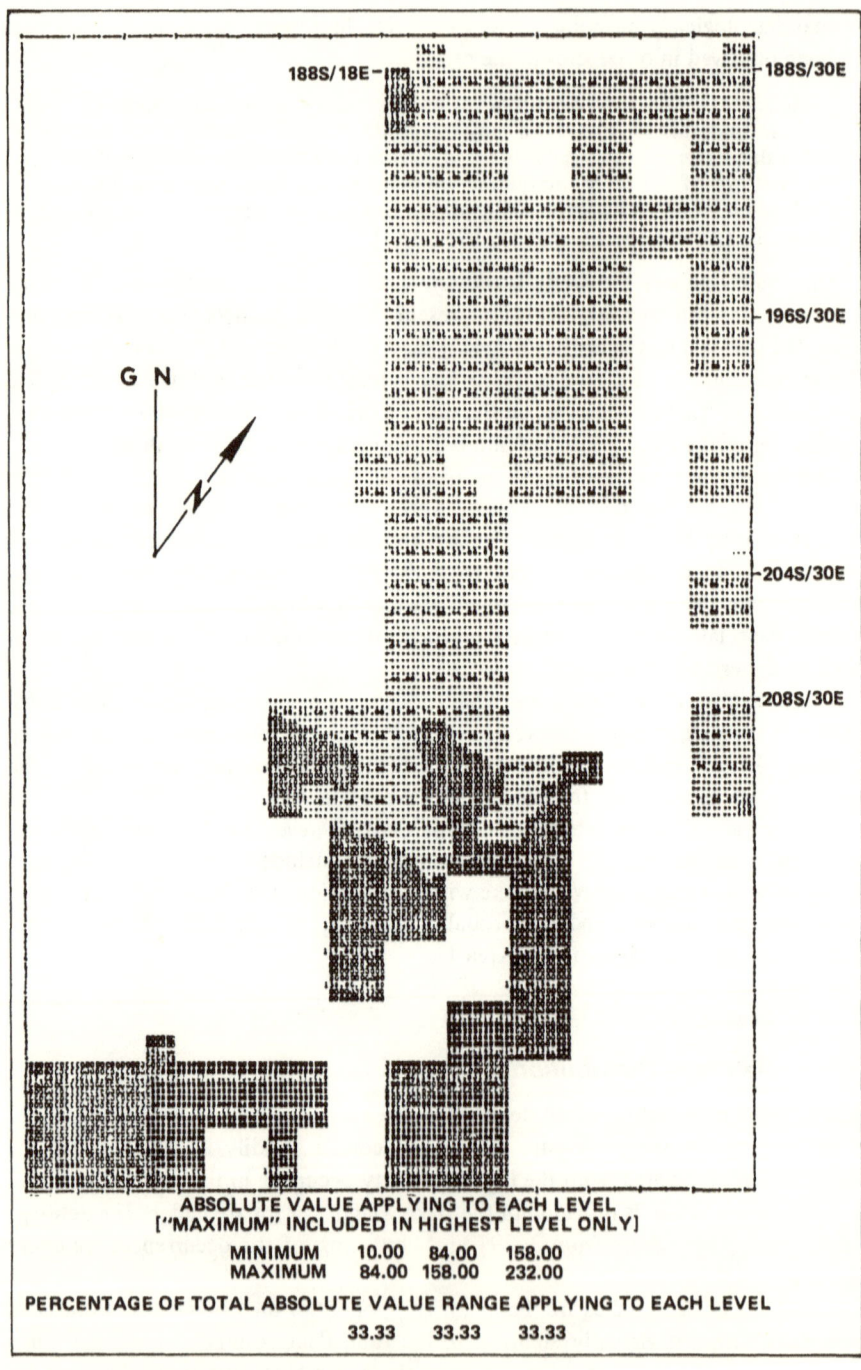

Figure 40. SYMAP distribution of total debitage counts for Area 2.

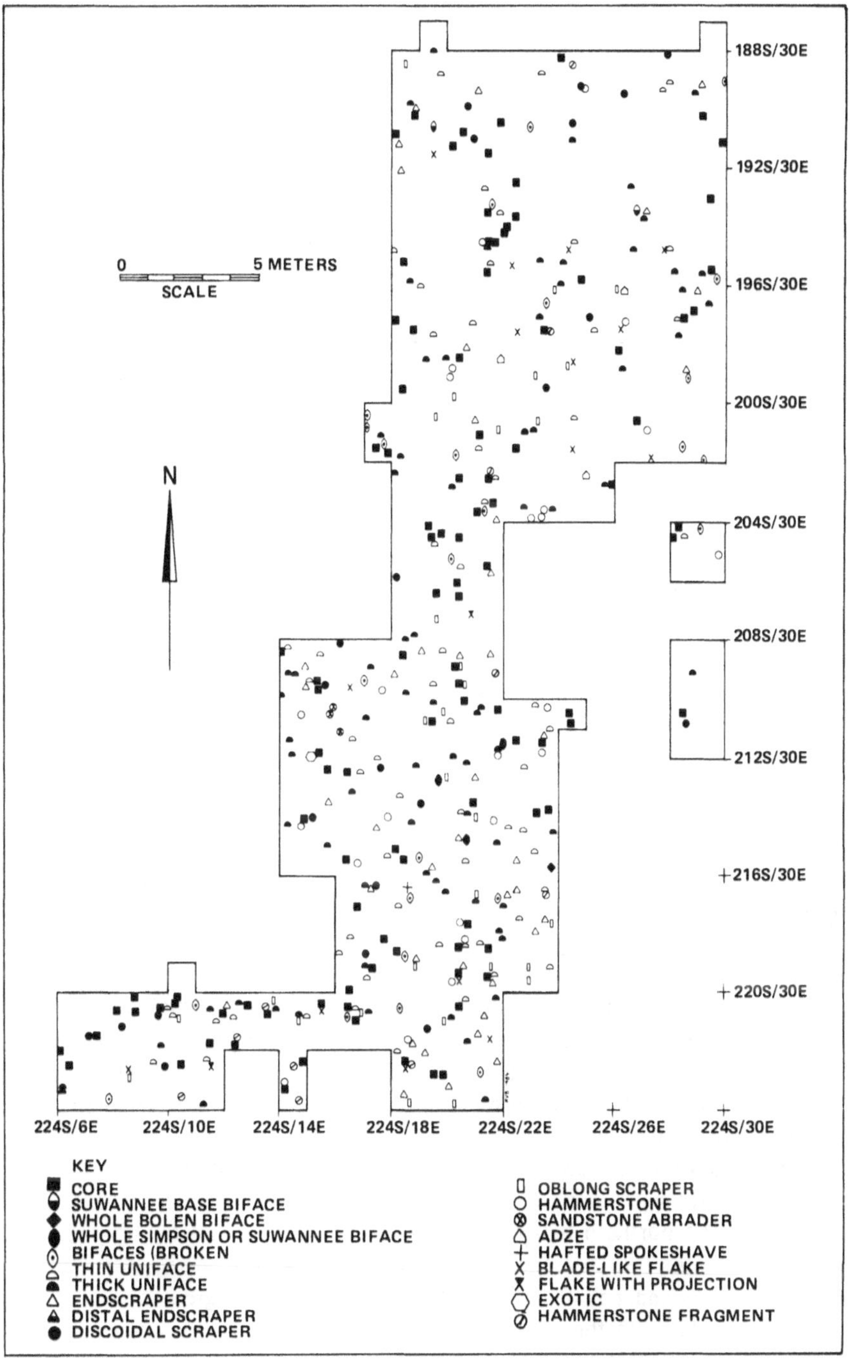

INTRA-SITE SPATIAL ANALYSIS / 109

Figure 41. Area 2 artifact proveniences.

Secondary decortication flakes are the second most numerous flake type, but counts are much lower than for non-decortication flakes, ranging from 1-44 per square meter. Again, higher densities are located in the southern half of the area with relatively small (1-4 m^2) clusters containing the highest densities. The distributions of the remaining flake types—cortex fragments, shatter and primary decortication—are low in density with the highest counts fewer than eight flakes per square meter. As with the distributions described above, the higher counts are located in the southern half of the area. Considering the low totals, these distributions are difficult to interpret.

The distribution of the uniface fragments and resharpening flakes recovered in the debitage from Area 2 has values from one to four flakes per square meter. Possible "clusters" may be marked by fragments in contiguous squares. Again, the higher concentrations are located in the southern half of the area.

The distribution of biface fragments is also widespread, but it is much less dense. Utilized flakes in Area 2 range from 0-7 per square meter. Although the distribution is widespread across the area, the density is highest in the southern half.

Tool Distribution

The distribution of all artifacts in Area 2 is shown in Figure 41. The distribution of cores and core fragments in Area 2 shows linear clusters that are well spread across the area. During the excavation two possible caches of hammerstones were recovered; one containing a pair of hammerstones while another had three. The remaining specimens are dispersed. The density of hammerstones is greater in the southern half of the area.

The bifaces are less common in Area 2 (and 3) than in Area 1, and the distribution looks more dispersed than clustered. Of particular interest are the locations of pieces of a refitted preform. The tip was recovered near the eastern edge of the southern half of the area, while the base was recovered approximately 14.5 m to the northeast. As with the refitted biface in Area 1, this separation may be accounted for by throwing or tossing, although 14.5 m seems excessive. Other cultural and natural possibilities may exist, but cannot be proven.

The distribution of the thick and thin unifaces is clustered and it is difficult to discern any real patterning. As with the hammerstones, two possible clusters of thick unifaces appeared in the northern and southern halves of Area 2. This pattern is not present in the thin uniface map, although the density appears greater in the southern half of the area.

The distribution of endscrapers again reveals a denser distribution in the southern half of the area with two to four possible clusters, each containing three to ten specimens. The northern half of the area mostly contains isolated occurrences of distal fragments. Two possible subareas can also be seen in the distribution of oblong scrapers and possibly discoidal scrapers. A distinct group of eight oblong scrapers is isolated in the northern half of the area (along with a single specimen located in the northwest corner). A second group exhibits a linear distribution that virtually covers the southern half of the area and contains the majority of this type.

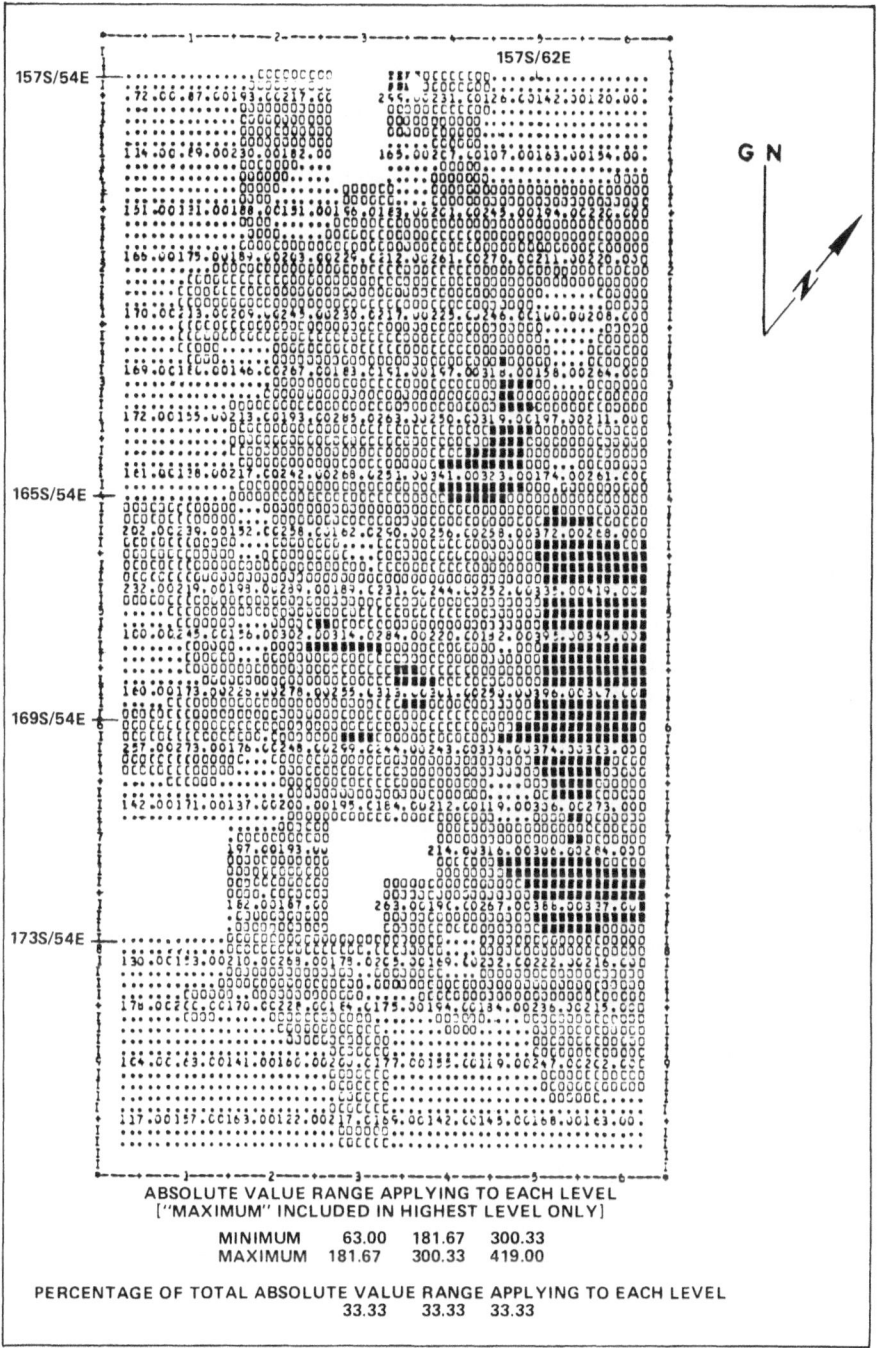

Figure 42. SYMAP distribution of total debitage counts for Area 3.

Similarly, three groups of discoidal scrapers containing two to four artifacts are located in the northern half of the area, while the south half contains two or three clusters with three to five specimens each.

The remaining tool types from Area 2 include sandstone abraders, blade-like flakes, adzes, a flake with projection, a hafted spokeshave, and an exotic specimen. Of particular interest are the two sandstone abraders that likely represent a cache located in the approximate center of the area near the western edge. Another sandstone piece with multiple grooves is located within a meter of the other two near one of the exotic specimens.

Area 3

Debitage Distribution

The distribution of all debitage in Area 3 ranges from 63-419 flakes m^2 (Figure 42). The map shows that the western edge of a large flake concentration has been uncovered. The lowest range of counts ring the northern, western, and southern edges of the area. Medium counts generally cover most of the remaining area with the exception of the eastern edge where some high density areas are located—an elongated area measuring approximately 16 m^2. A few additional concentrations are located near the center of the area. These are relatively small, generally 1-3 m^2.

As in the previous two areas, non-decortication flakes dominate the flake assemblage with counts ranging from 40-328 flakes m^2. The distribution of secondary decortication flakes ranges from 6 to 82.

The distributions of the remaining flake types differ from the general pattern noted above. Counts are low, ten flakes per square meter or less for shatter and primary decortication flakes. The distributions of these two flake types show a few isolated occurrences of medium to high density areas covering a few meters well-distributed across a low density background.

The counts for cortex fragments are somewhat higher ranging from 0-24 m^2, but the distribution is dominated by low counts. Only a few small occurrences of medium to high density counts are observed. Overall, the counts for these remaining flake types are so low that no meaningful interpretation can be made.

Uniface fragments and resharpening flakes range from 0-5 m^2, most likely reflecting the overall density of the area. Moreover, the distribution is widespread. The distribution of biface fragments, on the other hand, is clearly less dense with the highest occurrence being 2 m^2 with only three units having this value. The remaining number are isolated occurrences, some of which include a few (2-4) contiguous units. Utilized flakes in Area 3 are quite numerous with at least one in almost every square. A single square in the southwest corner contained the highest count.

Tool Distribution

The distribution of all artifacts in Area 3 is shown in Figure 43. The distribution of cores and core fragments forms a linear arrangement of interconnected groups. Although cores and core fragments are found throughout the area, they appear to be concentrated in the eastern half. Hammerstones (including fragments)

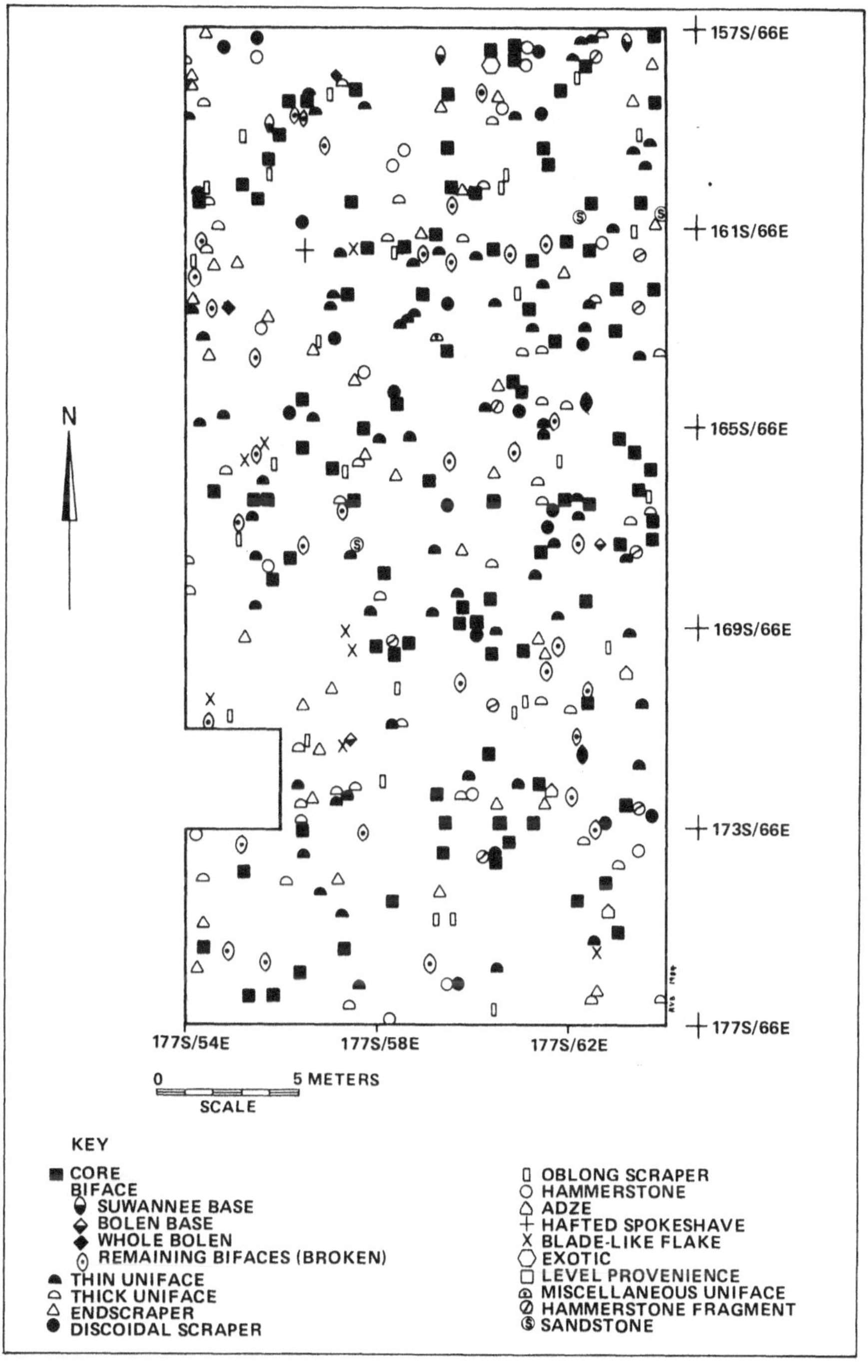

INTRA-SITE SPATIAL ANALYSIS / 113

Figure 43. Area 3 artifact proveniences.

are also well dispersed and, like the cores, appear to be concentrated in the eastern half of the area.

Small groups of bifaces, generally between two and five specimens per square meter, are dispersed across the area in linear or arced patterns. Suwannee and Bolen points are generally spatially segregated. The thick unifaces are grouped in linear clusters which often contain several artifacts and are several meters long. Some linear clusters can also be observed in the distribution of thin unifaces, but they are shorter in length and fewer. Some linear patterns are apparent, but, again, these generally cover the area. One large cluster of discoidal scrapers in the northern half of the area covers over 40 m^2 with a few remaining specimens dispersed along the edges. Some clusters of oblong scrapers are apparent on the map, but it is difficult to discern any real patterning.

The distribution of blade-like flakes, three adzes (located in the southeast portion of the area), sandstone, a hafted spokeshave, a miscellaneous uniface and a large piece of exotic stone. Although none of the pieces of sandstone recovered in Area 3 exhibited any signs of use, two of the specimens were located in adjacent units near the northeastern corner of the area. The third specimen is located more centrally. The single exotic specimen is the large stone, described earlier, that due to its size and location near a cache of hammerstones near the northern edge of the area is inferred to have functioned as an anvil.

INTER-AREA COMPARISONS

In the previous discussion we suggested fine grained spatial patterning on an intra-area level by analyzing the distribution of individual artifact classes. The overall distribution of every tool class in each area (Figures 39, 41, 43) is complex, overlapping, and represents an unknown number of occupations. Given our current understanding of the site formation processes, it is not surprising that no clear cut pattern emerged at this level of analysis.

Of the three areas, Area 1 exhibits the greatest potential for fine-grained structural analysis. Some possible artifact associations can be identified, but their exact meaning cannot be confidently determined. Still, some tentative generalizations can be offered concerning these distributions.

The three areas are generally similar in the spectrum of tool types they contain; however, they differ in the relative frequencies of those tool types. A list of all tools by area is given in Table 12 and a comparison of the percentage of tool types by area is given in Figure 44. Examination of this graph suggests that Areas 2 and 3 are quite similar in percentages of different tool types while Area 1 differs from the other two. This pattern is readily apparent from examination of the cumulative frequency of tool types in each of the areas (Figure 45).

To determine if the observed differences between the areas are statistically significant, a chi-square analysis was done for the total counts of each class by area (excluding all classes with fewer than ten artifacts). These results are summarized in Table 13. All pairwise combinations were calculated on a single class of tools, between

Table 12. Artifact Counts by Area

	Area 1		Area 2		Area 3	
1. Bifaces	51	(17.9%)	31	(7.1%)	43	(11.3%)
2. Endscrapers	46	(16.1%)	41	(9.5%)	37	(9.7%)
3. Oblong Scrapers	8	(2.8%)	30	(6.9%)	28	(7.4%)
4. Discoidal Scrapers	21	(7.3%)	22	(5.1%)	18	(4.7%)
5. Thick Unifaces	74	(26.0%)	77	(17.8%)	69	(18.2%)
6. Thin Unifaces	26	(9.1%)	63	(14.6%)	45	(11.9%)
7. Blade-like Flakes	9	(3.15%)	15	(3.4%)	8	(2.1%)
8. Hafted Spokeshaves	1	(0.35%)	1	(0.2%)	1	(0.2%)
9. Adzes	0		3	(0.6%)	3	(0.7%)
10. Flakes with Projections	1	(0.35%)	2	(0.4%)	0	
11. Exotics	2	(0.7%)	1	(0.2%)	1	(0.2%)
12. Cores and Fragments	39	(13.7%)	107	(24.8%)	97	(25.6%)
13. Hammerstones and Fragments	7	(2.5%)	35	(8.1%)	24	(6.3%)
14. Sandstone Abraders	0		3	(0.6%)	3	(0.7%)
15. Miscellaneous	0		0		1	(0.2%)
TOTALS	285	(100.0%)	431	(100.0%)	378	(100.0%)

two areas at a time. To control for the difference of the size of the excavated areas, the calculation was done in relation to all other tools in an area. Significant differences are found between Areas 1 and 2 for bifaces ($p < .001$), endscrapers ($p < .01$), thick unifaces ($p < .01$), cores and core fragments ($p < .001$), and hammerstones and fragments ($p < .01$); and between Areas 1 and 3 for cores and core fragments ($p < .001$) and oblong scrapers ($p < .01$). Significant differences were obtained between Areas 2 and 3 only for bifaces ($p < .05$).

Artifact Distribution

Cores and Hammerstones

Perhaps the most obvious difference among the three areas is the relative abundance of cores, core fragments and hammerstones. Cores and core fragments form a smaller part of the assemblage in Area 1 (about 14%) than they do in Areas 2 and 3 (about 25%). Likewise, an examination of core density among areas indicates higher values for Areas 2 and 3 than for Area 1. This same trend is generally represented if different types of cores are examined. Although the individual counts may be too small to be statistically valid, Areas 2 and 3 contain relatively more unidirectional, multidirectional, and bifacial cores. Micro-cores are absent from Area 3, but the overall counts for this category across the site are very low. Finally, the different core types tend to be heavier in Areas 2 and 3.

We suggest that clusters of hammerstones in Areas 2 and 3 are actually caches where they were stored for reuse. Because the presence of hammerstones is also consistent with the greater abundance of cores in Areas 2 and 3, it seems reasonable to suggest that the areas were used for core reduction or tool manufacturing.

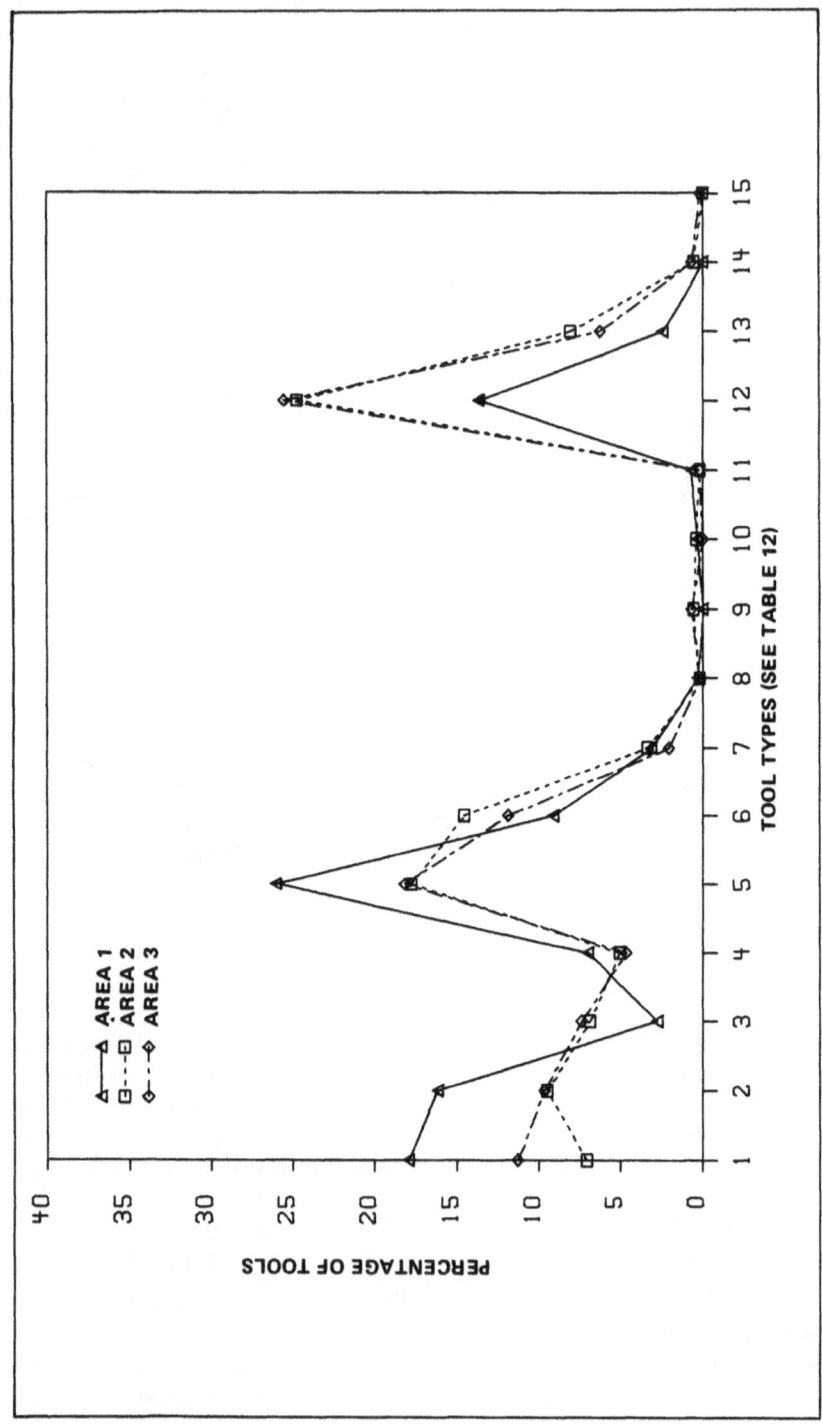

Figure 44. Percentage of tool types by area.

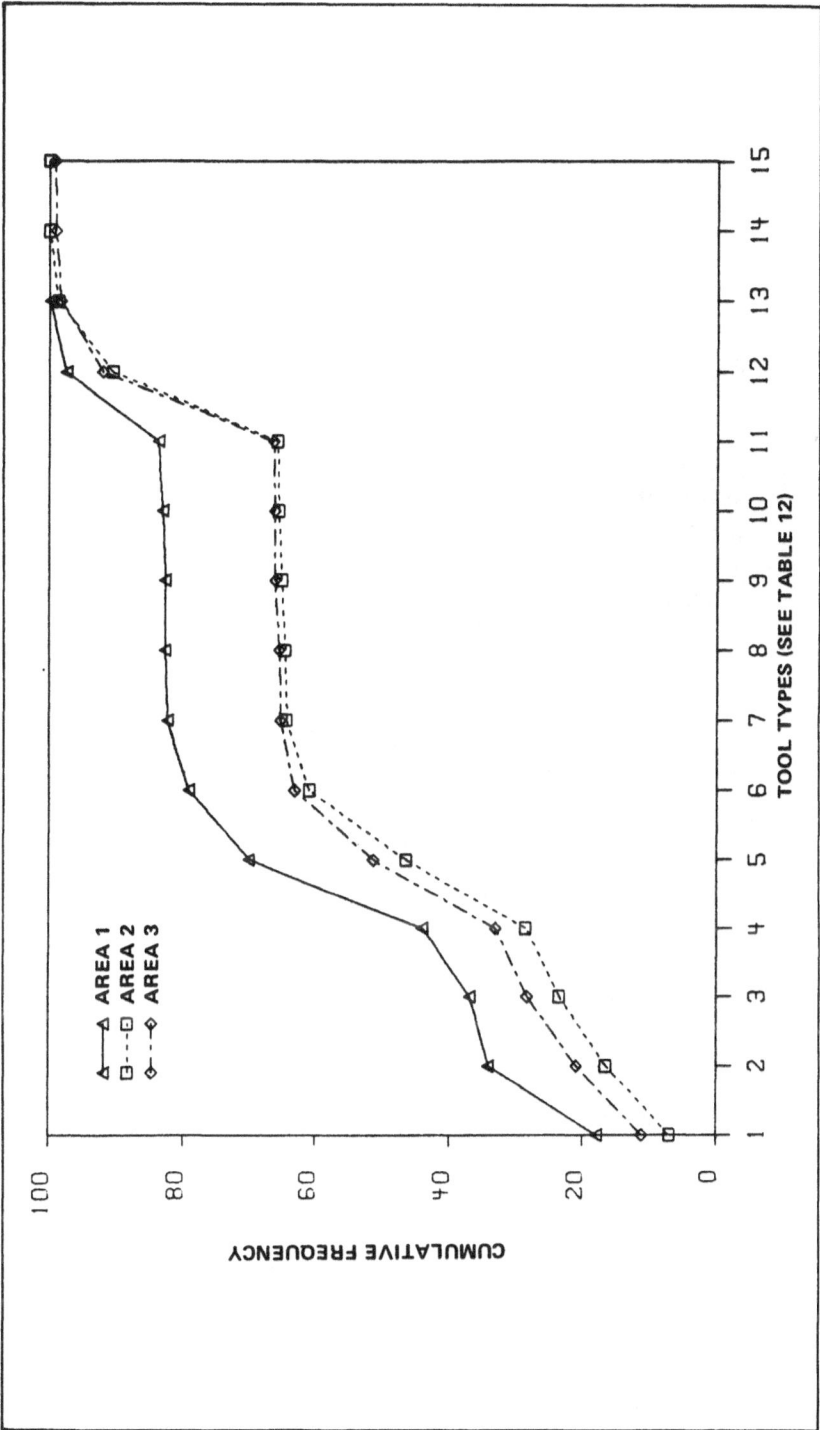

Figure 45. Cumulative frequency of tool types by area.

Table 13. Pairwise Combinations of a Single Tool Class Between Areas

	Area 1	Area 2	Area 3	Area 1	Area 2	Area 3	Area 1	Area 3
Bifaces	51	31	43	51	31	43	51	43
All remaining tools	234	400	335	234	400	335	234	335
Total	285	431	378	285	431	378	285	378
	$\chi^2 = 19.38, df = 1, p < .001$			$\chi^2 = 4.24, df = 1, p < .05$			$\chi^2 = 5.67, df = 1, p < .05$	
Endscrapers	46	41	37	46	41	37	46	37
All remaining tools	239	390	341	239	390	341	239	341
Total	285	431	378	285	431	378	285	378
	$\chi^2 = 7.06, df = 1, p < .01$			$\chi^2 = .0175, df = 1, p < .05$			$\chi^2 = 5.99, df = 1, p < .05$	
Thick Unifaces	74	77	69	74	77	69	74	69
All remaining tools	211	354	309	211	354	309	211	309
Total	285	431	378	285	431	378	285	378
	$\chi^2 = 6.76, df = 1, p < .01$			$\chi^2 = .020, df = 1, p < .05$			$\chi^2 = 5.71, df = 1, p < .05$	
Thin Unifaces	26	63	45	26	63	45	26	45
All remaining tools	259	368	333	259	368	333	259	333
Total	285	431	378	285	431	378	285	378
	$\chi^2 = 4.76, df = 1, p < .05$			$\chi^{22} = 1.28, df = 1, p < .05$			$\chi^2 = 1.31, df = 1, p < .05$	
Blade-like Flakes	9	15	24	15	8	23	9	17

All remaining tools	276	416	692	276	416	786	276	370	646
Total	285	431	716	285	431	809	285	378	663
	$\chi^2 = .055, df = 1, p < .05$			$\chi^2 = 1.35, df = 1, p < .05$			$\chi^2 = .7054, df = 1, p < .05$		
Cores and Core Fragments	39	107	146	39	97	204	39	97	136
All remaining tools	246	324	570	246	281	605	246	281	527
Total	285	431	716	285	378	809	285	378	663
	$\chi^2 = 13.12, df = 1, p < .001$			$\chi^2 = .0745, df = 1, p < .05$			$\chi^2 = 14.29, df = 1, p < .001$		
Oblong Scrapers	8	30	38	8	28	58	8	28	36
All remaining tools	277	401	678	277	350	751	277	350	627
Total	285	431	716	285	378	809	285	378	663
	$\chi^2 = 5.89, df = 1, p < .05$			$\chi^2 = .0604, df = 1, p < .05$			$\chi^2 = 6.696, df = 1, p < .01$		
Discoidal Scrapers	21	22	43	21	18	40	21	18	39
All remaining tools	264	409	673	264	360	769	264	360	624
Total	285	431	716	285	378	809	285	378	663
	$\chi^2 = 1.55, df = 1, p < .05$			$\chi^2 = .0502, df = 1, p < .05$			$\chi^2 = 1.99, df = 1, p < .05$		
Hammerstones and Fragments	7	35	41	7	24	59	7	24	31
All remaining tools	278	396	674	278	354	750	278	354	632
Total	285	431	716	285	378	809	285	378	663
	$\chi^2 = 9.97, df = 1, p < .01$			$\chi^2 = .9346, df = 1, p < .05$			$\chi^2 = 5.52, df = 1, p < .05$		

Note: $p < .05$ at $\chi^2 = 3.84$ for all calculations.

Table 14. Biface Types by Area

	Area 1	Area 2	Area 3	Total
Completed lanceolates				
base	3	3	3	
tip	2	0	0	
whole	1	2	2	
	6 (37.5%)	5 (31.2%)	5 (31.2%)	16
Preforms				
base	8	3	4	
tip	9	4	11	
mid/body	0	3	0	
whole	3	0	0	
	20 (44%)	10 (22%)	15 (33%)	45
Lozenge bifaces				
base	2	2	9	
whole	0	5	3	
	2 (9.5%)	7 (33.3%)	12 (57%)	21
Other bifaces				
base	5	2	2	
tip	9	3	3	
mid/body	4	3	2	
	18 (54.5%)	8 (24%)	7 (21%)	33
Notched points				
base	3	0	2	
whole	2	1	2	
	5 (50%)	1 (10%)	4 (40%)	10

Bifaces

As Table 12 shows, bifaces are disproportionately distributed among the areas with almost 18 percent of the assemblage from Area 1, approximately 7 percent of Area 2, and about 11 percent from Area 3. These figures represent only total bifaces; however, if the class is broken into types as in Table 14, differences among areas become even more apparent.

Completed lanceolates (either broken or exhausted) were apparently discarded in equal proportions in each of the three areas. Area 1 generally contains higher frequencies of preforms, other bifaces, and notched points. Only in the category of lozenge bifaces does Area 1 contain the smallest percentage. Although the differences here may be attributed to the size of the excavated areas, it is believed that Area 1 does exhibit a pattern of biface distribution different from that of Areas 2 and 3. Although biface manufacture took place in all three areas, different stages of manufacture are apparently represented in each.

The differences among the three areas are best seen in the relative frequencies of preform and other biface categories. Only three whole preforms were recovered, all in Area 1. Preforms could have been finished in Area 1 as opposed to Areas 2 and 3

INTRA-SITE SPATIAL ANALYSIS / 121

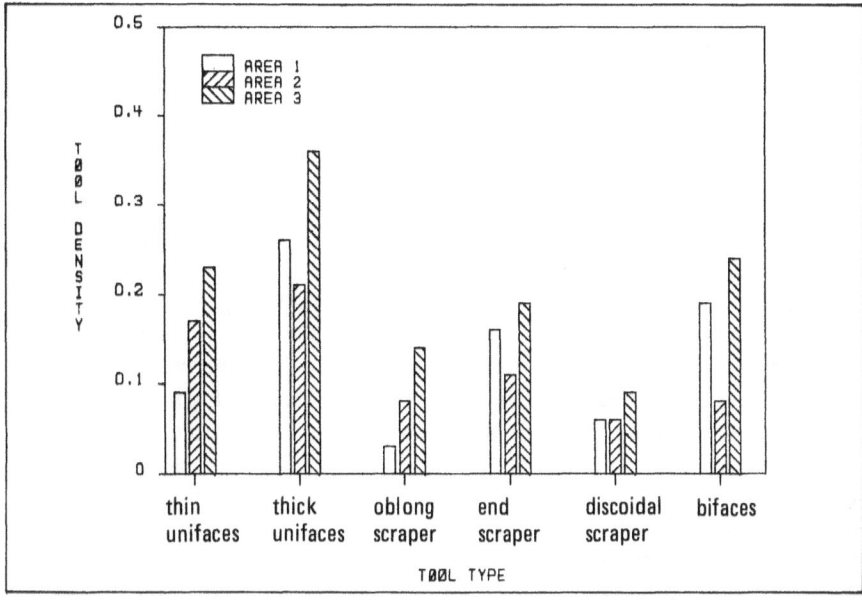

Figure 46. Tool types per square meter.

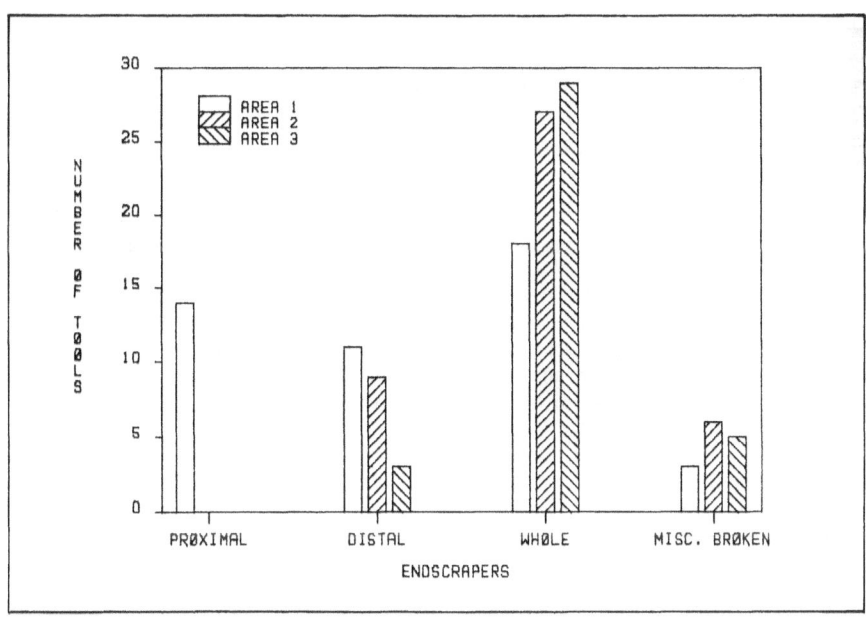

Figure 47. Number of endscrapers and endscraper fragments by area.

where earlier stages of biface manufacture took place. Perhaps blanks were brought to these two areas and initially thinned and shaped, while final shaping and preparation for hafting took place in Area 1. Retooling bifaces could also have taken place, but it should be pointed out that unlike endscrapers the proximal ends of completed points were located in all three areas and not localized in Area 1.

Curated Unifaces

Endscrapers make up 16 percent of the assemblage from Area 1, but only approximately 10 percent of the collections from Areas 2 and 3. The most significant difference is between Areas 1 and 2 ($p < .01$) (Table 13).

Area 3 contained the greatest density of endscrapers followed closely by Area 1 (Figure 46). Again, this may be misleading, since this figure better reflects the fact that Area 3 contains greater numbers of whole endscrapers (Figure 47). Relatively few broken or distal portions of endscrapers were recovered from Area 3. Area 1, on the other hand, contains more broken pieces, including proximal and distal ends. Moreover, all of the proximal or butt ends of endscrapers that were recovered during the excavations came from Area 1. Similarly, proportionally more distal fragments were recovered. Distal (bit) ends of endscrapers were recovered from all three areas suggesting that they were being utilized in all parts of the site. This, of course, assumes that breakage was a result of use, and that no broken tools were removed from the areas.

Of particular interest is the distribution of proximal or butt ends. Remembering that none of these pieces could be fitted to the other fragments, and assuming that this is representative of the site as a whole, then these proximal ends may represent portions of endscrapers removed from their hafts and then abandoned. Area 1 may represent the primary locus for retooling endscrapers (see Keeley, 1982:799).

These proximal ends may never have been used at the site. Such behavior is consistent with Binford's expectation that heavily curated gear will not be discarded or repaired in the field, but will be returned to the residential camp (Binford, 1977:33-34; Binford, 1979:263). As Keeley noted, "once hafted" tools tend to accumulate in archaeological contexts neither necessarily when nor where they were last used.

> Within a site, retooling debris can accumulate at certain special locations. One of the most obvious is around domestic hearths under shelter where warmth, light, and conversation are amenities, and where a wide variety of tools, facilities and materials are likely to be at hand. . . . (H)afted tools may be retooled when it is convenient to do so rather than when it is necessary (Keeley, 1982:802-803).

The implication is that this activity would take place in the vicinity of a living area, such as Area 1 with its more favorable topographic setting.

The distribution of the remaining curated unifaces is somewhat more difficult to interpret. Significant differences in the number of oblong scrapers are found between Area 1 and 3, while no significant differences are found between Areas 1 and 2 and 2 and 3. Since these are curated tools, it is difficult to know how many of them were actually used at the site before they were discarded there. Though the life history of these curated unifaces is unknown, the nature of curated tools would largely imply that they were utilized at more than one site. Consequently, it would seem unlikely that all of the oblong scrapers (or many of the curated unifaces in general) recovered at the site were manufactured, used and discarded there. On the whole, it is possible that these may actually represent discarded tools brought to the site, exhausted, and replaced by others; and may never have been used at Harney Flats.

A small number of the oblong scrapers recovered from Areas 2 and 3 appear to be manufacture rejects, while many more appear to be heavily resharpened or exhausted. Consequently, at least in terms of the greater number of oblong scrapers, their presence in Areas 2 and 3 reflects discard or disposal areas rather than use.

Expedient Unifaces

The majority of the expedient unifaces recovered are divided into thick and thin categories, which are arbitrary distinctions and may or may not have any behavioral or functional meaning. Area 1 contains relatively greater numbers of thick unifaces in relation to the other tools than Areas 2 and 3. Thin unifaces, however, exhibit a different distribution among the areas. No significant differences are found in the counts between Areas 2 and 3 or 1 and 3, but significantly greater counts are found in Area 2 than in Area 1.

Given the nature of expedient tools, these unifaces were probably manufactured, used in daily tasks, and discarded within the same general location. As opposed to the curated unifaces, these expedient tools might be representative of some of the tool using activities that occurred on the site. The results of use-wear analysis (Ballo, 1985) indicate that the expedient unifaces were predominantly used on more resistant materials (e.g., wood). Combined, these unifaces make up about one third of the assemblage within each area, suggesting these activities were well represented across the site.

Although differences among the activities that took place in the three areas may be represented by the different counts of thick and thin unifaces, they are difficult to interpret. When the distribution of the expedient unifaces is viewed in relation to the remaining assemblage in each area, however, some possibilities arise. Given the range of activities possibly represented by the assemblages in Areas 2 and 3 thus far, we suggest that the expedient unifaces from these areas were used in manufacturing tools and hafts from wood. Those specimens recovered from Areas 1, however, may have been utilized for maintenance or subsistence tasks associated with daily living.

Debitage

A summary of the flake counts by type for each area (Table 15) shows a similarity in the percentages of flake types within each area. Non-decortication flakes predominate in all three areas, consisting of 80-83 percent of the debitage. Secondary decortication flakes constitute the second largest percentage (12-17%). The other three flake types—primary decortication, cortex fragments, and shatter—

Table 15. Flake Counts by Area

	Area 1	Area 2	Area 3
Non-decortication	13,844 (82.9%)	19,593 (79.9%)	30,652 (79.5%)
Secondary decortication	2,023 (12.1%)	3,956 (16.1%)	6,542 (16.9%)
Primary decortication	165 (0.98%)	350 (1.4%)	477 (1.4%)
Cortex fragments	567 (3.3%)	351 (1.4%)	561 (1.4%)
Shatter	96 (0.57%)	258 (1.0%)	315 (0.81%)
TOTALS	16,695 (100%)	24,508 (100%)	38,547 (100%)
	59 per m^2	64 per m^2	196 per m^2

make up the remaining amounts. With the exception of cortex fragments from Area 1, these categories account for about 1 percent each.

The primary difference among the areas is the greater density of flakes in Area 3 with some slight differences in the percentages of individual flake types among the three areas. The percentage of non-decortication flakes is slightly higher in Area 1 than Areas 2 and 3, while the opposite is true for the percentages of secondary decortication flakes. This is consistent with the suggestion that the earliest stages of tool manufacture or core reduction at the site were located in Areas 2 and 3. While this may be the case, the predominance of non-decortication flakes in all areas implies late stage reduction (tool manufacture, maintenance and resharpening, or core reduction) for the site as a whole.

Very little, if any, primary or initial reduction appears to have taken place at Harney Flats, because the site is located within a "quarry cluster area" where a number of different chert sources are present (Upchurch, 1984). A strong likelihood exists that a quarry source was in the vicinity of the site (in the flats?) and may have been exploited during the occupation. Primary reduction probably took place at the quarry location itself, and the chert was transported from there in various core or flake blank forms.

The Remaining Assemblage

The remaining tool types in the assemblage are represented by too few specimens within any one type to allow statistically significant differences in distributions to be found, but some interesting points regarding some of the types can be made when their distributions are compared to the rest of the assemblage.

Blade-like flakes have similar distributions in each of the areas, and can be seen as expedient tools that were used when needed in all three. All six adzes recovered came from Areas 2 and 3 and may have been used for heavy duty tasks such as procuring and working wood to be further modified. Similarly, sandstone abraders were recovered from Areas 2 and 3, but those from Area 3 showed no evidence of use. Finally, specimens of metamorphic rock were recovered from all three areas. They are unusual since they are not of local origin: we assume they were used in activities in the areas from which they were recovered.

Discussion

Three or four possible clusters of cores contain small or fragmentary ones as opposed to the larger, heavier ones found in the other two areas. If Area 1 were a living area, then relatively isolated places for core reduction could be expected. These clusters could also represent disposal areas rather than activity areas. The core and core fragment clusters are generally located in the vicinity of units with relatively high debitage counts, perhaps reflecting the arc or doughnut dispersal patterns representing discrete places of lithic reduction. Some spatial separation is also recognized between cores and bifaces, suggesting a separation of activities.

Area 1 contains a high density of thick unifaces. If thick and thin unifaces represent expedient tools, and their individual positions accurately reflect the locations of use and discard, then their corresponding activity areas are well dispersed across the area.

Area 1 also contains a high density of endscrapers within three small clusters. These might well be discrete loci where the retooling of endscrapers occurred, however, there is no way to demonstrate this. The meaning of a very low density of discoidal and oblong scrapers cannot be inferred from their distribution.

Perhaps the only real behavioral event that can be confidently inferred from Area 1 is from the presence of the cache of two exotic stones. We do not know if these stones were used within the area, but this seems likely, as other caches in Areas 2 and 3 include tools that were most likely used in their respective areas. Therefore, these stones may represent "site furniture" associated with activities within the living area.

Although there is evidence that Area 1 was a living area, it is frustrating not to be able to better define its particular structure. Living areas within sites are usually defined by the presence of structural remains, hearths, or storage pits. Unfortunately, no direct evidence of any such features was uncovered during the excavations. Assuming such evidence existed, and we had excavated enough of the area to locate it but didn't, it seems likely that none was preserved. The fact that no such features were located during any of the other Highway Salvage excavations in this area reinforces this possibility. In general, the lack of organic preservation contributes much to our inability to define fine-grained spatial structures in the site as a whole.

The remaining two areas especially Area 3 show less patterning than Area 1. Areas 2 and 3 may well exhibit a "blending and smearing" (Ascher, 1968) of patterns through time. Simply, individual patterns of artifact association may not appear in areas of intense utilization, especially over a long period of time. That is not to say that no fine grained structure is present at Harney Flats; some patterns can be observed, as evidenced by the presence of caches. For the most part, however, fine grained structure cannot be recognized. We can discuss the overall activities within an area, but cannot say much about how they are patterned within it.

Aside from the high debitage density in Area 3, there are distinct differences in the patterns of flake distribution among the areas. While Area 1 contains small discrete areas of relatively high flake density, this pattern is absent in Areas 2 and 3, which exhibit a more regular distribution of debitage, increasing towards one end of the area. In both Area 2 and Area 3, a single, relatively large, oval cluster contains the highest flake density. This pattern is consistent with an interpretation of these areas as loci of specialized activity, where episodes of manufacturing activity repeatedly took place. Moreover, the distribution of cores and core fragments is also quite regular across the two areas.

Bifaces are not well represented in either Area 2 or 3. Most of those found were interpreted as early stage manufacture failures. Exceptions to this would be broken, completed point bases, probably brought to the site and discarded in anticipation of retooling. For the most part these appear evenly distributed across the area.

No real patterning is seen in the distribution of the thick and thin unifaces, but it is postulated that their locations represent general areas of use and subsequent discard. In contrast, the locations of the curated unifaces are probable discard areas rather than use areas. The pattern in Area 2 suggests it consists of two subareas. The distributions of some of the other tool classes in Area 2 also suggest this, but it is possible that this may simply be a function of the shape of the excavation.

The other possible cluster of tools is a probable cache of abraders in Area 2. Two other abraders are felt to be associated with the cache. One is a small piece of sandstone with numerous grooves and the other is an exotic stone. This group of specimens is interpreted to represent "site furniture" associated with activities within the area.

Area 3 contains the highest density of virtually every artifact type and perhaps represents the most intensively utilized area within the excavated portion of the site. The observed spatial patterning of most tool classes within the area is likely a composite of many discrete tool distributions accumulated over the course of many separate occupational episodes.

Structural Patterning

Evidence for structural patterning at Harney Flats can be seen in the differences among tool assemblages recovered from the three block area excavations (Figure 48). Microtopographic relationships among the three areas and the availability of raw material are also seen as important factors influencing the nature of this site structure.

While the assemblages of Areas 2 and 3 are believed to represent activities primarily associated with tool manufacture and core reduction, Area 1 had a significantly different assemblage composition and has been interpreted as a living area. Area 1 is situated in the most favorable topographic setting, on the highest and flattest portion of the site, with Areas 2 and 3 situated farther downslope. Retooling endscrapers is suggested to be a primary activity in Area 1, as is biface finishing.

Refurbishing tool kits is postulated to have been a primary activity at the site. Therefore, as a group, the curated unifaces most likely represent exhausted tools

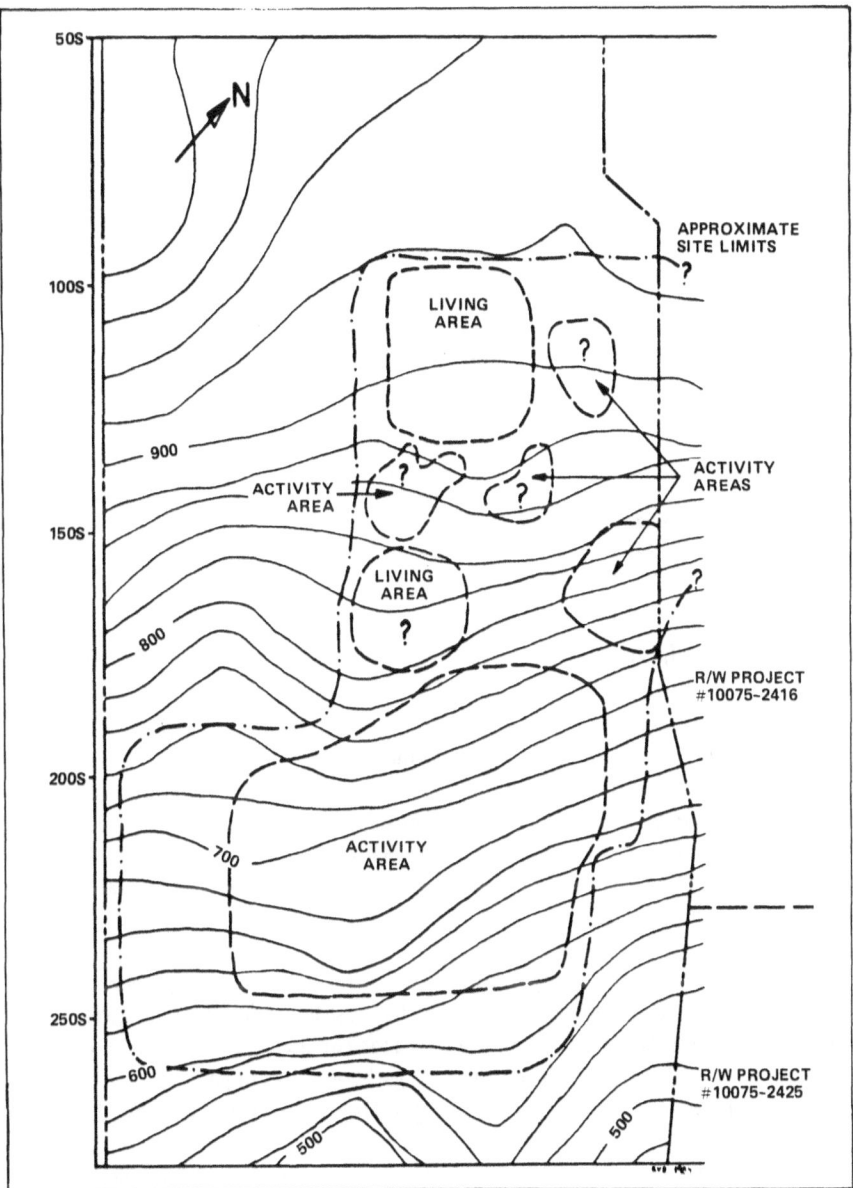

Figure 48. Schematic map of spatial structure at Harney Flats.

which were replaced by new tools manufactured from the readily available raw material. The curated unifaces (particularly in Areas 2 and 3) may not be tools that were brought to the site for long-term use, but rather nearly exhausted tools that were brought to the site and subsequently replaced using the abundant, high quality, local materials. No one is likely to bring useless tools to Harney Flats for the sole purpose of discarding them, but one's survival potential is increased if a complete tool kit, even one with nearly exhausted implements had been brought. Once new ones were manufactured, the old ones could be discarded. Support for this is seen in the large number of expedient unifaces that undoubtedly were used at the site.

This expectation is consistent with our current understanding of the manufacture, use, and discard of tools in hunter-gatherer societies. Moreover, such a pattern of discard of curated unifaces at lithic source areas has been noted elsewhere (see Gardner, 1974:105; Gramly, 1980:829). A similar distinction has been made between the use of hafted/curated tools and expedient tools relative to lithic resource availability.

> For example, if a group is occupying a site near a source of lithic raw material, they may prefer to employ expedient implements while conserving or even ignoring hafted tools. The assemblage at such a site would contain large amounts of waste and a relatively large number of big, minimally retouched tools. This same group occupying another location where raw material was more difficult to obtain may preferentially employ its hafted implements so that the assemblage deposited would contain little waste and a high proportion of small, intensely worked tools. Although the assemblages from these two sites would be quite dissimilar, they might nevertheless be the remains of the same group and could even be of the same suite of activities. In addition, a group about to leave a site with abundant lithic raw material may extensively retool in anticipation of future shortages of suitable stone at sites occupied next in their seasonal round (Keeley, 1982:803-804).

The implicit assumption in this discussion is that at least two of the three areas at Harney Flats were occupied contemporaneously (i.e., Areas 1 and 2 or Areas 1 and 3). One way to test this might be through the refitting of broken artifacts. We might expect that tools broken in one area would have their "refit" piece present in another area, as is the case at Debert (MacDonald, 1968:133; see also discussion by Schiffer, 1983:688). The few conjoinable tool fragments found at Harney Flats were found within single areas, but refitting attempts were done only on bifaces and endscrapers.

The contemporaneous occupation of the three areas within the site has not been demonstrated. Nevertheless, it still remains the most logical alternative, given similar structural patterns observed at other archaeological sites, as well as in our current understanding of the organization of hunter-gatherers sites in general.

Finally, the nature of the data recording at Harney Flats will allow further examination of spatial patterning. One of the first steps in this direction would be an intensive refitting study. The refitting of chipped-stone artifacts is now beginning to be seen as an important analytical tool (see discussion by Hoffman, 1983) in the identification of potential activity areas such as loci of manufacturing, use and resharpening, or discard (see Cahen et al., 1979). Moreover, refitting studies can help further assess postdepositional disturbances. Additional attempts at quantitative analysis are also anticipated in this area.

CHAPTER 6

A Comparative Overview of Early Man Sites

This review of selected early man sites in North America presents many disparate data collected by a host of investigators over an extended period of time and from a number of diverse environmental regions.

Many of these early sites were found to be similar in terms of their lack of bifacially worked artifacts, except projectile points. On the other hand, unifacially flaked tools predominated at sites ranging from Blackwater Draw in New Mexico to Debert in Nova Scotia to Harney Flats in Florida. When taking into account that these unifacial implements are seldom recovered from later Archaic assemblages, this indicates that unifaces were the hallmark of the Paleo-Indian era and represent what Hayden (1982) terms "stylistic homogeneity."

In addition to unifacial tools, another commonly shared trait of Paleo-Indian people was their marked preference for high quality silicate materials (Funk, 1977: 325; Frison and Bradley, 1980:14; Ritchie, 1953:250; Witthoft, 1952:473; Wormington, 1957:68) and their fine workmanship on these materials (Frison, 1978; Wheat, 1971). Data collected by Wilmsen (1970) regarding various Paleo-Indian sites strongly suggest early man employed intensive selective criteria in his search for stone materials suitable for conversion into tools. Others have even suggested that specific individuals traveled from 320-650 km to obtain lithic materials from high quality sources directly or through trade (Hester and Grady, 1977:92). Moreover, it is postulated that knappers might have been few in number, leading one to believe they were important personages who may have bargained for power and influence. These same investigators also speculated that knappers were the most likely candidates for special status such as headman or shaman (Hester and Grady, 1977:94).

Most Paleo-Indian sites, including Harney Flats, also contain some exotic raw materials (Adovasio *et al.*, 1980; Byers, 1955; Funk, 1967; Hester *et al.*, 1973; Ritchie, 1953; Soday, 1954; Witthoft, 1952).

> Chalcedonies and cherts were often imported into sites where the materials do not occur naturally even though less desirable stones have been locally available in quantity. This procurement of exotic material must have entailed some effort (Wilmsen, 1970:66).

Another possible explanation for the presence of exotic materials on these early sites is borrowed from the study of Australian aborigines who develop social and ritual ties with stone materials originating from totemic sites. In this instance, a man sees the stone as part of his own being and carries some form of it for use at different localities even though functionally superior material is locally available. Some of this stone material at such sites as Lindenmeier (Colorado) may have been linked within a similar network that served to bind widely dispersed bands (Wilmsen, 1974:119).

In contrast to these characteristics of the Paleo-Indian traditions, subsequent Archaic traditions (especially from Middle Archaic times onward) tended to manifest values toward the opposite extreme with an increase in stylistic regionalization and variety. Many local materials, such as rhyolite, quartzite, and other coarse-grained rocks found in Eastern North America were utilized. Probably one of the most striking differences between the Paleo-Indian and Archaic assemblages is the decline in the high quality of lithic workmanship. As a consequence of these type changes, it is inferred that less interaction between peoples from neighboring areas occurred during the Archaic and that territories became more bounded (Hayden, 1982:115).

In any event, the rapid and apparently successful movements of Paleo-Indians across almost the full range of environments represented throughout the Americas, may well have constituted the most impressive feat of early man. His actions reflect "not only the viability of his subsistence modes, but also his organizational talents, initiative, and flexibility which were in no way inferior to those displayed by Western European nations after A.D. 1492" (Butzer, 1982:302).

PALEO-INDIAN SUBSISTENCE

The idea that Paleo-Indian subsistence was dependent on extinct megafauna, such as mammoth and bison, is the most widely held view of early man in the Americas (Haynes, 1980:11; Leonhardy, 1966:53; Mason 1962:234; Sellards, 1952:117). Willey (1966) characterizes these early cultures as being represented by lanceolate points and other lithic tools. The typical projectile points are fluted Clovis and Folsom, the single-shouldered Sandia, and several Plano types that are integrated parts of complexes which reflect a way of life dependent on hunting large game animals, many of which are now extinct.

> The big-game hunting pursuit is the most characteristic and diagnostic feature of culture shared by these particular early Americans. There can be no question that it was an activity of great and, probably primary importance. Viewed in perspective of all of Pre-Columbian New World History, it imparted a design, a style to their lives (Willey, 1966:38).

Many proponents of the big-game theory believe that a relatively homogeneous Paleo-Indian culture spread throughout the Americas until it was no longer capable of coping with the dramatic decline of large mammals. In short, Paleo-Indian peoples were forced to adopt a new life way as the postglacial progressed or to become extinct, just as did the Pleistocene megafauna they presumably preyed upon (Mason, 1962:243; Graham et al., 1981).

Although most of the early Paleo-Indian sites have been found in the West, it is assumed that these sites would serve as a model for the entire continent, since extinct fauna in the East somewhat resembled specimens found at western kill sites. For example, a similarity of artifact assemblages (lithic materials) was noted between Suwannee sites in Florida and Llano complex sites from the West (Neill, 1964:234).

There is increasing evidence, however, that is contrary to this simplistic view of Paleo-Indian subsistence. Much data regarding early man have come from kill sites (Wormington, 1957). Paleo-Indian habitation sites are hidden by changing vegetational cover, altered drainage patterns, water sources no longer in existence, and sites near the coastal plain which have been flooded by rising sea levels and high water tables (Albanese,1977; Gramly, 1981; Hemmings, 1972). Moreover, habitation sites (compared to kill sites) are frequently covered by culturally sterile soil deposits. If more sites of this kind are found, they would probably reveal a much wider range of faunal and floral materials (Kunz, 1969:28).

While it is unfortunate that workers in the field of Paleo-Indian culture have been preoccupied with such topics as gross projectile point typology, chronology, and extinct megafauna (Wilmsen, 1970:81), archaeologists are now developing a more accurate model of Paleo-Indian subsistence. The stereotypical view of Paleo-Indians as vagabonds who spent most of their time in relentless pursuit of large Pleistocene herbivores needs to be corrected.

Paleo-Indians of western North America effectively exploited their environment and were not solely dependent on large animals, but rather used small game, plants, and insects as part of their diet. As Kunz maintains (1969:29), "Rabbits are much easier to drive than bison, and women and children can be employed in rabbit drives. A sizeable amount of meat can easily be obtained in this manner, as witnessed by the present day Hopi." Perhaps the reason for the recovery of so many large mammal bones (as opposed to the relative scarcity of fish, birds, and small vertebrates) results from the less fragile nature of their hard parts, the hazards of burial, and the edibility of smaller bones.

Carbonized and dessicated plant remains are not as common as could be desired (Brothwell and Brothwell, 1969:13), although there are numerous manifestations of plant use by Paleo-Indians. Grasses were once more luxuriant than they now are in western North America and produced edible seeds that could have been utilized for food. A seed grinding slab was recovered from an early occupation of the Levi site. The collecting and grinding of seeds was added to the hunting and trapping of a wide variety of game animals during the Plainview occupation of the site as early as 9,300 B.P. (Alexander, 1963:526). A small milling stone was found at Elida, a Folsom campsite near the Clovis site (Warnica, 1966:355). Probably the earliest grinding stone in North America, however, comes from Blackwater Draw and is significant because it documents a varied economy at an early date, as well as provides incontrovertible evidence for the gathering of plant foods (Hester, 1972:92). At Baker Cave (10,000-8,000 B.P.) in southern Texas, sixteen plant species were found in a hearth which included sunflower, grasses, oak, Mormon tea, buckthorn, cattail, and a variety of herbaceous plants as well as wood, charcoal, flowers and fruits (Hester, 1979). Shafer (1977:194) characterized the late Pleistocene environment on the ecotone between the southern High Plains and the eastern Woodlands as optimal for foraging. Plant foods were the basic staple with hunting being only a supplemental activity carried out mainly for social reasons rather than for nutritional needs. In Eastern North America, too, a substantial amount of data on subsistence of early man has been compiled. From this research it is apparent that Paleo-Indians in the East were not necessarily associated with the same faunal complexes as in the West (J. B. Griffin, 1952:354).

The early fluted point hunters occupied diverse habitats in the East from about 12,000-10,000 B.P., from the Gulf Coast to the Bay of Fundy, from Florida to Minnesota, from upland mountain areas to the Mississippi flood plain, with considerable variation in vegetational cover and animal life. They were not carnivorous but omnivorous, limited only by technology and food taboos (J. B. Griffin, 1977:12).

Gardner (1972) brings to light some of the difficulties precipitated by the historic dominance of the Plains in Paleo-Indian studies. As a result of the assumption fluted points (regardless of the environmental context) are indicative of migratory big-game hunting. Eastern American archaeologists have concentrated almost exclusively on point distributional activities (Brennan, 1982) and comparisons with western finds. While hunting may have been practiced in the East, the nature of the fauna could not have supported a life style predicated on constant nomadism and hunting of megafauna. To the contrary, small bands probably exploited a wide, but restricted eco-space, in a defined territory scheduled on the basis of tool kit depletion and social needs with periodic returns to a home base (Gardner, 1972:11). So, despite the apparent similarities in technologies, the economic basis for Eastern Paleo-Indians was somewhat different than those of the so-called big-game hunters of the Great Plains. There are a number of studies which clearly indicate that the Eastern Paleo-Indians began moving toward a highly efficient gathering economy (usually associated with the Archaic period) at an early date (Muller, 1978:284).

In more northern regions of North America, concentrations of populations at such sites as Debert in Nova Scotia (MacDonald, 1968), Bull Brook in Massachusetts (Byers, 1954; 1955), Holcombe Beach in Michigan (Fitting *et al.*, 1966), and Parkhill in Ontario (Roosa, 1977) were reoccupied seasonally. Caribou (*Rangifer* spp.) appears to have been the most suitable quarry and would have provided sufficient amounts of protein to maintain settlements of this size. The caribou, moreover, were predictable enough in their migratory habits to allow for the development of a central hunting camp that was reoccupied regularly as opposed to scattered kill sites (MacDonald, 1971:36). Cunningham, (1973:126) describes a technique that may have been employed by Paleo-Indians when hunting herding animals such as caribou:

> Paleo-hunters did not doggedly pursue migratory prey for other than short periods of time. Rather, it seems that while bands could not follow the herds, they could guess at the probable path of traveling animals and wait at some narrow valley or at a likely river crossing where the animals could become mired, thereby rendering them relatively helpless, and the hunters could be ready when the animals arrived to secure enough game to provide food for some time.

There is a notable lack of evidence, however, for hunting activities focused on Pleistocene megafauna by the Paleo-Indians of Eastern North America (Marshall, 1982:18). Eastern Woodlands people were more likely to hunt deer and smaller mammals rather than mammoth, mastodon, or bison. The later Paleo-Indian groups in this region—such as at the Quad, Shoop, and Williamson sites—appear to have made a more intensive utilization of vegetable and aquatic foods (Butzer, 1971:513). "With the exception of the Kimmswick site, however, the human and megafaunal [mastodon] remains are never physically associated, as they are in the better known Clovis localities" (Meltzer and Smith, 1986:4).

Fishing was in evidence at the Shawnee-Minisink site in the Upper Delaware Valley of eastern Pennsylvania some 10,640 years ago (McNett and McMillan, 1974). Wild hawthorn pits were found in the same hearth with charred fish remains (Marshall, 1982; McNett et al., 1977).

Although the principal foods exploited at Meadowcroft Rockshelter in Pennsylvania were white-tailed deer and wapiti (*Cervus canadensis*), Adovasio et al. (1977: 157) postulate that the seasonal availability of plant foods may have dictated the nature of Paleo-Indian occupation there. Some of the plant foods found include charred and uncharred hackberry (*Celtis* sp.), walnut (*Juglans* spp.), and hickory (*Carya* spp.), goosefoot (*Chenopodium* spp.), blueberries (*Vaccinium* spp.), and blackberries (*Rubus* spp.). Charred nut fragments were also recovered from the Williamson site in Virginia, providing further evidence that plant collecting was one of many subsistence activities of early man (Benthall, 1972:17).

There was an intensive occupation of the southeastern United States during the early postglacial period. At many sites with tool industries containing fluted points; however, they are proportionately fewer numbers when compared to other tools than is true of periglacial sites like Holcombe, where projectile points and bases account for more than 25 percent of the total assemblage. This might suggest that there was, in the Southeast, less emphasis on hunting and more on collecting than there was in the Northeast at the same time (Fitting, 1968:443).

Results from Dalton period sites in the Southeast more or less corroborate this theory. For example, at Rodgers Shelter in Missouri, fish, turtles, rabbit, squirrel, raccoon, terrestrial rodents, deer, bison, elk, turkey, hickory nuts, and black walnuts were evidenced (McMillan, 1976:224). If artifacts in the lowest levels of Stanfield-Worley Bluff Shelter in Alabama, Modoc Rock Shelter in Illinois, and Graham Cave in Missouri were deposited by Dalton peoples as is now presumed, then their subsistence was based on recent species. The exploitation of extinct Pleistocene fauna is not documented at any of these sites (Goodyear, 1982a:391). In the Early Archaic levels at Russel Cave, Alabama, a variety of animals were found including turkeys, squirrels, porcupine, turtles, and snakes (Weigel et al., 1974). Based on data from a number of sites in Arkansas, it appears Dalton peoples had stable territories, a rich ceremonial life, social mechanisms for long distance trade, and a successful hunting and gathering exploitation (Morse, n.d.:17).

Although early man in Florida probably utilized a wide variety of foodstuffs, this certainly did not preclude his hunting various forms of megafauna. Enough provocative evidence exists to confirm man's contemporaneity with extinct Pleistocene species in Florida as well as to suggest that on occasion he pursued some of these species as prey.

The first, and most controversial, evidence came from the Atlantic coast where a mastodon tusk, which allegedly was engraved by man, was recovered at Vero (Sellards, 1916). Another intriguing discovery was made in the Wacissa River in north Florida of a young female bison (*Bison antiquus*) with a fragment of a chert projectile point imbedded in the fronto-parietal area of her skull (Webb *et al.*, 1983:81). A giant land tortoise (*Geochelone* sp.) excavated from Little Salt Spring was apparently impaled by a man wielding a wooden stake (Clausen *et al.*, 1979). In 1981, another giant land tortoise was recovered in the Hillsborough River at underwater site 8Hi393c/uw, located several kilometers northwest of Harney Flats. One of the bones had been gouged, possibly by man, before fossilization occurred (Clayton, 1983:103).

Not far away from the Wacissa Bison Kill site on the nearby Aucilla River at a location known as Half Mile Rise, Serbousek and his associates recovered a number of extinct species (i.e., bison, bear, beaver, camel, and horse); as well as various lithic and bone tools, including a number of Paleo-Indian projectile points (Serbousek, 1983). The Half Mile Rise location, however, typifies the situation that exists at many river localities in north and central Florida. These findings seldom, if ever, demonstrate a definitive association between man and megafauna. So, it continues an unresolved question as to what role the animals played in the overall subsistence strategies of Paleo-Indian peoples in Florida.

In summary, the general hypothesis—based on a few dated kill sites on the Plains—that all Paleo-Indian peoples between 10,000 and 12,000 years ago were specialized hunters of herd animals is not confirmed by data collected from other natural regions of the continent (Bryan, 1977:360). The idea that Paleo-Indian groups wandered around the woods of Eastern North America for several thousand years in an unadapted condition is unacceptable. Paleo-Indian peoples may have entered the New World as cold steppe or tundra hunters, and they may have been big-game hunters on the Plains before entering the Eastern Woodlands, but less awe-inspiring local resources appear to have been of more importance once these peoples had arrived in the East (Fitting, 1968:442).

Early man had adapted to a multitude of environments and a plethora of resources, ranging from the open southwestern grasslands to the temperate forests of the Eastern Woodlands and Subarctic conditions of Nova Scotia. Nevertheless the recovered technology seldom reflects his varied subsistence and ecological adaptations. For the most part, Paleo-Indian assemblages, whether in New Mexico, Florida, Massachusetts, or Nova Scotia, manifest basically similar tool types (Richardson, 1978:286). In addition, a drastic change in subsistence did not occur from the Paleo-Indian period to the Early Archaic period but the transition was very gradual (Science Applications, Inc., 1979). Therefore, the idea of Paleo-Indian subsistence being almost totally dependent on big-game no longer seems tenable. "The restriction of the diet of these early hunters to big-game has been by certain archaeologists not by Paleo-Indians who were present 12,000 to 10,000 years ago" (J. B. Griffin, 1964:224).

SITE STRUCTURAL PATTERNING

To provide a perspective for viewing structural patterning at the Harney Flats site, we examined in more detail the structure of the following Paleo-Indian sites.

Debert

Eleven separate sections, for which discrete boundaries were intuitively defined, were excavated at the Debert site in Nova Scotia. Eight of these were concentrated within a strip 61 m by 183 m running across a ridge in the central portion of the site. The remaining three were scattered over another 8 ha. The overall pattern of occupation was described as nucleated with 92 percent of the artifacts and ten or eleven hearths being recovered from the central strip (MacDonald 1968:21). Each section was about 110 m^2 and contained one or two hearths and approximately 600 artifacts. One of the concentrations may have been twice as large as any other and could have resulted from successive occupations rather than a single contemporaneous one.

The central living floors at Debert show a different pattern, which is repetitive from one to another, but is not a smaller version of the overall pattern. On these floors, which average about 110 m^2 is a pattern of multiple hearths aligned along a north-south axis. Occasional small pits and depressions occur but no large features suggestive of semi-subterranean structures nor evidence of major supports for dwellings were found. In view of this and of the large size of the floors, simple open structures or windbreaks were more likely. Skin covers may have been used around the windbreaks, and some shelter may have been provided by natural tree-throw mounds. On the average, two to three hearths occurred on each floor, spaced from 1.83-6.10 m apart. The best-preserved floor was in section J, where artifacts clustered around the hearths and in a rim on the periphery. A second concentration, in the featureless area to the south of the hearths, was also excavated. This may have been an open area in front of the dwelling to take advantage of a sunny exposure such as was common in Naskapi dwellings (MacDonald, 1968:132-133).

MacDonald concluded that each floor represented a communal dwelling of several related families (30-40 individuals) and that each archaeological section, excluding the largest one, represented a single season's occupation. Interpreted activities in the center area are those of general maintenance tasks (wood working, bone working, and hide working), as reflected by a high percentage of endscrapers, *piece esquillees*, and flake tools. Projectile points and bifaces in general are relatively rare. Apparently tool maintenance was more frequently done than tool manufacture in this area.

The central area contrasted with two peripheral areas to the west slightly down slope and one to the north. Due to the high percentage of primary debitage, overall high flake to tool ratio, and emphasis on bifaces and points, these two areas were seen as tool manufacturing areas (1968:133).

A "lithic tempering hearth" uncovered in one of these sections contained large hammerstones and anvils that could be reused during successive occupations. In the remaining section north of the main area a unique occurrence of black pigment identified as pyrolusite was recovered in direct association with the artifacts, but none was found in culturally sterile test pits surrounding the section. There was little tool manufacturing on this floor. MacDonald concluded that Debert represented an occupation by a small band engaged in seasonal caribou hunting (1968:132-134):

> In terms of community pattern it was noted ... that eleven living floors were distinguished, of which eight clustered within a nuclear area, about three acres in extent. The central floors share the same basic pattern in terms of total floor area, of the number and distribution of hearths, as well as of the types and distribution of artifacts and varieties of lithic raw materials. Three sections on the peripheries of the site, D, E, and One, on the other hand, show the greatest number of distinctive features. It is considered that these represent special function areas rather than the occupation floors of different bands at another period. The occurrence of pigment in section One and the evidence for a chipping floor and lithic tempering hearth in section D support this view of areas of special activity (1968:131).

Holcombe Beach

Holcombe Beach is a relatively small Paleo-Indian site in Michigan with three major areas totaling 225 m^2, which had indications of differing activities in different areas of the site, and a significant distribution in the pattern of raw materials, flake types, and other artifacts (Fitting *et al.*, 1966). There were also a number of hearths—one with a calcined caribou fragment.

> ... it is possible to define a core area on the site where the main Paleo-Indian occupation occurred. Within this core area there appears to be a communal area where food preparation took place, at least for large game. The initial working and heat-treating of preforms also took place here. Surrounding this communal area are areas which appear to have been occupied by individual families. These areas are marked by a high occurrence of small retouch flakes indicating finishing or repair of artifacts, distinct chert profiles reflecting individual family chert preferences, and fired areas without calacined animal bone or debitage which could be interpreted as fires built by the family units for warmth (1966:81).

Fitting *et al* (1966:81) suggested there were five family areas at the site and postulated that three more existed in the unexcavated areas.

Summarizing later work at the site which revealed two additional floors and adjusting Fitting's original data, MacDonald (1971:36) postulated a site population of twenty-eight individuals. Of particular interest is MacDonald's interpretation of site function since he argued that the assemblage was that of a hunting camp based on his assumption that "so few processing tools associated with women's activities were found" (1971:36).

This may be nothing more than curating behavior manifesting itself in the tool assemblage, but if MacDonald is correct, his interpretation of a male dominated hunting party contrasts with Fitting's interpretation of a small band of families occupying the site for a single short period.

Although there are some basic differences between Holcombe Beach and Debert, MacDonald saw a common pattern.

> ... it is difficult to draw comparisons between the two sites. Nevertheless, the pattern of specialized areas with lithic tempering hearths and high preform and primary flake frequencies on the one hand, and living areas with small hearths and predominantly retouch flakes and finished artifacts on the other, is common to both. It appears that Holcombe is a concentrated version of the Debert pattern in which the essential plan is maintained. The most important variation is that areas of specialized activity at Holcombe were central and that the living areas were peripheral, whereas at Debert this pattern was reversed. Thus the positioning of specialized areas is variable and may depend on local topography, whereas the concept of specialized areas is consistent (1968:132).

Thunderbird

The Flint Run complex consists of several Paleo-Indian and Early Archaic sites focused upon a series of jasper quarries in the Middle Shenandoah Valley of Virginia. Gardner proposed that Thunderbird was a base camp within the Flint Run complex. Community patterning was evident as early as the initial season at the site (1974:20). In one area of the site a series of postmolds was uncovered forming an outline of some 7.32 × 6.10 m. Gardner associated the alleged structure with the Paleo-Indian component, although he acknowledged possible problems with this association due to artifact mixing. Nevertheless, he postulated that a series of residential units could have existed along the terrace slope on the South Fork of the Shenandoah River.

> ... continued replication of this pattern, however, should be sufficient to confirm that Flint Run complex base camps indeed contain structures, and that the residential areas are spatially separate from the general work areas (1974:20).

Excavation revealed knapping activity areas in the Clovis levels which contained lithic concentrations that were divided into two categories based on size and density—small compact clusters with few or no tools in association, and larger areas with a wide variety of tools. The small clusters were interpreted as short term chipping activities of a single individual (Verrey, 1986), while the larger areas were thought to represent differences in stages of manufacture and possibly differing tool type manufacture. A few complete tools such as side scrapers, endscrapers, and gravers were also found in this area.

Concerning activities in the larger areas Gardner stated:

> The presence and character of this minor variety of material when considered in light of the nature of the rest of this area may point to two related episodes of quarry exploitation wherein a base-camp was established prior to the quarry visit. This chert may have been used at the site before tool-kit

refurbishment could occur. Otherwise it may have comprised an exhausted tool-kit that was discarded upon arrival at the site subsequent to the quarry visit when the tool-kit had been refurbished (1974:105).

Vail

The Vail site lies in the Megalloway River Valley of northwestern Maine and was exposed by the retreating water level of Aziscohos Lake. Eight artifact concentrations thought to represent habitation loci were recognized during the excavations. They were unevenly distributed over an area about 140 X 40 m along what is believed to have been the former channel of the Megalloway River. What is interpreted as a killing ground is located approximately 250 m to the west.

> Loci A-F lie in an arc bordering what were once shallow stream courses ... now filled and leveled with eroded islands and tree litter. Loci G and H lie off by themselves well to the south of the main portion of the encampment. Although Locus G occupies an almost imperceptible knob or swell and might have been selected by Paleo-Indians for its improved drainage, Locus H has no such advantage (Gramly, 1982:46).

The largest locus (E) comprised approximately 85 m^2 while the smallest locus (H) covered only about 26 m^2 (4.5 X 6 m). This latter area contained 276 artifacts (after refitting) that Gramly believes were related to a single occupation, based on the relatively low counts. Since the full range of tools discarded at the other loci were represented at locus H, he states that it is representative of the site as a whole and "no extraordinary activities appear to have been performed on the spot" (Gramly, 1982:48).

Individual maps with all plotted artifacts are given; with the exception of the postulated number of reoccupations for each loci (except H) no real differences are noted among them.

> The artifact plot for Locus H ... shows no neat patterns or juxtapositions of tools and waste. The smallest activity area, then, is the locus itself, which measures 4.5 m X 6 m. The lack of segregated activities strongly suggests that many tasks were performed indoors. Foot traffic, sweeping, rummaging around, and opportune disposal may have scrambled artifacts resulting from separate events (Gramly, 1982:53).

The artifactual remains recovered from the postulated killing ground consist of ten broken and intact fluted points, seven of which were located within a 6 X 8 m area. Six of the recovered tips conjoin bases recovered at the main encampment and form the basis of the inference of the area being a killing ground. An additional 700 m^2 were examined by raking, and no additional artifacts were found.

No organic remains were recovered, and the inference of ambushed caribou at Vail is based largely on environmental evidence and that caribou bones have been recovered from three other early sites in the Northeast. Gramly believes that caribou could have been ambushed as they crossed the stream, and that this was the primary function of the camp.

PALEO-INDIAN SETTLEMENT PATTERNS

It is important to study past human behavior in the context of communities, and the settlement provides the best locus for such a perspective (Chang, 1972:1). Settlement patterning has been defined by Willey (1953:1):

> ... as the way in which man disposed himself over the landscape on which he lived. It refers to dwellings, to their arrangement and to the nature and disposition of other buildings pertaining to community life. These settlements reflect the natural environment, the level of technology on which the builders operated, and various institutions of social interaction and control which the culture maintained. Because settlement patterns are, to a large extent, directly shaped by widely held cultural needs, they offer a strategic starting point for the functional interpretation of archaeological cultures.

This section covers what Emyrs Jones (1966) has termed the distributional aspect of settlements. In other words, where are the areas settled by Paleo-Indians and what areas did they avoid? The assumption is that an archaeological settlement pattern is not chaotic, but the result of political, economic, and ecological forces working themselves out on the landscape (Butzer, 1982:22).

The known distribution of Paleo-Indian sites in North America may be biased. For example, Kunz (1969:27) has indicated that kill sites are much easier to find than are sites of extended occupation. This results from habitational sites not being as subject to the erosional forces of nature (at least for the Paleo-Indian period) and being covered with culturally sterile soil deposits, making them much more difficult to find. This has resulted in most open sites having been found accidentally during construction activities which have largely destroyed the contextual information contained within them.

A notable exception to the rule of disturbed, mixed component, primarily surficial Paleo-Indian occupations is Templeton—6LF21—in Washington, Connecticut, which was found by looking "... where the context was the best, and not where the artifacts had already been plowed from their original context" (Moeller 1980: 13). Although none of the surface collections from this terrace of the Shepaug River had yielded any Paleo-Indian artifacts, soil corings revealed that the fine grained sand was the deepest where the artifacts were the scarcest. Acting under the assumption that the best context is where the disturbance is the least, the excavators uncovered an undisturbed single component dated to $10,190 \pm 300$ years B.P., 8240 B.C., (W-3931) between .80 and 1.5 m below surface.

> Attempts at predictive modeling of site locations using distributional studies of fluted point surface finds from distant and adjacent regions have focused upon appropriate hunting, fishing, and gathering areas accessible in immediately post-glacial times. While these must of necessity have been extremely important and extensive *in toto*, the temporal extent of Paleo-Indian and their non-subsistence needs are ignored. An attempt should be made 1) to consider crucial non-subsistence resources with limited distributions and 2) to concentrate the search in those areas most likely to have conditions conducive to long term *in situ* preservation of artifact and ecofact associations (Moeller, 1984:241).

Funk (1977:16) maintains that rarity of known Paleo-Indian sites is not only due to the long-term operation of natural processes that result in the loss of archaeological resolution, but also the low density of aboriginal peoples possessing "simple" technologies in the relatively unfavorable environment of the late glacial and early postglacial time. According to Bryan (1977), most human occupation sites were located either near the coast or along major river courses during the Pleistocene, in the same locations as many later sites. However, both of these resource-rich habitats (the littoral and the riverine) are difficult for archaeologists to investigate, as eustatically rising sea levels have drowned the entire late glacial/early Holocene shoreline of the Atlantic and Gulf Coasts. Moreover, most of the major rivers, even hundreds of miles inland, have aggraded to the rapidly rising postglacial sea level, inundating other likely occupation localities in the water table of floodplain terraces (Bryan, 1977:160-162; see also Hemmings, 1972). For example, along the upper east coast of North America, beaches were 100 to 150 km farther east and ocean levels may have been as much as 90 m lower. Peat borings indicate that the now submerged continental shelf from ten or eleven millenia ago was a fairly level plain interspersed with lakes and lagoons and supported such vegetation as spruce, pine, and fir and was probably capable of supporting a significant human population (Kraft, 1977).

Keeping these limitations in mind, we know, from the sites that have been studied, that site size and artifactual density appear to have been influenced by the physiographic features on or near which archaeological sites are located. Almost all Pre-Columbian inhabitants of the Americas returned to favored localities. If the area was broad and open, the sites tended to be only approximately reoccupied on subsequent visits, resulting in a thin scatter of artifacts over a wide area. If, on the other hand, the feature (e.g., a floodplain) is very narrow, then the spatial restraints force a return to more nearly the same location each time—resulting in a smaller site with a higher density of artifacts (Mato and Gunn, n.d.: A31-32). Although the preceding explanation is somewhat simplistic, it does serve to demonstrate that landform affects not only site selection, but also the density of cultural remains left at the site. Paleo-Indian peoples preferred certain physiographic settings for various site activities.

Virtually all sites producing Paleo-Indian artifacts in the Southeast are situated on hilltops or ridges overlooking some type of water source (White, 1980:1; Gardner, 1977:262). Paleo-Indian peoples often set up their camps on ridges or slopes overlooking water spots, thus allowing them to keep these places under constant surveillance (Hudson, 1976:40; Jochim, 1976:49; J. Wood, 1978). Broster (1982: 102-103) indicated that one of the reasons the Pierce site in Tennessee was selected was because it provided an extensive overview of the South Fork of the Forked Deer River. In the Ohio Valley, Cunningham (1973) has confirmed the placement of Paleo-Indian sites on higher terraces and knolls overlooking broad expanses of alluvial bottom land, generally away from the river and close by the precipitous hills of the region.

In central New Mexico, Paleo-Indian sites are generally found on ridges overlooking playas (basin-shaped depressions with interior drainage), which provided graze for herbivores hunted by the Indians (Judge, 1973:248). Folsom sites, in particular, were either at or within an average of 100 m from an overview upon which a good lookout over a hunting area was possible (Judge, 1973:196). A similar situation existed at West Athens Hill (a Paleo-Indian quarry-workshop-habitation site) overlooking Athens Flat in New York (Funk, 1977). This area was repeatedly visited by Indians, not only because of the high quality flint, but also because it provided an unobstructed view of game in the adjoining flats.

Fifteen hundred fluted point locations were correlated with various physiographic features in northeastern North America to demonstrate an early Paleo-Indian preference for low-lying plains with a terrain of moderate local topographic relief in major river valley areas (Jackson, 1983:397). The primary settlement locations for northeastern Paleo-Indian sites seemed to be in spruce woodland and spruce parkland vegetative communities, which usually occur in low-lying plains and river valleys (Curran and Dincauze, 1977). These same parklands and woodlands were once the preferred habitats of migratory herbivores such as bison and caribou, suggesting that the disposition of early Paleo-Indian sites may be reflective of a primary exploitive pattern (Jackson, 1983).

Another apparently important consideration in Paleo-Indian site selection was the location of game trails or crossings. In the Ohio Valley, Cunningham (1973) noticed that many Paleo-Indian sites were strategically situated near natural routes and trails leading to and from the river lowlands—indicating that these people situated themselves where large fauna might pass in their seasonal migration cycles or while randomly seeking forage. In addition, he observed that many of the sites were located near "licks" or saline springs, probably to stalk game attracted to those areas (Cunningham, 1973:125). At Debert in Nova Scotia, MacDonald (1968:120) found that the site was primarily occupied for intercepting game moving between two microenvironments. The Vail site in Maine also seems to corroborate findings that the proximity of a killing ground was a primary determinant in the choice of a place to erect dwellings (Gramly, 1981:39). At Blackwater Draw in New Mexico, the once-extant pond served as a favored hunting site for the Paleo-Indian inhabitants of the Llano Estacado. During the Clovis period, there is good evidence that mammoths were ambushed, killed, and butchered as they stood in the shallow water at the edge of the pond (Hester et al., 1973:178). The Domebo site in Oklahoma, where a mammoth was found in association with cultural materials, was once a spring-fed marsh with a luxuriant growth of vegetation where the animal had grazed (Leonhardy, 1966:42). The attraction of the water holes and lush grazing areas is a common element in the choice of western kill sites (Wheat, 1971:24).

In his comprehensive study of site locations in New Mexico, Judge (1973:311) concluded that proximity to a hunting area was one of the major environmental variables common to all Paleo-Indian sites. Wood's (1978) model for describing optimal location strategies supported the contention that base camps would be located near major hunting and potential trap areas. To the contrary, Jochim (1976:54) postulated that the lower the mobility of the resource, the more reliable it would be for the hunter-gatherers to establish a base camp nearby, whereas such highly mobile resources as game animals would be less important in the specific location of the settlement. In essence, the base camp would be near secure resources, while satellite extraction stations would be established near the more mobile, highly prestigious resources (e.g., big game) (Jochim, 1976:63).

Proximity to water was another major factor in the selection of suitable site locations (Butzer, 1971). Along with an overview and a prime hunting area, Judge (1973) found this to be a major variable common to all Paleo-Indian sites within his area of study, although Paleo-Indians may not have considered fresh water essential to the selection of a campsite (Judge, 1973:124). According to Wood's (1978) model, Paleo-Indian base camps would have been located near running water. Another factor applicable to water location in mountainous areas of the west, but not in the southeastern coastal plain, was the vertical distance to water (Kvamme, 1982). Western sites are generally discovered on more level ground or at least on less precipitous slopes.

Although we do not know the specific criteria used for site selection by Paleo-Indians, site catchment analysis indicates less concern with band spacing and population density as determinants of site location, and instead emphasize such considerations as the availability, abundance, spacing, and seasonality of plant, animal, and mineral resources (Roper, 1979:120). Additional variables which affect site selection include position of natural shelters, degree of exposure, dry ground, available fuel resources, and factors impeding or facilitating human movements, e.g., coasts, swamps, canyons, and vegetational patterns (Butzer, 1971).

In an ideal situation, where the centers of distribution of all resources coincide with conditions of adequate shelter and an overview, the base camp is located at the central point. But in reality, the spatial distribution of resources does not coincide, making it more difficult to predict site locations, especially across regions (Jochim, 1976). For example, Haynes (1980:115) discovered a distinct difference in the location of eastern and western Clovis sites. He found that most stratified Clovis sites in the west were associated with small tributary streams and springs, whereas those in the east were related to buried stream terraces.

While Haynes' description of differing regional settlement strategies is woefully inadequate, Carbone's (1983) recent study may shed light on explaining the differences between general settlement patterns in the east and west. He postulates that

> ... a homogeneous environment would be seen as coarse grained (grain refers to the size of areas of ecological diversity in the environment) whereas a heterogeneous environment would be fine grained. In terms of adaptation, coarse grained environments lead to greater specialization whereas fine grained environments lead to generalization. The late glacial and early postglacial environments in eastern North America, and especially in the southeast, were highly fine grained, probably in contrast to the western environments. Thus, the fine grained nature of the environment demanded a rather generalized adaptive strategy for the eastern Paleo-Indian populations, again in contrast to the seemingly more specialized western tradition (Carbone, 1983:13, 14).

Due to the diversity of subsistence strategies, patterns of settlement and locations of sites would be spatially more varied in the Southeast than in the West. For wherever man settles, he tends to maintain forest edge (the tendency for increased variety and density at community junctions is known as the edge effect) communities in the vicinity of his habitations (Odum, 1971:158).

In Florida, Paleo-Indian sites (i.e., mostly isolated point finds) have long been associated with water, especially large springs and spring-fed rivers (Neill, 1964; Simpson, 1948; Dunbar and Waller, 1983). Similarly, the typical Florida Paleo point is widely distributed along the beds of a number of North Florida rivers including the Aucilla, Withlacoochee, Suwannee, Santa Fe, Ichetucknee, and Oklawaha (Milanich and Fairbanks, 1980). An avid amateur archaeologist and diver, Ben Waller, has found more Paleo-Indian projectile points in the Santa Fe River in north-central peninsular Florida than in any other location in the state. He finds most of the Paleo-Indian artifacts in broad, shallow areas .3-.6 m feet deep at what he believes to have been game crossings where hunters had an excellent opportunity to ambush prey while its movements were restricted by water. The shallow areas also presented the hunter with the opportunity to float his victim downstream to a ledge where he could begin his butchering (Waller, 1972:14).

A recent study of Clovis/Suwannee point distributions suggest that major concentration of Paleo-Indian sites in Florida would be within regions of Tertiary age limestone outcrops (i.e., the Northern Panhandle and Central Gulf coast karst regions). Most of the sites located elsewhere are found near or in sinkholes, spring caverns, or other karst features which expose limestone (Dunbar and Waller, 1983: 19). Clausen et al. (1979:613) propose that the intervening dry periods would have exercised control over the distribution of habitation sites on the inland portions of the peninsula. This would explain the concentrations of Paleo artifacts in solution features, spring runs, and the major drainages of the peninsula. In other words, during Paleo-Indian times when the climate was much drier than today, there would have been little or no stream flow (Clausen et al., 1975).

Dunbar and Waller (1983:23-24) delineate eleven specific site clusters: 1) Lake Jackson/Lake Lafayette Cluster (Leon County); 2) Aucilla/Wacissa Cluster (Jefferson and Taylor Counties); 3) Upper Suwannee/Withlacoochee North Upland Valley Cluster (Columbia, Hamilton, Suwannee and Madison Counties); 4) Waccasassa Cluster (Levy County); 5) Lower Sante Fe/Ichetucknee Cluster (Alachua, Columbia, Gilchrist, and Suwannee Counties); 6) Paynes Prairie/Orange Lake Cluster (Alachua and Marion Counties); 7) Silver Springs/Oklawaha Cluster (Marion County); 8) Chain of Lakes Cluster (Lake County); 9) Tsala Apopka/Panasoffkee/Withlacoochee south Cluster (Marion, Citrus, and Sumter Counties); 10) Brooksville/Lecanto Upland Cluster (Hernando and Citrus Counties); and (11) Hillsborough/Harney Cluster (Hillsborough County).

In addition to the presence of a water source, the availability of quality lithic materials was another important consideration in Paleo-Indian site selection (Funk, 1972). With regard to the Flint Run complex in Virginia, Gardner notes "a jasper deposit because of its fixed position (secure resource), served as a point where any segment of the population could readily predict the other segments would return to" (Gardner, 1977:260). Other investigators believe that Paleo-Indian sites will be found fairly close to every locality where the characteristic outcrops of high quality chert occur (Benthall and McCary, 1973:132).

Early Archaic sites have been found in many of the same environmental settings as the older Paleo-Indian sites, especially along the major drainages—which one would expect of a transitional period of changing environmental variables and perhaps population increases—but it is also clear that Early Archaic activity or habitation sites are preserved in other localities as well (Claggett and Cable, 1982). After 8,500 B.P., according to Milanich and Fairbanks (1980), changes in settlement pattern and subsistence were evident between the Paleo-Indian and subsequent Early Archaic cultures. Many archaeologists, nonetheless, are of the opinion that very little change took place between these two periods in North American prehistory in the Southeast (Gardner, 1974:24; Science Applications, Inc. 1979). From the standpoint of lithic technology (which in most instances is our only tangible evidence), a definite shift occurs not between Paleo-Indian and Early Archaic, but between Early Archaic and Middle Archaic tool assemblages (Hemmings, 1972:11). Clearly much more data are needed from stratified early man sites before this problem will be satisfactorily resolved.

CHAPTER 7

Context of Paleo-Indian in Central Florida

Prior to Simpson's (1948) initial illustration of Paleo-Indian points from Florida, Sellards (1916, 1917) at Vero Beach and Gidley (1926) at Melbourne proclaimed that man had been in the peninsula since the Pleistocene based on findings of human skeletal remains in alleged association with Pleistocene faunal remains. Hrdlicka (1922) discounted Sellards's conclusions, based on his belief that the earliest peoples had arrived in Florida no more than 5,000 years ago. Although Hrdlicka's reasons were incorrect, so were the assumptions made by Sellards and Gidley. J. W. Griffin (1952) and Rouse (1950) have refuted the theories of these early investigators. Griffin asserts that

> ... the Vero and Melbourne finds represent an early Indian population, older than Hrdlicka would have granted, but more recent than the Pleistocene dating of some geologists. Strictly speaking, the Vero and Melbourne remains are not those of Paleo-Indians but rather those of an Archaic occupation that occurred sometime after 8,000 or 9,000 years ago" (1952:323).

Unfortunately, just as in the other South Atlantic states, most Paleo-Indian sites reported in Florida have been isolated point finds and possible kill sites (Science Applications, Inc., 1979:II-28). Rayl's (1974; see also Hoffman, 1983) investigation of a purported mammoth kill in Silver Springs Run near Ocala, where conclusions are tenuous at best, seems to be typical of these kinds of sites. Another such site was found in the Itchetucknee River in northern Florida. In this instance, a chert scraper was recovered *in situ* below a partially articulated mastodon skeleton. Three fossilized ivory points were also located in the vicinity of these faunal remains (Simpson, 1948:14).

Two notable Paleo-Indian sites in the state are underwater ones. Little Salt Spring contains both Paleo-Indian and Archaic components. The most unique Paleo-Indian implement recovered, however, was a nonreturning oak boomerang, which may be the oldest example of this type of weapon in the world and is the first found in the Western Hemisphere (Clausen *et al.*, 1979). At another nearby sinkhole, Warm Mineral Springs, a human burial was accompanied by a worked shell spear thrower (atlatl) spur. Other early artifacts from the site include a polished bone needle, a fossilized shark's tooth that had been intentionally pressure-flaked along the edge, and Greenbriar-type points with lateral and basal grinding (Cockrell and Murphy, 1978).

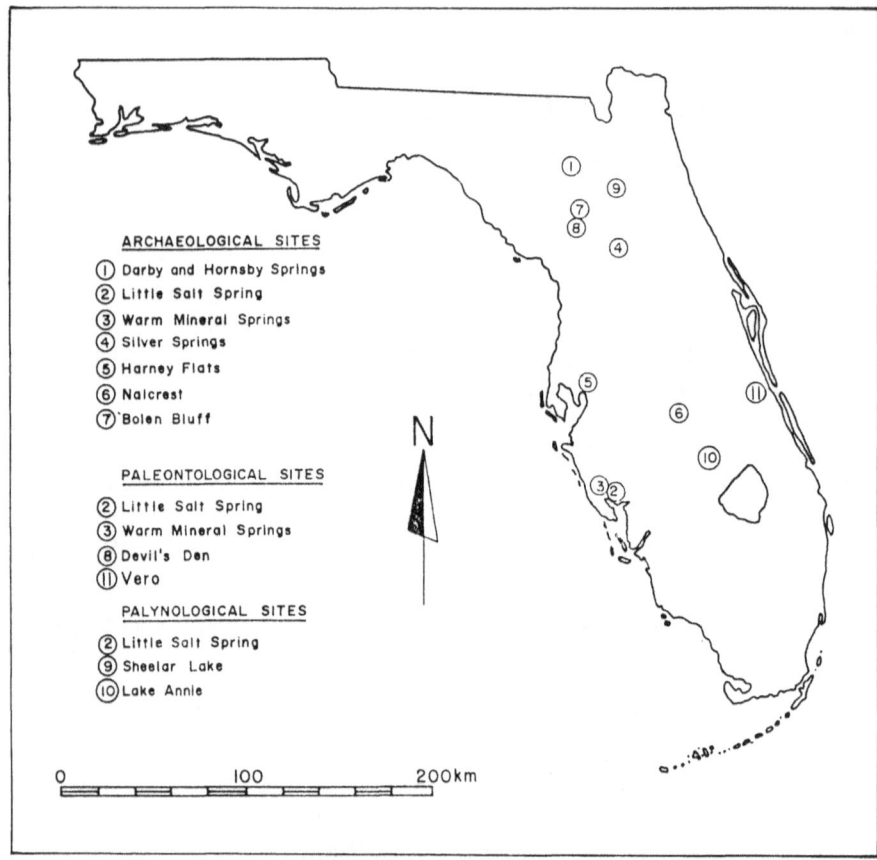

Figure 49. Site locations in peninsular Florida.

Prior to the excavations at the Harney Flats site, the only systematically investigated Florida terrestrial location that produced *in situ* Paleo-Indian diagnostic tools was the Silver Springs site (Neill, 1958) in Marion County (Figure 49). A Suwannee point recovered from the lowest level of the site was described by Goggin (1952:65) as being weakly fluted on one face. Although archaeologists at this time considered fluting to be the major trait used to distinguish Paleo-Indian points from subsequent forms, Neill (1971), noted that the "fluting" on this particular point resulted from the removal of two or three spalls and was not a typical channel flake scar. Other artifacts in the Silver Springs assemblage included a chopper, a plano-convex side scraper, two sandstone abraders whose suggested function was for sharpening bone awls or for grinding the edges of projectile points, and a possibly-worked piece of fossil shell (Mason, 1962), elongated knives, snub-nosed (end) scrapers, retouched flakes, utilized flakes, graver perforators, and ornaments (Neill, 1964). Hemmings (1975:148) reinvestigated the Silver Springs site and described it as a campsite, but was unable to locate any additional diagnostic materials from the Paleo-Indian or Early Archaic periods.

EARLY RADIOCARBON DATES

Four sites in Florida have produced early dates which fall into the accepted time range for the Paleo-Indian period; however, none of these has been explicitly associated with Suwannee remains. The only Florida land site with a Paleo-Indian period radiocarbon date is from Darby and Hornsby Springs. In this case, excavation in a limestone solution cavity adjacent to Hornsby Springs revealed some chert flakes and mastodon teeth within a sandy muck deposit, capped by a freshwater shell marl stratum that was radiocarbon dated to 9880 ± 270 B.P., 7930 B.C. (Dolan and Allen, 1961:40). The significance of this date is uncertain since no diagnostic remains were associated with the dated stratum. Since Suwannee remains were recovered elsewhere around the springs, they imply that this date is associated with the Suwannee material: "this dating is significant because it establishes the latest date before the worked lithic material and the vertebrate remains could have been associated" (Dolan and Allen, 1961:35). Unfortunately, no further description is given of the artifacts.

The three remaining early dated sites are underwater ones, but none has produced diagnostic Suwannee projectile points. At Little Salt Spring in Sarasota County a series of dates spanning the Paleo-Indian and Archaic Periods were obtained from a 60 m deep sinkhole: one from a wooden stake allegedly used to kill a giant land tortoise (*Geochelone* sp.), which was dated to 12,030 ± 200 B.P., 10,080 B.C. (TX-2636), 9,920 ± 160 B.P., 7970 B.C. (TX-2461) from a hickory nut, and 9,080 ± 250 B.P., 8830 B.C. (TX-2594) from a carved oak mortar (Clausen et al., 1979). The spring also yielded a socketed antler projectile point with the tip of the dart still preserved in its base. At nearby Warm Mineral Springs, a 70 m deep sinkhole, a human "burial" was radiocarbon dated to 10,310 ± 145 B.P., 8360 B.C. (I-7213) (Cockrell and Murphy, 1978). Greenbriar projectile points appear to have been associated with this site. A date of 11,170 ± 130 B.P., 9220 B.C. (Beta 5942) was obtained for a bison kill location in the Aucilla River using the distal end of a bison humerus found within 1 m of a bison skull. Embedded in the skull was a distal fragment of a chert projectile point of unknown type (Webb et al., 1983). Although these dates indicate the presence of man in Florida as early as 12,000 years ago, none can be confidently assigned to a diagnostic content (i.e., Suwannee or Clovis).

PROJECTILE POINT CHRONOLOGIES

Examination of Table 16 indicates a general agreement of point chronologies and dates although Milanich and Fairbanks (1980) would extend the Paleo-Indian period in the state from 12,000 to 14,000 B.P., which is earlier than the earliest known date of 12,000 B.P. for this period. The ending date postulated in the table

Table 16. Early Man Chronologies in Florida

Bullen (1975, 1976)	Milanich and Fairbanks (1980)	Purdy (1981a)
1. Paleo-Indian (12,000–10,000 B.P.) a. Early—Clovis b. Late—Simpson, Suwannee, and Santa Fe?	1. Paleo-Indian (14,000–9,500 B.P.) Clovis, Suwannee, and Simpson	1. Paleo-Indian (12,000–10,000 B.P.) Simpson and Suwannee
2. Dalton (10,000–8,000 B.P.) a. Santa Fe, Dalton and Tallahassee b. Greenbriar, Bolen, Union Side-Notched	2. Late Paleo-Indian or transitional (9,500–8,500 B.P.) Bolen, Greenbriar, Santa Fe, Beaver Lake, Dalton	2. Late Paleo-Indian or transitional (10,000–9,000 B.P.) Bolen, Greenbriar, Hardaway Side-Notched, and Nuckolls
3. Early Preceramic Archaic (8,000–7,000 B.P.) Hamilton, Arredondo Kirk serrated Middle Preceramic Archaic (7,000–5,000 B.P.) Newnan and Florida Archaic Stemmed Late preceramic Archaic (5,000–4,000 B.P.) Layfayette, Clay, Culbreath	3. Early Archaic (8,500–7,500 B.P.) Arredondo, Hamilton Florida Morrow Mountain, Florida Spike, Savanna River, Kirk Serrated and Sumter Middle Archaic (7,000–5,000 B.P.) Newnan, Hillsborough Late Archaic (5,000–4,000 B.P.) Layfayette, Clay	3. Preceramic Archaic (9,000–4,500 B.P.) Kirk and Arredondo (earlier forms), Newnan, Florida Archaic Stemmed (later forms)

ranges between 8,000 and 9,000 B.P., which would include within the Paleo-Indian period most side and corner-notched points (e.g., Bolen and Greenbriar) that have come to be diagnostic of the Early Archaic (e.g., Big Sandy I, Palmer, and Taylor) elsewhere in the Southeast. These chronologies apparently follow Bullen's original Florida sequence except his Dalton period is replaced with Late Paleo-Indian. This portion of Bullen's chronology was primarily based on the excavations at Stanfield-Worley Bluff Shelter where everything found in Zone D was included typologically as part of the "Dalton complex" including both Dalton and notched (i.e., Bolen-like) projectile points (Bullen 1975:52–53).

Recently, Goodyear (1982a) strongly criticized the presumed association of Dalton and Early Archaic side- and corner-notched points by arguing that this association is a product of disturbances in caves and shelters, and that excavations in open sites have indicated a stratigraphic and typological distinction between Dalton and later notched point complexes. He synthesizes data from the Southeast to date notched point assemblages from 10,000–9,000 B.P. and Dalton from 10,500–9,900 B.P.

Disregarding for the moment whether the notched forms should be labeled Late Paleo-Indian or Early Archaic, Goodyear's synthesis suggests that an approximate ending date for Suwannee can be placed at 10,000 B.P. This, of course, is based on the assumption that various notched forms existed as "... basically synchronous horizon 'styles' across the eastern United States" (1982a:390). Although the ending date for Suwannees can be reasonably assumed, the beginning date and their relationship to the fluted (i.e., Clovis) point horizon, so prominent in the East, is still unknown.

The fluted Clovis point is known, albeit rarely, to occur in Florida (see Goodyear et al., 1983:46). Fluting, or the lack thereof, is also of importance here. Summarizing Neill's observations, Goodyear et al. (1983:46) state that if they are fluted, Suwannees are only fluted on one side (which suggests that this removal was not important to haft designs), and that in other states lanceolate forms which are not strongly fluted and are identified as Clovis, actually resemble Suwannees in Florida. This may indicate that the two types are basically contemporaneous. If this is true, however, it raises the question of why so few fluted points are found in Florida. The explanation may be that in Florida we have a unique regional expression of Paleo-Indian material culture contemporaneous with the better known "western traditions."

On the other hand, fluted points may represent an essentially pre-Suwannee horizon as suggested in the chronologies in Table 16, but they have not been found in a closed pre-Suwannee context. On the basis of the available stratigraphic evidence (including Harney Flats), it appears that Suwannee is the basal cultural stratum in Florida. Perhaps Florida remained largely unoccupied (for environmental reasons?) when Clovis peoples inhabited other areas of the Southeast. The few Clovis points in Florida may represent limited forays into the peninsula with the first long term habitation in the state beginning with later Suwannee occupations. If true, and assuming that fluted points date roughly from 11,000-10,500 B.P. [e.g., Goodyear (1982a:369)], then Suwannees may be bracketed between the beginning dates for notched forms and the ending date for fluted forms (i.e., 10,500-10,000 B.P.). This range corresponds with the recently postulated temporal placement of the Dalton horizon from 10,000-9,900 B.P. (Goodyear, 1982a). Contemporaneity with Dalton culture may be the case because Daltons, with the exception of the serrated Tallahassee, are rare in Florida (Goodyear et al., 1983:46).

Suwannee and Clovis

Although the Suwannee point is generally considered the predominant Florida Paleo-Indian artifact manifestation, its exact temporal position in the state and its chronological association with respect to the North American fluted point horizon have never been resolved. We will address the evidence for early cultural sequences in Florida by demonstrating the stratigraphic priority of Suwannee in the state and the dating of this sequence. Florida site locations discussed in the text appear in Figure 49.

Since Suwannee points were first recognized by professional archaeologists, they have been presumed to be Florida's earliest point type (Goggin, 1950:46; Williams and Stoltman, 1965), and the most characteristic Paleo-Indian tool in Florida

(Goodyear et al., 1983; Milanich and Fairbanks, 1980:39). Simpson (1948) was the first investigator to describe and illustrate this particular biface, and Goggin (1949: 20) was the first to use the term Suwannee as a unique type series (Neill, 1964). The Suwannee point has been compared to many early tool forms including Clovis (Goggin, 1949; Mason, 1962; Neill, 1964, 1971; Wormington, 1957), Dalton (Williams and Stoltman, 1965), Folsom without flutes (Simpson, 1948), Plainview (Goggin, 1949; Wormington, 1957) and Quad (Bullen, 1975). While most investigators (Bullen, 1975, 1976; Goggin, 1949; Hemmings, 1972; Mason, 1962; Milanich and Fairbanks, 1980; Purdy, 1981a) consider the Suwannee point to be a separate pre-Dalton tool form, Williams and Stoltman (1965) place it in the Dalton period, and postulate that the two forms (Dalton and Suwannee) were contemporaneous. In terms of range distribution, Suwannee points have been found in a horizon-like distribution from South Carolina (Science Applications, Inc., 1979) to Charlotte Harbor and Vero Beach in south Florida (Bullen, 1975). The heaviest known concentrations occur in the Sante Fe and Itchetucknee rivers of north-central Florida (Dunbar and Waller, 1983:22).

Bullen (1975:55) characterized Suwannees as usually large and fairly heavy, lanceolate-shaped, slightly waisted points with concave bases, basal ears, basal grinding, and waisted edges or sides. After examining the Simpson collection, he (1962b) concluded that fluting is rare. Another closely related projectile point, apparently in terms of age and form, is the Simpson. Some archaeologists are even of the opinion that Simpson points may have been Suwannees that were snapped at the base and later reworked (Milanich and Fairbanks, 1980). Bullen defines Simpson (1975: 56) as a wide bladed, relatively narrow waisted, fairly thin, concave based, medium to large-sized point with grinding apparent in the haft area. Basal ears are present, but are not as developed as in the Suwannee point. Basal thinning also occurs, but is not well developed. Workmanship ranges from fair to good. Points of this shape, if well fluted, could be termed Cumberland. The major stylistic difference between Suwannee and Simpson Points is that the latter are more waisted, have less prominent ears, and are generally smaller.

Excavations during the 1950s and early 1960s provided evidence for the stratigraphic relationship of lanceolate bifaces to later notched and stemmed points in Florida. Perhaps the most noted of these was at Silver Springs (Neill, 1958) where excavations showed Suwannees at the lowest level (88-93″ b.s.) of a stratified sequence with no other point types present. This work proved to be very important, as Mason's (1962:239-240) synthesis of Eastern Paleo-Indian archaeology relied on Neill's work to demonstrate that lanceolate points (Suwannees) came before stemmed or notched Archaic types. Subsequent work by Bullen (1958) on two sites at Bolen Bluff suggested a similar sequence. One Arredondo (30-35″ b.s.) and two Bolens (24-30″ b.s.) were recovered from the lowest levels of the excavations of these two sites. These points were associated with a number of well made unifacial tools all of which were found below stemmed Archaic forms (Bullen, 1958:24-25). Two Suwannees were also recovered from the excavation, but these were located in upper stemmed point levels; and Bullen (1958:17-18) is careful to state that these were out of their proper stratigraphic position. In his 1958 report Bullen first summarizes his evidence for the Florida stratigraphic sequence of Suwannee, Bolen, and stemmed forms in the state.

Bullen also conducted work at Dixie Lime Caves (Bullen and Benson, 1964) near Ocala that yielded a similar sequence with a Bolen point found stratigraphically below stemmed points. However, no Suwannee points were recovered. Excavations at Darby and Hornsby Springs (Dolan and Allen, 1961) in Alachua County also yielded some evidence of early occupations. Of interest here is one of several excavation pits at Darby Springs which yielded a Suwannee point at 114 cm below the surface and a Bolen between .75-.91 m below the surface. These results are similar to the sequence postulated by Bullen. The stratified sequence at Harney Flats confirms the sequence of Suwannee succeeded by notched and then stemmed forms in Florida.

Although these sequences are consistent with others elsewhere in the Southeast, no radiocarbon dates associated with these diagnostics exist. Thus the dates for early Florida chronologies are based on correlations with radiocarbon dated sequences from outside the state (see Bullen, 1975:2), and lead to ambiguities in dating some projectile point types—in this case the Suwannee—which are primarily Florida types.

Dalton and Early Archaic

The next cultural stage in Florida is termed the Dalton period (10,000-8,000 B.P.) by Bullen (1975, 1976) and the Late Paleo-Indian or Transitional by Milanich and Fairbanks (1980) and Purdy (1981a). Bullen recognized two discrete lithic traditions—the Dalton tradition proper (represented by Santa Fe, Tallahassee, and Dalton points [e.g., at the Terra Ceia Bay site (Warren and Bullen, 1965)] and a notched tradition manifested in Greenbriar, Bolen, and Hardaway points [e.g., at the Nalcrest site (Bullen and Beilman, 1973)].

Both Bullen (1976) and Hemmings (1972) maintain that Dalton—especially Bolen—should not be placed under the Paleo-Indian rubric. Tallahassee and Santa Fe points differ from Suwannee and Simpson points by virtue of having transverse parallel or collateral flaking. While this may appear to be a difference in degree and not in kind, sharpening by serration or beveling are definitely not Paleo-Indian traits (Tuck, 1974:74; Goodyear et al., 1983).

Bullen formally defined Bolen points (Bullen, 1975:51) as a small to medium sized, side-notched point with a ground base, dating to about 9,000 B.P.; blade edges are usually straight, but some are excurvate; serrations are rarely present. The Bolen Beveled point (Bullen, 1975:52) is identical to the Bolen point, except it is alternately beveled and usually has serrated blade edges.

Other than scattered surface and river bottom finds, Bolen points have been recovered at the Bolen Bluff and Dixie Lime Caves with a few well made unifaces. Apart from this, little else is known about these sites as only limited excavations were conducted, and these were apparently focused on gathering stratigraphic information.

One particular site, probably associated with this time period, is the Nalcrest site (Bullen and Beilman, 1973). A number of tool types comprising a microlith tool complex were recovered from underwater near the edge of Lake Weohyakapka in Polk County. Bullen and Beilman (1973:9-11) compared the site typologically with the Brand site (Goodyear, 1974), a Dalton period site in Arkansas. Some of the recovered tools included small cores, tiny side scrapers or drills, spurred chips, concave end scrapers, small Waller knives, and small ovate scrapers (Bullen and Beilman, 1973:4). More recently, Milanich and Fairbanks (1980:48) have interpreted it as a special use site where a single resource, requiring specialized tools, was exploited. Cane and grasses are postulated to have been collected and processed with the microlith assemblage to produce items such as baskets and mats.

In conclusion, the current status of early man knowledge in Florida consists of sketchy and purely descriptive findings. More and better data oriented to specific research problems are needed before a further synthesis of early man activities can be made.

PALEOENVIRONMENT

One is prone to assume that the landscape and climate of today are eternal conditions and to forget that man inhabited the earth during the ice ages and has witnessed the development and extinction of many species as world climate fluctuated through wide extremes (Jennings, 1957:6).

Sea Level

Based upon the amount of water contained within continental glaciers, fluctuations in sea level provide a means of discerning many of the major events in glacial history. In examining eustatic changes in sea level (i.e., fluctuations contingent upon the volume of water held in glaciers and disregarding tectonic effects), it is possible to infer paleoenvironmental conditions. Oscillations of sea level since the upper Miocene in Florida have ranged from 80 m above present Healy (1975) to 160 m below present (Ballard and Uchupi, 1970). These sea level changes have resulted in massive environmental modifications (Alexander and Crook, 1974; Davies and LeGrand, 1972; Webb, 1974), as well as major changes in the size of the Florida peninsula (Figure 50).

Milliman and Emery (1968) have conducted studies of sea level changes along the North Atlantic coast covering the past 35,000 years. Based on dates from eighty radiocarbon samples, their findings revealed the following pattern: 1) near the end of the Altonian period (35,000-30,000 years ago), sea level was near its present stand; 2) during the cool Farmdalian interstade of Wisconsin glaciation from 30,000-21,000 years ago, sea level gradually fell; 3) at the time of the Woodfordian stade [including the Wisconsin maximum at about 20,000 B.P. (Whitehead and Doyle, 1969)], sea level dropped rapidly to about 130 m below present; 4) the last major eustatic change was the Holocene transgression (14,000-7,000 B.P.), which resulted from rising seas during the Two Creeks ice recession at about 11,600 B.P.

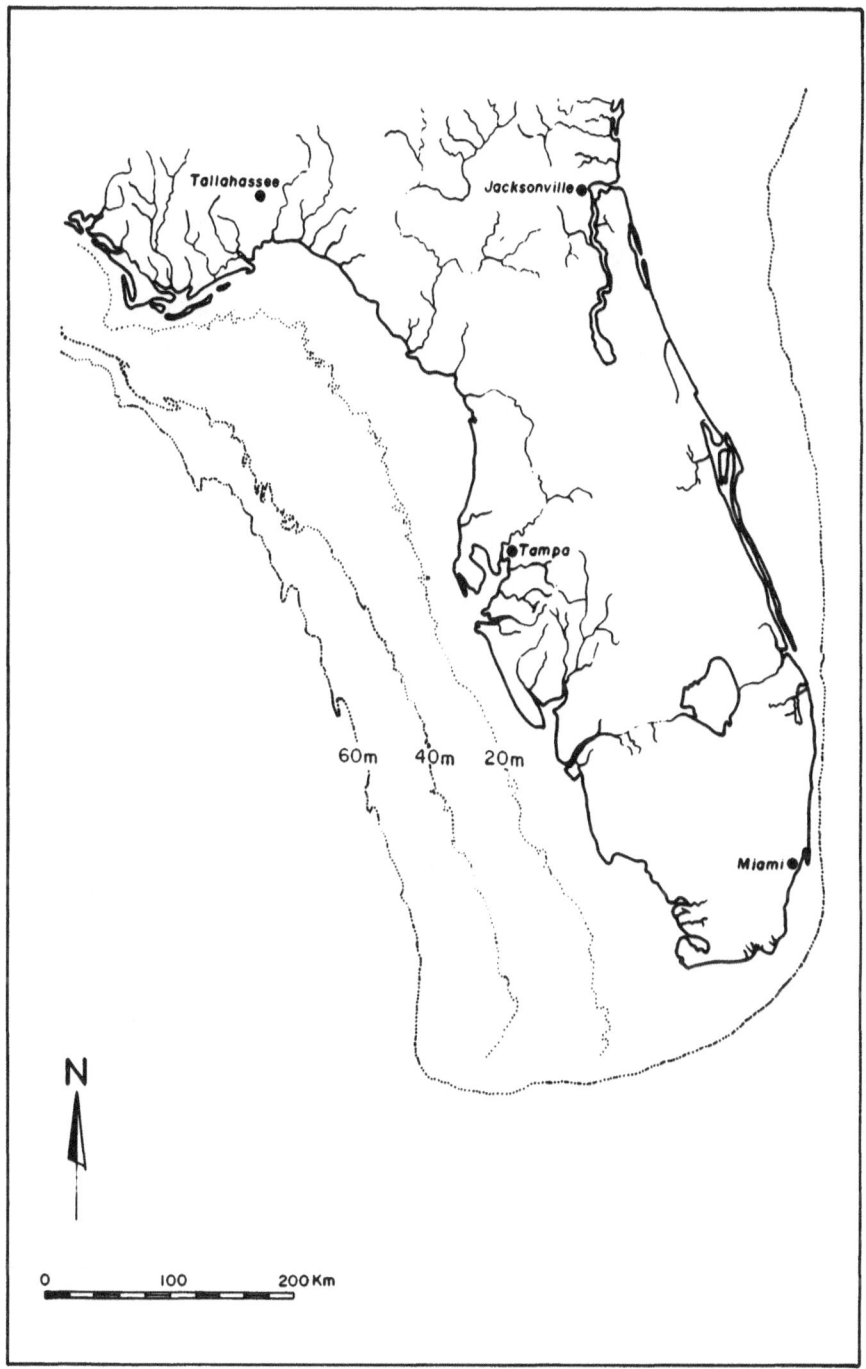

Figure 50. Late Pleistocene/Early Holocene sea level.

(Emiliani et al., 1975). Previously Broecker et al (1960) had noted a major fluctuation in climate at this time as revealed in their studies of ocean surface temperatures and deep sea sedimentation rates. Their data seem to be corroborated by other investigators who discerned a drop in water temperatures in the central Caribbean from $23.5°-22°C$ sometime between 12,000 and 11,000 B.P. (Emiliani, 1966).

Although the Milliman and Emery (1968) curve is the most widely accepted indicator of sea level, three major changes have led to a reconsideration of its utility south of Cape Hatteras (Science Applications, Inc., 1981:1-45). First, recent studies (Dillon and Odale, 1978) have demonstrated evidence of down-warping of the shelf north of central New Jersey, indicating that some of the data used by Milliman and Emery came from a subsiding shelf. Second, many of the cores which were used to denote a deep stand of sea level on the southeastern shelf (e.g., bedrock and algal rock) probably should be eliminated, since they no longer are considered reliable shallow-water indicators (MacIntyre et al., 1975). Third, shells lying on the sea floor and subject to movements by currents were also unreliable sources of data used to formulate the Milliman and Emery curve (Blackwelder et al., 1979).

More reliable sea level indicators found below the sea floor in intertidal deposits such as oyster shells and marine peats are not as likely to be displaced after deposition and have begun to be used in the reconstruction of sea level. In particular, Blackwelder et al. (1979) collected dates from several in-place indicators obtained by coring on the shelf south of Cape Hatteras. As a result of their findings, recent workers have proposed a new sea level curve much shallower than that of previous researchers (see Table 17).

The implications of sea level studies are especially critical for interpreting settlement patterns and subsistence activities of Paleo-Indian cultures. A number of investigators have previously indicated the importance of locating and evaluating submerged terrestrial sites which are now situated on the continental shelf of the Gulf of Mexico and the Atlantic Ocean (Bullen, 1955; Hester, 1980; Goodyear et al., 1983; Ruppé, 1980; Salwen, 1962; Warren and Bullen, 1965).

In Florida, Suwannee points of the Paleo-Indian period have been dredged from the Gulf of Mexico, perhaps verifying early man's presence on the continental shelf (Neill, 1964). At the Turtlecrawl Point site, (which dates to approximately 9,000 B.P.) in Pinellas County, Florida, the changed nature of the settlement pattern is

Table 17. Sea Level Stands 8,000 to 16,000 Years Ago

Years Before Present	Florida Cultural Periods	Sea Level in Meters Below Present Stand
8,000	Early Archaic	12
10,000	Paleo-Indian	23
12,000	Paleo-Indian	35
14,000	?	44
16,000	?	56

Adapted from Science Applications, Inc. 1981.

clearly demonstrated, as the site now rests beside a coastal estuary, whereas it was beside a freshwater stream when first occupied (with sea level 12-20 m lower) Goodyear *et al.*, 1980).

Although it has not been conclusively demonstrated, utilization of both marine and freshwater shellfish resources by Paleo-Indian peoples may have occurred (Emery, 1967). He postulated, based on the discovery of a 10,850 year old oyster bed on the Atlantic shelf (Emery and Edwards, 1966), that oysters (*Crassostrea virginica*), which thrive in protected marine waters with low salinities such as inland sides of barrier beaches or in estuaries (Edwards and Emery, 1977), may have been especially important along the North Atlantic coast. Emery (1967) later described an oyster "midden" found near Chesapeake Bay in 43 m of water. Subsequent to these findings, core samples have revealed two periods in the past when oysters were relatively abundant in the Atlantic—10,200 years ago when the shoreline was 55-65 m lower than now, and again 8,700 years ago when seas were 30-40 m lower than present (Edwards and Merrill, 1977).

Sea level advances have affected much more than just the size of the peninsula. Changing ground water salinities influenced the succession of plants in coastal areas. Sea level variations also affected inland sites where Tertiary Limestones at or near the ground surface were exposed to prolonged karst erosion (Brooks, 1967) resulting in a highly permeable system of underground flow. Increased permeability within this limestone resulted in more rapid changes in the potentiometric surface as it fluctuated in response to discharge and recharge rates within the Floridan aquifer. Changes in the potentiometric surface, then, affected the rate of flow at artesian springs throughout the state. Some investigators believe that rising sea levels were responsible for both Warm Mineral Springs and Little Salt Springs having been transformed from cenotes to flowing springs:

> The simplest explanation of this transformation at both springs is that post-Wisconsin sea level, around 8,500 B.P., had reached a point closely approximating present MSL; and the springs, responding to a potentiometric water level similar to that existing at present, began to flow. However, *other factors* such as increased amounts of precipitation in the recharge area in central and northern Florida may also have contributed to the higher potentiometric level in the Floridan (artesian) aquifer (Clausen *et al.*, 1975:26).

Whatever the reason, when Paleo-Indian and Early Archaic peoples occupied the area around Harney Flats between 9,000 and 12,000 years ago, the weather in peninsular Florida was much drier than now (Brooks, 1973; Brown, 1981; Watts, 1980). The climate could probably best be described as an interpluvial period coeval with the cool Northern Hemisphere temperature regime of late glacial times (Coleman, 1982:144).

Paleoflora

Fossil pollen provides excellent material for reconstructing terrestrial plant communities that have existed since the Pleistocene epoch. Once pollen studies are conducted and evaluated, biotic communities and climates can be inferred by describing what plant forms were dominant in the past (Odum, 1971:160). When reviewing these studies of early vegetational communities, one should know that precise reconstructions (based on ancient pollen assemblages) are difficult because the prehistoric communities differed from modern vegetational communities, and they cannot be interpreted through comparison (Wright, 1981). Many environmental reconstructions done in the past have been shortsighted in assuming a simple southward displacement of all existing phytogeographic zones. These studies must be reconsidered in light of a growing body of data which indicates a different distribution and greater abundance of many plant species south of the ice sheet than now occur in arctic and boreal regions (Davis, 1969).

As the glaciers oscillated between advances and retreats, temperatures on the North American continent ranged from those of cooler glacial periods to warmer intervals, similar to the present. Even as late as 14,000 B.P. much of Eastern North America was covered in tundra and spruce/pine woodland. By 9,000 B.P. the tundra and spruce was replaced by deciduous and coniferous vegetation (Davis, 1969). The unglaciated areas of the Southeast along the coastal plain were characterized by evergreen forest of conifers and dicotyledons (hardwoods). Refugia of mixed hardwoods such as elm, black gum, sweetgum, oaks, and hickories were common in bottomlands (Whitehead, 1965). Butzer (1971) postulated a humid temperate climate for the southeastern United States during the very late Wisconsin period.

Although it is agreed that full glacial conditions were never felt in peninsular Florida, different theories have been proposed regarding late Pleistocene temperatures in the Southeast. Although Brooks (1973:559) found no evidence of a significant temperature change over the past 16,000 years in Florida, most other investigators have indicated a reduction in the mean summer temperature of more than 10°C during the late glacial/early Holocene, due to the more southerly location of the Laurentide ice sheet (Gates, 1976; Watts and Stuiver, 1980). Winter temperatures, however, are believed to have been milder at this time, especially absolute minimum temperatures, due to the ice sheet acting as a shield to prevent Arctic cold fronts from reaching the region (Bryson and Wendland, 1967). The temperature decline in the summer, coupled with warmer winter temperatures resulted in a more uniform distribution of rainfall throughout the year (Coleman, 1982:149). In short, a marked decrease in seasonal fluctuation occurred, with a compression of winter and summer temperature ranges (especially the extremes), and increased aridity (Carbone, 1983:6). The climate at this time may have been similar to that of Mexico City today where average monthly temperatures vary from only 12.2-17.7°C throughout the year (Miller and Thompson, 1979).

These climatic factors account for pollen remains of boreal species such as spruce not being found south of Sheelar Lake in north-central Florida (Watts and Stuiver, 1980). Similarly, the low endemicity of tropical flora in Florida seems to indicate that the climate was not suitable for growing tropical West Indian species (Dillon, 1956). Thus, pollen studies generally confirm that Florida had a more temperate climate at this time.

Evidence from Lake Annie (Watts, 1975) revealed that from 37,000-13,000 years ago south central Florida experienced extremely dry conditions, with the primary plant cover consiting of rosemary (*Ceratiola*) scrub on sand dunes. Wright (1981) suggests that Florida underwent a period of maximum aridity between 18,500 and 14,600 years ago. Where sufficient soil moisture was available, some sclerophyllous oak stands may have coexisted with prairie-like vegetation.

The cool and dry glacially-influenced climate of Florida ended about 14,600 years ago (Watts and Stuiver, 1980). Sediments from Sheelar Lake, of this age, revealed a preponderance of mesic vegetation in the form of oak (*Quercus*), beech (*Fagus*), hickory (*Carya*), ironwood (*Ostrya*), and other broad-leaved trees indicating greater rainfall (Watts, 1980). Pollen samples from Lake Annie show that dune species disappeared about 13,000 years ago. Apparently, sufficient moisture was available for the development of oak scrub prairie, even though general aridity with restricted availability of water continued to prevail. The coarse, sandy soils covering much of the region must have made it difficult for mesic forests to survive during droughts or periods of lowered water tables. Under these circumstances, discrete vegetational communities would be strongly influenced by the water retaining potential of various types of soil (Watts, 1980:405). Watts was unable to find a modern analog for this type of vegetation in present-day Florida. He dated the beginning of the Holocene in peninsular Florida somewhere between 13,000 to 12,000 years ago, primarily based on a high count of pine pollen at Lake Annie. By 12,000 B.P. the climate continued to be dry, but not cold (Watts, 1980:400; Watts and Stuiver, 1980:327).

Pollen from Little Salt Spring (about 100 km south of Harney Flats) and from other sites in the state indicated a relatively dry climate in central Florida from 12,000-9,000 B.P. (Brown, 1981; Wright, 1981:121). Due to lower water tables, resulting from the more arid climate, a flora unlike that of today was found throughout peninsular Florida (Long, 1974:29). Mesic forests were once again on the decline as xerophytic species of oak became the most prevalent tree genera. By 10,410 B.P., termed the hypsithermal of the Southeast by Watts, local sclerophyllous oak forests with patches of open prairie and savanna prevailed in the landscape. Ragweed (*Ambrosia*) and other composites and grasses were also abundant during this period (Watts, 1980). By 9,500 B.P., temperatures were gradually approaching those of today (Edwards and Merrill, 1977:36).

Although drier conditions prevailed when Paleo-Indians inhabited the Florida peninsula 12,000-9,000 years ago, a number of factors may have improved their chances of finding sufficient water. First, cooler summer temperatures led to an increased density of air at lower atmospheric levels (Miller and Thompson, 1979:125). This resulted in higher mean atmospheric pressure which in turn, served to load and compress the aquifer. This decreased the amount of pore space in the limestone forcing more water out of the aquifer and slightly increasing flow levels from artesian springs (Rosenau et al., 1977). Second, Brooks (1967) calculated the rate of solution of karst terrain in Florida at .028 m^3 of rock (largely $CaCO_3$) per .093 m^2 of land over an 8,000 year period. This suggests that 10,000 years ago the aquifer had not been eroded to its present extent, and as a result could hold less water. The lower storage capacity of the aquifer, when fully charged, must have resulted in an increased flow. Third, if Watts' scenario of a much higher proportion of grassland to woodland is valid, such vegetational differences would have significantly increased the amount of available runoff, as a change from trees to grasses usually decreases evaporation and transpiration, and also reduces the amount of water trapped by surface soils (Miller and Thompson, 1979:325). Losses through evapotranspiration are even less in or near barren dune-covered areas than in grasslands (Wetterhall, 1965:10). Another factor which conserved water was lower summer temperature resulting in reduced evaporation rates. Excess runoff caused by lower rates of evaporation could have effectively charged both water table and artesian aquifers in Florida with substantially smaller amounts of precipitation than now occur in the Tampa Bay region. With the passage of time, increasing amounts of rain fell on the peninsula. Paleobotanical evidence from Little Salt Spring and hydrological data from Warm Mineral Springs (Lazarus, 1965:56) revealed wetter conditions from 9,000-8,000 B.P. Within this time span many of Florida's relatively shallow perched water table lakes and ponds, like Lake Thonotosassa near Harney Flats, began forming (Watts and Stuiver, 1980).

Nevertheless, this was to be a relatively short-lived transformation. Studies in central Florida and southern Georgia indicate that during the mid-Holocene (8,000-5,000 B.P.) the region reverted to a drier climatic regime, as evidenced by sclerophyllous oak forests intermixed with scrub and savanna, and patches of blue stem (*Andropogon furcatus*) prairie (Watts, 1971). Greater extremes between summer and winter temperature, similar to those of today, were first established at around 7,000 B.P. when the melting of the Laurentide ice sheet was completed (Science Applications, Inc., 1981:115).

Higher water tables became more or less permanent features when precipitation in dramatically at about 5,000 B.P. This change was revealed in a shift in vegetation in which pine became much more common in upland areas, especially Longleaf pine (*Pinus palustris*), which probably has been the dominant plant species for the past 5,000 years along the entire southern coastal plain (Long, 1974:33; Watts, 1971). Cypress (*Taxodium* sp.) swamps also began developing around the newly formed lakes during this period (Wright, 1972:277). In addition, a more diverse flora of mesic broad-leaved trees such as beech (*Fagus* sp.), wax myrtle (*Myrica* sp.), loblolly bay (*Gordonia* sp.), holly (*Ilex* sp.), saw palmetto (*Serenoa repens*) and sweet bay (*Magnolia virginiana*) were beginning to appear 5,000 years ago. These species represent the first appearance of Florida's modern flora (Watts, 1980).

Paleofauna

The fossil record and distribution of fauna indicate that significant ecological shifts have occurred throughout the Quaternary period in southeastern North America. Vertebrate sites are especially useful in sampling specific local areas, whereas pollen profiles represent a much broader range of regional information. Therefore, climatic models based on pollen types alone are best verified and supplemented by studies that focus on interpreting terrestrial faunal remains (Science Applications, Inc., 1981:I-73).

Pleistocene avifauna were similar to their modern-day counterparts, which indicates that they probably inhabited similar environmental areas. Perhaps this is a result of the southern origin of most birds, for environmental changes were demonstrated to have been milder in the south during the Pleistocene (Selander, 1965). Likewise, freshwater fish thus far recovered from Pleistocene strata (especially post-Nebraskan remains), are indistinguishable from living species (Miller, 1965:71). The same may be said of most reptilian fauna, which have remained virtually unchanged since the latter half of the Cenozoic era (Auffenburg and Milstead, 1965).

On the other hand, some species of reptiles, such as the giant land tortoise and the large box turtle have become extinct in Florida within the past 10,000 years. Modern relatives of the giant land tortoise cannot withstand freezing temperatures, and the animals are too large to burrow and hibernate. As a consequence, the northern limits of their range must have fallen south of the frost zone. Thus, their fossilized remains would indicate that mild (non-freezing) winters, similar to those of today in extreme southern Florida, occurred from Charleston, South Carolina southward during the late Pleistocene (Science Applications, Inc., 1981:1-81).

Freshwater mollusks are another class of animals sensitive to climatic shifts. They were often collected for food by early man (Evans, 1978). A variety of mollusks were also available to Florida's earliest inhabitants as indicated by fossil shells, very similar to contemporary species, recovered from within Pleistocene contexts.

Rancholabrean megafauna (late Pleistocene mammals) existed from 500,000 years ago, beginning with the immigration of the first bison into North America, until sometime after 10,000 B.P. The majority of conspicuous changes in mammalian fauna, therefore, occurred after the Wisconsin glaciation (Hibbard *et al.*, 1965). Although most recent mammals were present during the Pleistocene, they are a poor and colorless remnant of the earlier faunal assemblage (Simpson, 1929). The Melbourne bone bed in Florida has produced fossils of more species of large animals than live in all of North America today (Ray, 1958). Late Pleistocene faunal remains are not uncommon in Florida.

Fossils from Devil's Den, Little Salt Spring, Warm Mineral Springs, and Vero indicate a variety of animal species were present in peninsular Florida during the late Pleistocene/early Holocene. Devil's Den (Martin and Webb, 1974), located approximately 165 km north of Harney Flats, is a sinkhole. Based on the ecological requirements of the fauna recovered, it was surrounded by a mesic forest located in the midst of a predominately xeric open woodland. Many of the fossil vertebrates (Table 18) were deposited by trapfall at Devil's Den around 7,000-8,000 B.P. and were discovered in a lateral passage some 21 m below the modern water surface (Martin and Webb, 1974). In addition to the mammals listed in the tables, remains of domestic dog (*Canis familiaris*) were found in a higher stratum at Devil's Den. Although it is possible these dog bones also date to 7,000-8,000 B.P., this cannot be verified. Nonetheless, domestic dog remains more than 10,000 years old have been found in other parts of North America such as Jaguar Cave in Idaho (Lawrence, 1968) and at Agate Basin in Wyoming (Walker and Frison, 1982). In

Table 18. Faunal Remains from Selected Sites in Peninsular Florida

Extinct Species	Devil's Den	Little Salt Spring	Warm Mineral Springs	Vero
Sloth (*Megalonyx* spp.)	X	X	X	X
Dire wolf (*Canis dirus*)	X			
Spectacled bear (*Tremarctos floridanus*)	X			
Sabercat (*Smilodon floridanus*)	X		X	X
Mastodon (*Mammut americanum*)	X	?		X
Horse (*Equus* sp.)	X			X
Pecarry (*Platygonius compressus*)	X			*Mylohysus* sp.
Bison (*Bison* sp.)	X			
Giant land tortoise (*Geochelone crassicutata*)		X		*G. sellardsi*
Box turtle (*Terrapene carolina putnami*)		X		
Mammoth (*Mammuthus* spp.)		X		X
Llama (*Paleolama mirifica*)				X
Giant Armadillo (*Dasypus bellus*)				X
Capybara (*Hydrochoreus aesopi*)				X
Tapir (*Tapirus haysii*)				X
Extant Species				
Panther (*Felis concolor*)			X	
White tailed deer (*Odocoileus virginianus*)	X	X	X	
Florida cooter (*Chrysemys floridana*)		X		
Gopher tortoise (*Gopherus polyphemus*)		X		
Eastern diamondback rattlesnake (*Crotalus adamanteus*)		X		
Rabbit (*Sylvalagus* spp.)	X	X		
Wood stork (*Mycteria americana*)		X		
Bobcat (*Lynx rufus*)	X			
Striped skunk (*Mephitis mephitis*)	X			
Black bear (*Ursus americanus*)	X			
Raccoon (*Procyon lotor*)	X			
Gray fox (*Urocyon cinereoargenteus*)	X			
Muskrat (*Ondatra zibethicus*)	X			
Squirrels (*Sciurus* spp.)	X			
Oppossum (*Didelphis marsupialis*)	X		X	

Note: After Clausen et al., 1979; Cockrell and Murphy, 1978; Martin and Webb, 1974; Science Applications, Inc., 1981.

the interior of the southern coastal plain, the earliest dog remains from a well-stratified site date to 7,200 B.P. (Hemmings, 1980).

The Vero site (Weigel, 1962), located near the Atlantic Ocean directly across the peninsula from Tampa Bay, contained the widest variety of late Pleistocene megafauna of the four. The extensive samples of grazing ungulates and sloths indicate more grasslands than now appear in coastal Florida, although the presence of mastodon suggests some patches of woodland were present. Freshwater animals were also well-represented. In an area such as this, early man would have had ample access to abundant herds of large game as well as freshwater fish (Science Applications, Inc., 1981).

In sum, although many of the animals recovered from Devil's Den, Little Salt Spring, and Warm Mineral Springs were not proved to be directly associated with man, it is certainly likely that he must have been in the vicinity of these water holes when the animals were. The variety of vertebrate species represented suggests that the deep south, with its subtropical and temperate fauna, was one of the richest and most diverse environments in all of Eastern North America (Carbone, 1983:16; Meltzer, 1983:4).

CONCLUSIONS

Although human occupation in Florida may date as early as 12,000 B.P., it is unknown whether these early occupations were associated with a Clovis or Suwannee material culture, or, if the technologies were contemporaneous. Due to the rarity of early sites and the factors affecting preservation, no radiocarbon dates exist for the few known Suwannee sites. Evidence does suggest that the ending date of the Suwannee complex can be postulated to be approximately 10,000 B.P.; although the beginning date remains unknown.

Presently, plausible arguments exist for postulating either the contemporaneous existence of Clovis and Suwannee or a pre-Suwannee Clovis occupation. Regardless, we tentatively suggest that the Suwannee component at Harney Flats dates between 10,000 and 11,000 B.P. based on several lines of evidence. First, there is a close stratigraphic relationship between Suwannee and Bolen. Second, there is an absence of Clovis points at the site. Finally, environmental conditions in the area, particularly water availability, were more favorable closer to 9,000 than to 12,000 years ago.

Although we are just beginning to understand the environmental changes that took place during the earliest occupation of Florida and the Southeast, we believe that the environmental uniqueness of the Florida peninsula is probably the important key in learning the relationship between Suwannee and Clovis adaptations. More studies of environmentally sensitive indicators (e.g., pollen horizons) must be integrated with studies of sea level fluctuations to increase our understanding of prehistoric adaptations. Finally, the relationship between Suwannee and Bolen complexes is also an important problem that needs further study. At present the identification of notched point assemblages in Florida as late Paleo-Indian is at variance with the data from elsewhere in the Southeast.

CHAPTER 8
Developing Models of a Band Society

Direct observations on preserved tangible artifacts and features, must be utilized to determine the nature of the social, political, ideological, and other intangible or nonpreserved aspects of prehistoric life. Starting with the assumption that Paleo-Indian peoples were hunter-gatherers and organized as bands (Lee and Devore, 1968; Willey and Phillips, 1958), archaeologists have constructed a series of models based upon technologically similar, ethnographically studied societies. The organizing principles of these models are abstractions from functionally integrated realities selected because they fit the archaeologically observed traits. Due to the diversity of alternative solutions available for solving the problems necessary for human survival and the permutations for combining these solutions to suit particular stimuli unique to a given series of circumstances throughout the history of an individual band, all models must be fine-tuned to fit every shred of tangible evidence as it becomes available. The crucial test of any model is that it not only explains all of the observed traits, but it must also lead to logically deduced traits which can be confirmed by future research.

TERRITORIALITY AND SITE PLACEMENT

In his earliest model, Binford (Binford and Binford, 1966) considers the dichotomy between maintenance and extractive tasks and proposes that these activities were differentially distributed across the landscape relative to resources. Based upon artifact assemblages and locational variables, two general site types can be identified: base camps and work camps. Since then, far more detailed principles of hunter-gatherer organization have been advanced, which presume that early prehistoric bands of the Tampa Bay area were territorial or at least they occupied exclusive territories (i.e., habitats or areas used regularly) (Williams, 1974:4; Wobst, 1974:151). The functional basis of territorial divisions is that essential resources are apportioned to all segments of a population and:

> Spatial allotments to each band unit appear to be demarcated in such a way that access to several different plant producing areas is assured. Compensation is thus made for fluctuations in area productivity, and consequently each group has an appreciably better chance of meeting its requirements for this type of resource (Wilmsen, 1974:8).

Similarly, Jochim (1981:170) notes the boundaries of territories are often related to potential resource zones.

A common feature of territories or home ranges of hunters and gatherers is that very often they seem to be centered on rivers, waterholes, or lakes, partly because these features form stable resource concentrations, and partly because they offer easy travel possibilities. In many areas, a watershed formed the approximate extent of the territory. Another common feature is that territories often crosscut many different habitats and thus contain a variety of different resources, thereby, providing greater subsistence security. The spatial arrangement of different habitats and resources therefore would be quite important in determining the size and shape of territories (1981:170).

While there are territories, the inhabitants using these places change frequently due to the fluidity of the regional population as a whole. Moreover, there is a flexibility in the composition of membership of the band that results in some variability in group size which enables the band to react to environmental change and to redistribute people over the land (Jochim, 1981:159-160). This results in rather open communities that are able to break into small groups, mix, and reassemble. This may have been particularly true in Paleo-Indian times given the assumed extremely low population densities.

Another aspect of modern day hunter-gatherer adaptations is regional mobility (Binford, 1983:204-208; Jochim, 1981:148-151). Generalizing from his experiences, Binford argues that hunter-gatherers must monitor large amounts of territory to provide a secure set of options for future decision making. Their security depends on their ability to make good judgments about where to move, and this is only possible if they have knowledge about areas beyond their current living area. Therefore, mobility contributes to security by allowing groups to collect information about resources occurring in other areas.

A third characteristic of band societies is their reliance on stable and abundant food sources, which often consist of wild plant foods (Lee, 1968:39-43). Modern hunters depend for most of their subsistence on sources other than meat—generally wild plants, shellfish, and fish. Nevertheless, they are still willing to devote considerable energy to obtaining less reliable, more highly valued, more prestigious food sources such as medium and large sized mammals (Lee, 1968:43). Jochim (1976:11) has proposed two major goals that guide resource selection among hunters and gatherers. One is the attainment of a secure amount of food and raw materials (i.e., the meeting of nutritional and manufacturing needs); the second is the limitation of energy expenditure to within a predefined range. Relevant factors affecting food selection and exclusion include such variables as seasonality, ease of exploitation, and distance traveled.

The arrangement and accessibility of resources are critical factors in determining hunter-gatherer site locations. Moreover, many factors must be considered in resolving the different "pulls" (Jochim, 1976:50) that resources may exert on determining site location.

> Fixed resources are more important to settlement decisions than are mobile ones. Fixed resources are predictable in space and thus more reliable to

procure.... As a result, hunter-gatherers demonstrate a hierarchical nesting of their activities in space around their camps, with procurement of the most reliable and fixed resources nearby and exploitation of more mobile and unreliable resources at greater distances. (Jochim, 1981:153).

Hunter-gatherers tend to locate their camps near secure resources (e.g., water, firewood, plants) that can be easily exploited, while they obtain the less secure resources like game animals by hunting over a wider area surrounding the camp.

Another feature of band adaptation, probably related to fluctuating group size, is the apparent need for periodic aggregation; this function may be as much social as economic.

Although environmental factors may facilitate such decisions, the apparent need for periodic aggregation in band societies may be related as much to social as it is to economic needs.

> Periodically, band segments come together into full band units to engage in a variety of functional and social actions. Finally several bands would sometimes meet in ecologically favorable places and cooperatively carry out a wide range of exploitative and social activities (Wilmsen, 1970:80).
>
> Although the ecological factors promoting aggregations among observed hunter-gatherers are well described and hence easily extended to archaeological interpretations, the social and ritual components of aggregations should not be minimized (Conkey, 1980:609).

Reciprocal exchange is probably one of the most important social functions that has been documented (Wilmsen, 1974:25-26; Wobst, 1974:152). The stated purpose and apparent functions of these aggregations are manifold and varied: provision of mates, exchange of foodstuffs, cooperative exploitation, trade in nonfood items, performance of ritual and curing, and sharing of information. Most significant at this point, however, is the generality of the desire for some periods of aggregation (Jochim, 1976:19).

AN ETHNOGRAPHIC MODEL OF TECHNOLOGICAL ORGANIZATION

Binford (1979:261) defines technological organization in terms of how a group views their gear "with regard to the planned execution of their adaptive strategies." Gear is organized toward goal-oriented subsistence decisions which are made to anticipate future conditions. Binford's example was based on his ethnographic work with the Nunamiut Eskimo, who organize their gear into three basic classes: personal gear, site furniture, and situational gear (Binford, 1978).

Personal gear includes that part of the Nunamiut technology carried by each individual in anticipation of future conditions or activities. When an expedition away from the village was planned, personal gear was organized to anticipate the goals of the expedition, the need for food and warmth, and any possible misfortunes or mishaps. Items included varied depending upon the purpose of the trip and the season. Nunamiut personal gear was heavily curated: implements were recycled, reused, and many maintenance expenditures were made on them (Binford,

1977:33-34). Such gear was always inspected before going into the field and either repaired or replaced. Consequently, Binford asserts that the discarding of personal gear was related to its use-life and that worn out items were generally discarded in a residential camp, not in the field where the activity took place.

The second category, site furniture, was considered part of the site and generally available for use by any of the inhabitants. The items in this category exhibited a low use-ratio and were usually cached at the site. The most common examples were hearth stones, anvils, tent weights, support sticks, and lithic raw material (Binford, 1979:264). One feature of many of the items of site furniture was that they were "laterally recycled," that is, they were previously used in a different context. Worn out items, such as pots, would be transferred from a household at a residential location to be used as "site furniture" at a hunting stand.

The final category consists of situational gear for specific and frequently unanticipated activities. Situational gear is expedient in nature (Binford, 1977), as opposed to curated, and is usually limited by the available raw material. This may come from caches, personal gear modified for reuse, material resources from the immediate environment, or material scavenged from previous occupations.

The basic classification of the Harney Flats lithic assemblage was structured around these three general categories. Although the technology of modern day Eskimo may not be a proper analog for that of prehistoric central Florida peoples, the organizing principles of Binford's scheme should be applicable to any technology. At a basic level all hunter-gatherers must organize their technology to anticipate future conditions in their subsistence-settlement strategies. We do not mean that the prehistoric inhabitants of Harney Flats necessarily viewed their gear in this way; Binford's model is used here as a heuristic device to provide some insight into the behavior of early man.

RESIDENTIAL BASES AND LOGISTICAL STRATEGIES

Binford (1980) has suggested two basic principles of organization employed by hunter-gatherers in carrying out their subsistence strategies. These two subsistence-settlement systems differ in their mobility patterns, and are seen as responses to different environments. One is a "mapping on" strategy, while the other is a "logistical" strategy. These different adaptations are employed by "foragers" and "collectors," respectively. Foragers "... move consumers to goods with frequent residential moves ..." while collectors "... move goods to consumers with generally fewer residential moves ..." (Binford, 1980:15). A distinctive characteristic of a foraging strategy is that foragers generally do not store foods, but gather foods daily. Foraging strategies are generally applied to homogenous or largely undifferentiated ecological areas such as equatorial forests. Some foragers, however, may be found in areas with very different occurrences and distributions of critical resources.

In settings with limited loci of availability for critical resources, patterns of residential mobility may be tethered around a series of very restricted locations such as water holes, increasing the year to year redundancy in the use of particular locations as residential camps (Binford, 1980:9).

With some foragers, residential mobility may vary considerably in both duration of occupation and distance between sites; the size of the group can also vary.

A logistical strategy, on the other hand, is an adaptation to a spatial or temporal incongruence of resources. Collectors move near one resource and procure the others by special work groups. Essentially, it is a compromise based on the known distribution of resources, and as a result site patterns are determined by this prior knowledge. Collectors have logistically organized food procurement strategies involving specialized task groups which provide for subsistence of the social group by frequent planned trips away from the main residence.

Logistical or relatively sedentary strategies are also particularly adaptive when continuously available food (primarily plants) is reduced as a function of decreased length of the growing season, as in temperate and colder climates. In short, Binford suggests that mobility may well relate to other properties of the environment rather than conditions of food abundance. Cool environments are associated with incongruent resource distributions, while warmer environments generally exhibit a greater congruence of critical resources.

Different types of sites can be expected from the different organizations. Foragers produce two types of sites: a residential base and a location. Residential bases are places where activities generally considered common to base camps are carried out, where members of a group return and sleep, and where most processing, manufacturing and maintenance activities take place. Locations are special purpose sites where only extractive tasks are carried out. Consequently, the archaeological visibility of locations may be very low, since occupation time is short and there is little accumulation of debris.

Collectors produce, in addition to residential and location sites, field camps, stations, and caches (Binford, 1980:5-12). Field camps are temporary residences for groups on logistical trips away from the residential camp. Types of field camps would vary with the kinds of resources sought. A station is a site where particular information is gathered, such as a vantage point for monitoring game movements. Caches are also common sites in a logistical strategy, since small groups must obtain large quantities of resources for larger groups [e.g., bulk quantities of food may be stored temporarily and facilities may be constructed for this purpose (Binford, 1980:12)]. Other resources, such as fuel for fire or lithic raw material, can also be cached. These site types are not independent, but rather can occur in various combinations, particularly in logistical systems. Moreover, a particular place may be used for different purposes at different times, depending on the relative placement of residential camps (Binford, 1982).

Collecting and foraging should not be viewed as mutually exclusive strategies, but as alternatives which may be employed in varying mixes in different settings (Binford, 1980:11). Some groups may move through seasonal phases where their particular strategies may change.

... in some systems people may be dispersed in summer, behaving like foragers by employing a mobility strategy designed for coverage, seeking to maximize the "encounter" with resources, yet during the winter they may be living from stores at a site which was positioned in terms of logistical concerns. Mobility patterning may be both geographically and regionally complicated (Binford, 1982:11).

The consequences of variable site utilization, and the consequences of long-term land use not discussed above, will ultimately have to be addressed in any settlement model. Because of the mobility patterns of hunters and gatherers, a "site" may be a piece of land occupied many times because its location has made it suitable for many purposes. Because sites can consist of the accumulated deposition of myriad occupational episodes they seem highly varied when viewed from the perspective of archaeological assemblages.

Residential bases vary in size for both foragers (1980:5, Figure 1) and collectors (1980:12, Figure 3). For example, Nunamiut Eskimo residential bases include a winter village site ("... a cluster of relatively substantial houses..." and a move to a summer site "... accompanied by a reduction in group size as the local group breaks down into family units, each establishing independent residential camps..." (1980:12). Binford implies that seasonal changes are primarily responsible for the timing of these periods of aggregation and dispersion of residential bases.

The environment has played the determining role in many models. Traditionally the primary explanation of differences between Paleo-Indian and Archaic settlement patterns has focused on a supposed readaptation from Pleistocene to Holocene environments. Caldwell's (1958) "primary forest efficiency" characterized the Archaic period as a time of more intense use of the local Holocene environment. More recently, Cleland's focal/diffuse model (1976) describes a switch from specialized adaptations centered on one or a few similar resources to an economy adapted to varied or scattered resources.

Another example is a hunter-gatherer settlement model proposed by Binford in which he used a concept called "effective temperature" (E.T.) developed by Bailey (1960) which refers to the length of the growing season of wild foods. He paired calculated E.T. values with ethnographic groups scaled according to their relative sedentism. As a result, he demonstrated an association between cooler climates and sedentism. Stationary residences are generally associated with logistical mobility strategies, and, conversely, logistical mobility makes possible increased relative stability. This is not surprising, but what is unusual is the strong association between colder climates and sedentary residences (Binford, 1980:14). This is in contrast to the general assumption that sedentism results from abundance. On the contrary, sedentism can occur in food-scarce environments under conditions of very low human population densities.

CHAPTER 9

Settlement Systems and Technology: A Summary Model

Harney Flats spans three physiographic zones: the Gulf Coastal Lowlands, the Polk Upland, and the Zephyrhills Gap (in which the Hillsborough River Valley is entrenched). In the vicinity of the site, the Coastal Lowlands would have been an upland 30 m above mean sea level 10,000 or more years ago. The Polk Upland was even higher and much better drained than today, and probably did not provide an attractive physiographic setting for early man and other life forms. The Zephyrhills Gap, on the other hand, contained the Hillsborough River Valley, which was perhaps characterized by scattered patches of mesic forests. Although the flow of the river was probably less than now (if it flowed at all), there must have been permanent water holes perched atop the pockets of clay layers.

The site is located opposite a gap in the ridge that separates the Hillsborough River and the Palm River valleys. This gap may have been a corridor through which animals could have passed from the northern parts of Harney Flats prairie into the region of even moister soils of the Hillsborough River Valley. This area probably contained relatively greater amounts of water than most of the surrounding areas during the Paleo-Indian period. Because such low concave surfaces generally accumulate soil rather than lose it to erosion, these areas are usually moister (Spurr and Barnes, 1973:229). Given this, low inland basins such as Harney Flats were probably grasslands, perhaps interspersed with hummocks and open savannah woodlands, which could have served as grazing or browsing grounds for animals.

The elevation of the site on the sand ridge overlooking the flats would have provided a fine vantage point to observe animals in the basin and was favorably located to provide the basic economic requirements of a base camp: access to water, plants, animals, and suitable lithics for tool manufacture. Evidence that this site was actually utilized as a base camp is the diversity and quantity of implements recovered; the *in situ* manufacturing and reworking of stone tools; and the distribution of activity areas and refitted specimens.

Using the associations and contexts of the recovered artifacts within the reconstructed environmental setting in light of the preceding ethnographic models, we have fine-tuned them to explain what we cannot see. Although this is not a final statement and much work remains to be done, a crucial step in formulating a hunter-gatherer model for Southeastern Paleo-Indian is to understand all aspects of their lithic technology. Beginning with a firm footing in tool manufacture and curation, resource procurement, band mobility, site placement, and settlement patterns and systems, archaeological knowledge of early man will be advanced tremendously.

ACCESS TO RAW MATERIALS

While the mobility of Paleo-Indian groups in general appears well established, little is known about groups in Florida. Based on the development of a geological method of chert source identification by Upchurch, Strom, and Nuckels (Upchurch et al., 1981), a study of Paleo-Indian adaptation is now a possibility in Florida. Goodyear (Goodyear et al., 1983) has recently conducted a preliminary raw material study on a sample of twenty-seven Paleo-Indian lanceolate-shaped points from the Tampa Bay region. Although he expected that specimens of material from quarry clusters north of the Tampa Bay region would be found in the sample, no exotic cherts (i.e., from outside the Tampa Bay region) were identified. This is in contrast to the pattern reported from many other Eastern Paleo-Indian sites (however, see Moeller, 1980 for another example of local cobble chert utilization).

Reasons offered for this apparent anomaly include the small sample size, and the fairly continuous availability of chert along the central Florida Gulf Coast. As Goodyear notes, "... it may be the degree of curation was less such that tools were not used for long enough periods of time to travel as far as the person" (1983:61). In addition, the movement of Paleo-Indian settlement systems may not have been north to south along the state as projected, but rather east to west along the various drainages emptying into the Gulf of Mexico. An east to west pattern following drainages along the Gulf Coastal Lowlands and Polk Upland has already been postulated for the Archaic period (Daniel, 1985), and may have had its origins in the Paleo-Indian period. Now-drowned early sites exist in the Gulf of Mexico around Tampa Bay, and many sites representing the Paleo-Indian settlement system may be underwater.

No exotic cherts were observed in the sample from Harney Flats (Upchurch, 1984); only raw materials from the immediate vicinity of the site or the Tampa Bay area were identified. The implication of these studies is that the Paleo-Indian groups of Florida may not have exhibited the widespread mobility apparently existing elsewhere in the East. But a spatial and temporal incongruence may have existed between resources at some point in the yearly round necessitating a portable and flexible assemblage of stone tools. The overwhelming choices for raw material at Harney Flats were the limestone replaced cherts and not the locally available silicified corals (Upchurch, 1984), which is consistent with the results of Goodyear's study and reflects the pattern seen elsewhere in the East of selection of better cryptocrystalline raw material by Paleo-Indians. Elsewhere in the Southeast, archaeologists (Gardner, 1977) have postulated that the settlement pattern and geographical movements of Paleo-Indian groups were restricted by a dependence upon cryptocrystalline stone.

THE CURATED TOOLKIT: EVIDENCE OF MAINTENANCE AND RECYCLING

A certain regularity in tool form across North America has long been recognized for the Paleo-Indian period and the assemblage from this site is no exception. Certain classes of formal tools are considered to be personal gear, exhibited greater degrees of labor in manufacture, and are therefore believed to have been curated (Binford, 1973). These traits are manifested in tools being transported from site to site and maintained by resharpening and recycling. There is more evidence of tool maintenance than tool recycling in the Harney Flats assemblage, which is thought to be a consequence of the site's location in an area of raw material abundance. As a result, the need to transform one tool form into another would be less.

The hafted lanceolate bifaces are the most distinctive and perhaps the best made tools in the entire assemblage. Hafting itself implies portability and therefore curation. A pattern of tool maintenance has been observed in resharpening the blade and tip edges of the point. With a single exception, recycling of these bifaces was not noted; however, elsewhere Suwannee points have been recycled into endscrapers (Goodyear, Thompson, and Warren, 1968). Apparently such cases are rare, but they are interesting since they probably reflect an instance of personal gear being transformed into situational gear. Under situational contingencies, tool needs are immediate and therefore almost any readily available material is utilized. Instances of drafting personal gear into situational gear take place under conditions of low raw material availability and are most likely to occur at special purpose sites.

Another tool form thought to have been hafted is the endscraper. These tools appear to have been maintained rather than recycled. Evidence of maintenance in this class is variation in tool length, which probably reflects differing amounts of resharpening. The short, stubby specimens are believed to have been exhausted before discard, and are evidence that "retooling" (Keeley, 1982) was a primary activity at the site. Evidence of recycling endscrapers and other tool forms was absent in this assemblage, unlike at Debert (MacDonald, 1968:91) and Vail (Gramly, 1982:34) where endscrapers were transformed into *pieces esquillees* (bipolar cores) used for the production of small flakes (Goodyear, 1982b). Because use of these cores is believed to be related to relative scarcity of raw material, and since this was apparently not a problem at Harney Flats, no transformations would be expected, and indeed, *pieces esquillees* would be unnecessary.

The discoidal scrapers are similar in form to the endscrapers. The important difference between these two unifaces is that discoidal scrapers were probably not hafted, but were portable and could be hand held for use. Their circular or oval form allowed the working edge of the tool to be easily maintained by rotating and resharpening.

The final unifacial formal tool, the oblong scraper, represents a good example of flexibility in the assemblage. Although some could have been hafted, the majority appear to have been hand held. The variations in shape (Figure 24) are seen as representing dynamic stages of tool use and resharpening. The flexibility manifested in these forms suggests a tool designed to be capable of rejuvenation and of alteration into forms suitable for a particular occasion (e.g., pointed at one end for perforating or graving). Broken or shortened, exhausted oblong scrapers could have been transformed into large endscrapers. Like the transformations of Suwannee points to endscrapers, these recyclings probably took place when the need arose for a functional form that was not present in the tool kit and had been produced from an available one. This is most likely to have taken place at special purpose sites. Since raw materials were apparently readily available at Harney Flats, endscrapers could have been manufactured without having to be recycled from another form. We think that these recycled tools were probably made elsewhere, brought to the site when close to exhaustion, used until exhausted, and then discarded. Replacements were then manufactured and used on site (see Gramly, 1980).

Perhaps the best example of flexibility is the bifacial core, which was probably the most general purpose "tool" in the assemblage in that it could fulfill a number of different purposes. When properly reduced, it would function as a "handaxe." If large enough, it would serve as a core from which flakes could be removed. Ultimately, it could even have been transformed into a projectile point. Its most important property was undoubtedly its portability.

> To provide for all these tasks with flakes, one would need to carry an inconvenient number of them of various sizes, shapes, and edge angles, plus, perhaps, a core and hammerstone—not a very handy assortment to carry on the chase (Keeley, 1980:161).

LITHIC PROCUREMENT AND MOBILITY

Although technological organization provides a way of understanding how and why human societies created technologies as answers to their various adaptive problems, it is necessary to understand the influence of such factors as the degree of mobility, the availability of good raw material, and even the role of time (Torrence, 1983) in shaping prehistoric hunter-gatherer technologies. Some research questions, e.g., those concerning the organization of the technology (Binford, 1977; 1979), can be studied more effectively through technological analysis.

Within the discipline, most lithic analysts have pursued thus far two basic lines of inquiry. One is the technological approach, often with replication, where the techniques related to the manufacture of a chipped stone tool are reconstructed (e.g., Crabtree, 1966). The other approach concerns establishing the uses of stone tools through use-wear analysis (e.g., Hayden, 1980). Both of these avenues of research are necessary but not sufficient in themselves to allow an understanding of how and why prehistoric adaptations took place. The study of why certain tool designs were created and how these designs were implemented and manipulated within the total settlement system refers to the organization of the technology (Goodyear, 1982b:25-26).

This third approach—the investigation of the role of the lithic assemblage in the overall adaptation—has seen limited but important use in the analysis of particular sites (Claggett and Cable, 1982; Anderson and Schuldenrein, 1983) as well as in general cultural studies (Goodyear, 1979; Goodyear et al., 1983). Goodyear (1979), for example, postulates that Paleo-Indian groups used high quality cryptocrystalline material to create portable and flexible technologies to offset geographical incongruities between resources and consumers. Although proposed as general hypothesis, he claims that this statement is particularly applicable to the North American Paleo-Indian tradition. Certain technological adaptations are required in a highly mobile lifeway, and by viewing the Paleo-Indian stone tool assemblage from this perspective a better understanding of prehistoric adaptations can be obtained.

Goodyear argues that evidence for the high mobility of Paleo-Indian groups can be seen in the geographic distribution of exotic or non-local raw material used in the manufacture of stone tools. This phenomenon represents embedded strategies of raw material procurement. As groups move seasonally to different locales, they gather lithic raw material indigenous to that region. Only in an emergency were special trips made to get material.

> From my perspective, the presence of exotic cherts may be a fair measure of the mobility scale of the adaptation appearing as a consequence of the normal functioning of the system, with no extra effort expended in their procurement (Binford, 1979:261).

Based on this argument, Goodyear claims that most of the exotic lithic remains in Paleo-Indian sites in the Eastern United States are the result of mobility.

Given high group mobility, the procurement of needed resources can sometimes present problems. Since lithic raw materials and biotic resources do not occur evenly over the landscape, spatial or temporal incongruences will occur between the natural locations of raw material for stone tools and the places where such tools would be used for extracting and processing biotic resources. This logistical problem is solved by the creation of a portable technology.

The second major problem of a highly mobile lifeway is the need to adapt to the variable events that can arise on a daily basis. This problem, which Goodyear refers to as "situational contingencies," is best handled by flexibility.

> Another major constraint as well as source of variation in the situational response is the condition of the chipped stone tool kit from pose to pose. If the problem of geographic incongruencies can be solved through portable technologies, the problem of situational contingencies can be alleviated through flexible technologies. Flexibility means creating tools with lifespans long enough to be used on a number of occasions if necessary. With chipped stone tools this means designing tools which can be continuously and reliably rejuvenated. Flexibility also means the capability for redesigning tools as other tools and otherwise re-casting the raw material of the tool kit into wholly new tools or cores for the derivation of tools if necessary. If we place such requirements for flexibility as just defined within the additional and prior stricture of portability, I believe the form and variable condition of North American Paleo-Indian technologies become potentially more understandable (Goodyear, 1979:4).

The use of cryptocrystalline stone helps solve these adaptive problems because of the ease and precision with which it can be worked. Reliable flaking qualities allow tools to be fashioned for extended life spans and to be efficiently and reliably maintained. Furthermore, if necessary, such material can be transformed from one tool form to another.

To summarize Goodyear's hypothesis, the use of cryptocrystalline material is an adaptive strategy for making both portable and flexible tools that are necessary in a lifestyle characterized by high mobility.

ORGANIZATION OF TECHNOLOGY AT HARNEY FLATS

The apparent abundance of available raw material had a major influence on the assemblage at Harney Flats especially in the large number of unifaces, both curated and expedient, recovered. The presence of curated tools at a site may not necessarily indicate that they were utilized there, but rather that they were simply discarded and replaced by others. Indeed, the evidence of actual tool use at the site is probably best reflected in the expedient unifaces.

The many unifacial tools are consistent with the model of their use at sites near sources of lithic material, while curated tools are observed for use elsewhere (Keeley, 1982:803-804). Sites away from lithic sources (habitation or special purpose sites) should contain curated unifaces as opposed to the expedient forms. However, Binford has argued that

> ...if broken in the context of use (curated tools) are frequently transported to residential locations where they may be recycled or repaired for future use (1977:334).

The relatively large numbers of curated tools at sites near quarries may be evidence of the discarding of exhausted tools and their replacement by newly manufactured forms. A group about to leave a site near lithic sources may have retooled in anticipation of future travel in areas containing little or no suitable stone material (Gramly, 1980; Keeley, 1982:803-804). Consequently, curated forms may have been deposited at sites near lithic sources where they were replaced (such as at Harney Flats) and repaired or recycled at habitation sites where fresh raw material was not readily available. This model needs to be examined at other early sites in Florida.

Although a few of the larger expedient unifaces appear to have been hafted, this is not necessarily evidence of portability and curation, but rather represents a functional design for use in more robust activities. The larger size of these tools compared to the curated unifaces argues against their being curated beyond the length of the site occupation. Perhaps they were simply stored at the site like the large hammerstones.

The Harney Flats data provide some insight into the manufacturing processes of the Suwannee technology. At least three types of cores were recovered, suggesting that there were distinctions made in the manufacture and ultimate use of the flakes derived from those core types. The bifacial core is viewed as a curated tool like the unifaces, but which could be carried from site to site, and depending upon certain "situational contingencies," could be used to produce the functional equivalent of almost any tool type in the assemblage.

Overall evidence is present in the assemblage for the portable and flexible technology postulated by Goodyear. More evidence was found for tool maintenance, however, than for tool recycling. The curated tools reflect an assemblage with low diversity, (i.e., a general purpose tool kit containing tools that must be used for many different tasks). Due to the relatively high mobility of most hunter-gatherer groups, the gross number of artifacts which can be carried between residences is ultimately limited and the degree of tool specialization is restricted.

The particular nature of the Harney Flats site has allowed us to see different strategies of tool design. Although the curated portion of the tool kit is generalized and lacks diversity, there is a greater variety exhibited in the expedient unifaces. Functionally equivalent forms of curated and expedient tools are present in the assemblage, but the expedient ones are more a response to specific and immediate tasks, while curated tools are planned for long-term use and must meet different types of tool needs.

> We can expect many such tool-design parallels, that is tools of very different design being used for identical tasks; but this is not to say that they are functionally isomorphic, since they are clearly designed for very different intended roles within the technology (Binford, 1979:269).

In addition to the curated (personal gear) and expedient (situational gear) forms identified in the assemblage, there is also evidence for "site furniture." This is best represented by cached items such as hammerstones and sandstone abraders. While also being expedient gear, the many cores could also represent stored items awaiting reuse.

In sum, the organizational properties of the Paleo-Indian technology at Harney Flats are seen as being "location centered" (Binford, 1979:255). This perspective has allowed us to interpret a site where an assemblage has been influenced by readily available quantities of lithic raw material. Since the manufacturing of different tool types is seen as a principal activity at the site, inferences were made as to the intended roles of these tools from the perspective of the entire settlement system. Of course, a number of different site types must eventually be examined before we can fully understand how the technological options for planning and executing tasks in different places were made. Although Harney Flats has given us a good start, only by studying additional sites will the organizational variability within the Paleo-Indian cultural system be understood.

Our identification of the Harney Flats site as a residential base camp is primarily based on its relatively large size and internal site structure, including the presence of a living area separated from activity areas primarily associated with tool manufacture. Based on its location with easy access to many resources, it is also possible that it may have been a larger aggregation site for some social as well as economic functions. Of course, the indications of ritual or social activities at hunter-gatherer sites are very difficult to define archaeologically and have not been demonstrated here. If this is a large aggregation base camp, then special purpose and smaller scale camps inhabited by one or two families could also be expected as part of this settlement system.

This considered with the paleoenvironmental record provides a framework for the study of prehistoric hunter-gatherer adaptations in central Florida. The climate at the time of the earliest occupation of this site has been characterized as having decreased seasonality, reduced differences between winter and summer temperatures, and increased dryness in an environment composed of sclerophyllous oak woodlands with prairie-like openings. Water was generally restricted to low-lying segments of drainages and to locations in karst areas that penetrated the Floridan aquifer. Such places would also contain plants which in turn attracted game. Tentative evidence for some association between Paleo-Indian projectile points and these features is already known (Waller and Dunbar, 1977; Dunbar and Waller, 1983), although the types of site actually represented are not.

This heterogeneous or patchy, dry environment combined with a cooler climate would have tended to favor a logistically (collector) based settlement system with restricted mobility tethered to water sources. Settlement may not have been related as much to seasonal changes as is generally postulated for the succeeding Archaic period. Perhaps movement here was more related to scheduling of tool-kit replenishment, social needs, and the availability of water, to name just a few. Although the Florida peninsula would have been far larger than at present due to the lower sea levels, the territories defined on that basis of available water may have been oriented along drainages crossing the Gulf Coastal Lowlands and the Polk Upland borders and probably included land areas presently under Tampa Bay. This geographic orientation during the early Holocene may not have been north and south, but east and west with the mouths of rivers existing several kilometers farther west in what is now the Gulf of Mexico. Such an east-west orientation would naturally restrict mobility on the peninsula.

The Paleo-indian component at Harney Flats is a benchmark in early man studies in Florida and the Southeast. Until now Paleo-Indian studies in the state have largely been associated with a diagnostic projectile point style, a vague idea of other lithic artifacts, and inferences from early sites in other areas. The fieldwork emphasized opening large contiguous areas and mapping individual artifacts to study internal site structure. Broad scale patterning includes a living area and activity areas. Our study of the organization of the technology went beyond the traditional techno-functional stone tool study to understand the role of the lithic assemblage in the overall settlement system adaptation. This study has helped to reveal the generalized nature of the implements and indicates that tool form and function are not necessarily independent variables.

One of the most significant accomplishments was to prepare a strong foundation for defining Paleo-Indian settlement systems. Refinement of this model using more detailed spatial analysis, tool fitting, and use-wear studies must be encouraged for us to understand the adaptation of early man in Florida and other portions of the Eastern United States.

References Cited

ADOVASIO, J. M., J. D. GUNN, J. DONAHUE, and R. STUCKENRATH
    1977   Progress Report on the Meadowcroft Rockshelter—A 16,000 Year Chronicle. In *Amerinds and Their Paleo environments in Northeastern North America*, edited by Walter S. Newman and Bert Salwen, pp. 137–159. Annals of the New York Academy of Sciences, Vol. 288, New York.

ADOVASIO, J. M., J. D. GUNN, J. DONAHUE, R. STUCKENRATH, J. E. GUILDAY, K. LORD, and K. VOLMAN
    1980a   Meadowcroft Rockshelter, Retrospect 1977. *North American Archaeologist* 1:99-137.

ALBANESE, JOHN P.
    1977   Paleotopography and Paleo-Indian Sites in Wyoming and Colorado. In *Paleo-Indian Lifeways*, edited by Eileen Johnson, pp. 29-47. West Texas Museum Association, Lubbock.

ALEXANDER, HERBERT L. JR.
    1963   The Levi Site: A Paleo-Indian Campsite in Central Texas. *American Antiquity* 28:510-520.

ALEXANDER, TAYLOR R., and ALAN G. CROOK
    1974   Recent Vegetational Changes in Southern Florida. In *Environments of South Florida: Present and Past*, edited by P. J. Gleason, pp. 61-72. Miami Geological Society Memoir 2, Miami.

ALMY, MARION M.
    1981   Archaeological Excavations at the Curiosity Creek Site (8Hi480): An Inland, Short-term, Multi-period Aboriginal Occupation in Southern Hillsborough County, Florida. Manuscript on file, Florida Bureau of Archaeological Research, Tallahassee.
    1982   *Archaeological Excavations at the Cypress Creek Site (8Hi471): An Inland, Short-Term, Multi-Period Aboriginal Occupation in Northern Hillsborough County, Florida.* Interstate 75 Highway Phase II Archaeological Reports Number 4, Bureau of Historic Sites and Properties. Florida Division of Archives, History and Records Management, Tallahassee.

ALT, D., and H. K. BROOKS
    1965   Age of Florida Marine Terraces. *Journal of Geology* 73:406-411.

ANDERSON, DAVID G., and JOSEPH SCHULDENREIN
    1982   The Early Archaic Components at Rucker's Bottom Site, Elbert County, Georgia. Paper presented at the 39th Meeting of the Southeastern Archaeological Conference, Memphis.
    1983   Early Archaic Settlement on the Southeastern Atlantic Slope: A View from the Rucker's Bottom Site, Elbert County, Georgia. *North American Archaeologist* 4:177-261.

AUFFENBURG, WALTER, and WILLIAM W. MILSTEAD
    1965   Reptiles of the Quaternary of North America. In *Quaternary of the*

United States, edited by H. E. Wright, Jr. and D. G. Frey, pp. 557-568, Princeton.

AUSTIN, ROBERT J., and THOMAS E. JACKSON
 1983 *The Production and Analysis of Biface and Uniface Debitage: A Preliminary Report*. Paper presented at the 35th Annual Meeting of the Florida Anthropological Society, Tallahassee.

AUSTIN, ROBERT J., and DANA STE. CLAIRE
 1982 *The Deltona Project: Prehistoric Technology in the Hillsborough River Basin*. University of South Florida, Archaeological Report 12.

BAILEY, HARRY P.
 1960 A Method of Determining the Warmth and Temperateness of Climate. *Geografiska Annaler* 43:1-16.

BAKER, CHARLES M.
 1978 The Size Effect: An Explanation of Variability in Surface Artifact Assemblage Content. *American Antiquity* 43:288-293.

BALLARD, ROBERT D., and ELAZAR UCHUPI
 1970 Morphology and Quaternary History of the Continental Shelf on the Gulf Coast of the United States. *Bulletin of Marine Sciences* 20(3): 547-559.

BALLO, GEORGE R.
 1985 *Experiments in Use-Wear Formation on Stone Tools Made from Florida Cherts: A Study Supporting a Microwear Analysis of Paleo-Indian Lithic Artifacts from the Harney Flats Site, Tampa, Florida*. Unpublished Master's Thesis, Department of Anthropology, University of South Florida.

BENTHALL, JOSEPH L.
 1972 Test Excavations at the Williamson Site, Dinwiddie County, Virginia. *Eastern States Archaeological Federation Bulletin* 32:11-12.

BENTHALL, JOSEPH L., and BEN C. McCARY
 1973 Williamson Site: A New Approach. *Archaeology of Eastern North America*, 1:127-132.

BERRY, K. J., K. L. KVAMME, and P. W. MIELKE, JR.
 1983 Improvements in the Permutations Test for the Spatial Analysis for the Distribution of Artifacts into Classes. *American Antiquity* 48:547-572.

BINFORD, LEWIS R.
 1973 Interassemblage Variability: The Mousterian and the "Functional" Argument. In *Explanation of Culture Change: Models in Prehistory*, edited by C. Renfrew, pp. 227-254, Duckworth, London.
 1977 Forty-Seven Trips: A Case Study in the Character of Archaeological Formation Processes. In *Stone Tools as Cultural Markers: Change, Evolution and Complexity*, edited by R. V. S. Wright, pp. 178-188. Australian Institute of Aboriginal Studies, Canberra.
 1978 *Nunamiut Ethnoarchaeology*. Academic Press, New York.
 1979 Organization and Formation Processes: Looking at Curated Technologies. *Journal of Anthropological Research* 35(3):255-273.
 1980 Willow Smoke and Dogs' Tails: Hunter-Gatherer Settlement Systems and Archaeological Site Formation. *American Antiquity* 45:4-20.
 1981 Behavioral Archaeology and the 'Pompeii Premise.' *Journal of Anthropological Research* 37:195-208.

1982   The Archaeology of Place. *Journal of Anthropological Archaeology* 1:5-31.
1983   *In Pursuit of the Past.* Thames and Hudson, New York.
BINFORD, L. R., and S. R. BINFORD
1966   A Preliminary Analysis of Functional Variability in the Mousterian of Levallois Facies. In *Recent Studies in Paleoanthropology*, edited by J. D. Clark and F. C. Howell. *American Anthropologist* 68:238-295.
BLACKWELDER, B. W., O. H. PILKEY, and J. D. HOWARD
1979   Late Wisconsin Sea Level Curve for the Southeastern United States Continental Shelf. *Science* 204:618-620.
BORDES, FRANCOIS, and DON CRABTREE
1969   The Cordiac Blade Technique and Other Experiments. *Tebiwa, The Journal of the Idaho State University Museum* 12:1-21.
BRENNAN, LOUIS A.
1970   *American Dawn: A New Model of Prehistory.* Macmillan Company, New York.
1982   A Compilation of Fluted Points of Eastern North America by Count and Distribution: An AENA Project. *Archaeology of Eastern North America* 10:27-46.
BREW, J. O.
1946   The Use and Abuse of Taxonomy. In *Archaeology of Alkali Ridge, Southeastern Utah*, Papers of the Peabody Museum of American Archaeology, Harvard University 21:44-66. Harvard University Press.
BROECKER, WALLACE S., MAURICE EWING, and BRUCE C. HEZEN
1960   Evidence for an Abrupt Change in Climate Close to 11,000 Years Ago. *American Journal of Science* 258:429-443.
BROOKS, H. K.
1967   *Rate of Solution of Limestone in the Karst Terrain of Florida.* Florida Water Resources Research Center Publication No. 6, Tallahassee.
1973   Holocene Climate Changes in Peninsular Florida. *Geological Society of American Abstract* Vol. 5 No. 7.
1981   *Geologic Map of Florida.* Center for Environmental and Natural Resources, Institute of Food and Agricultural Services, University of Florida, Gainesville.
BROSTER, JOHN B.
1982   Paleo-Indian Habitation at the Pierce Site: Chester County, Tennessee. *Tennessee Anthropologists* 7:93-103.
BROTHWELL, DON, and PATRICIA BROTHWELL
1969   *Food in Antiquity.* Frederick A. Praeger Publishers, New York.
BROWN, JANICE G.
1981   *Palynologic and Petrographic Analyses at Bayhead Hammock and Marsh Peats at Little Salt Springs Archaeological Site (8SO188), Florida.* Unpublished Master's Thesis, Department of Geology, University of South Carolina, Columbia.
BRYAN, ALAN L.
1977   Developmental Stages and Technological Traditions. In *Amerinds and Their Paleoenvironments in Northeastern North America*, edited by Walter S. Newman and Bert Salwen, pp. 355-368. Annals of the New York Academy of Sciences, Vol. 288, New York.

BRYSON, R. A., and W. M. WENDLAND
1967 Tentative Climatic Patterns for Some Late Glacial and Post-Glacial Episodes in Central North America. In *Life, Land and Water*, edited by W. Mayer-Oaks, pp. 271-298. University of Manitoba Press, Winnipeg.

BULLEN, RIPLEY P.
1955 Archaeology of the Tampa Bay Area. *Florida Historical Quarterly* 34(1):51-63.
1958 *The Bolen Bluff Site on Paynes Prairie, Florida*. Contributions of the Florida State Museum No. 4, Gainesville.
1962a Indian Burials at Tick Island. *American Philosophical Society Year Book 1961*, pp. 477-480.
1962b Suwannee Points in the Simpson Collection. *Florida Anthropologist* 15:87.
1975 *A Guide to the Identification of Florida Projectile Points*, revised edition. Kendall Books, Gainesville.
1976 Some Thoughts on Florida Projectile Points. *Florida Anthropologist* 29(1):33-38.

BULLEN, RIPLEY P., and LAURENCE E. BEILMAN
1973 The Nalcrest Site, Lake Weohyakapa, Florida. *Florida Anthropologist* 26:1-22.

BULLEN, RIPLEY P., and CARL BENSON
1964 Dixie Lime Caves, Numbers 1 and 2, A Preliminary Report. *Florida Anthropologist* 17:153-164.

BUTZER, KARL W.
1971 *Environment and Archaeology: An Ecological Approach to Prehistory*. Aldine/Atherton, New York.
1982 *Archaeology as Human Ecology: Method and Theory for a Contextual Approach*. Cambridge University Press, Cambridge.

BYERS, D. S.
1954 Bull Brook—A Fluted Point Site in Ipswich, Massachusetts. *American Antiquity* 19:343-351.
1955 Additional Information on the Bull Brook Site. *American Antiquity* 20:274-276.

CAHEN, D., L. H. KEELEY, and F. L. NOTEN
1979 Stone Tools, Tool Kits, and Human Behavior in Prehistory. *Current Anthropology* 20:661-683.

CALDWELL, JOSEPH R.
1958 Trend and Tradition in the Prehistory of the Eastern United States. *American Anthropological Association, Memoir, Number 88*.

CALLAHAN, ERRETT
1979 The Basics of Biface Knapping in the Eastern Fluted Point Tradition: A Manual for Flintknappers and Lithic Analysts. *Archaeology of Eastern North America* 7:1-180.

CAMBRON, WARREN W., and DAVID C. HULSE
1967 *Handbook of Alabama Archaeology, Part 11, Uniface Blade and Flake Tools*, edited by David L. DeJarnette. The Archaeological Research Association of Alabama, Moundville.

CARBONE, VICTOR A.
1983 Late Quaternary Environments in Florida and the Southeast. *Florida Anthropologist* 36:3-17.

CARR, ARCHIE, and COLEMAN J. GOIN
1955   *Guide to Reptiles, Amphibians and Freshwater Fishes of Florida.*
        University of Florida Press, Gainesville.
CARR, WILFRED J., and DOUGLAS C. ALVERSON
1959   *Stratigraphy of Middle Tertiary Rocks in Part of West-Central Florida.*
        U.S. Geological Bulletin 1092, Washington, D.C.
CARTER, CLARENCE EDWARD (EDITOR)
1962   *Territorial Papers of the United States: The Territory of Florida 1839-1845* (Vol. 26). National Archives and Records Service, General Services Administration, Washington, D.C.
CAUSSEAUX, K. W., and H. C. ROLLINS
1979   *Summary of Hydrologic Data from Tampa Bypass Canal System, July 1974 to September 1976,* U.S. Geological Survey Open-File Report 79-1297.
CHANCE, MARSHA A.
1982   *Phase II Investigations at Wetherington Island: A Lithic Procurement Site in Hillsborough County, Florida.* Interstate 75 Highway Phase II Archaeological Reports Number 3, Bureau of Historic Sites and Properties. Florida Division of Archives, History, and Records Management, Tallahassee.
CHANG, K. C.
1972   *Settlement Patterns in Archaeology.* Addison-Wesley Modular Publications Module 24.
CHERRY, R. N., J. W. STEWART, and J. A. MANN
1970   *General Hydrology of the Middle Gulf Area, Florida.* Florida Bureau of Geology Report of Investigation No. 56, Tallahassee.
CLAGGETT, STEPHEN R., and JOHN S. CABLE
1982   *The Haw River Sites: Archaeological Investigations at Two Stratified Sites in the North Carolina Piedmont.* Commonwealth Associates, Inc., Report No. 23386, Prepared for Wilmington District Corp of Engineers.
CLAUSEN, CARL J.
1964   *The A-356 and the Florida Archaic.* Unpublished Master's Thesis, Department of Anthropology, University of Florida, Gainesville.
CLAUSEN, CARL J., H. K. BROOKS, and A. B. WESOLOWSKY
1975   Florida Spring Confirmed as 10,000-Year-Old Early Man Site. *Florida Anthropologist* 28:1-38.
CLAUSEN, CARL J., A. D. COHEN, C. EMILIANI, J. A. HOLMAN, and J. J. STIPP
1979   Little Salt Spring, Florida: A Unique Underwater Site. *Science* 203: 609-614.
CLAYTON, DANNY H.
1983   Unusual Marks Found on Giant Land Tortoise Remains in Hillsborough River. *Florida Anthropologist* 36:101-104.
CLELAND, CHARLES E.
1976   The Focal-Diffuse Model: An Evolutionary Perspective on the Prehistoric Cultural Adaptations of the Eastern United States. *Midcontinental Journal of Archaeology* 1:59-75.
CLEWELL, ANDRE F.
1971   *The Vegetation of the Apalachicola National Forest: An Ecological Perspective.* U.S. Forest Service Supervisor's Office, Tallahassee.

COCKRELL, W. A., and LARRY MURPHY
1978   Pleistocene Man in Florida. *Archaeology of Eastern North America* 6:1-13.

COE, JOFFRE L.
1964   The Formative Cultures of the Carolina Piedmont. *Transactions of the American Philosophical Society*, 54(5), Philadelphia.

COLEMAN, JAMES M.
1982   Recent Seasonal Rainfalls and Temperature Relationships in Peninsular Florida. *Quaternary Research* 8:144-152.

CONKEY, MARGARET W.
1980   The Identification of Prehistoric Hunter-Gatherer Aggregation Sites: The Case of Altamira. *Current Anthropology* 21:609-630.

CONOVER, C. S., and D. LEACH
1975   *River Basins and Hydrologic Unit Map of Florida.* Florida Bureau of Geology Map Series No. 72, Tallahassee.

CORNWALL, I. W.
1958   *Soils for the Archaeologist.* Phoenix House, London.

COVINGTON, JAMES W. (EDITOR)
1952   Regarding the Establishment of Fort Brooke. *Florida Historical Quarterly* 31:273-278.

CURRAN, MARY LOU, and DENA F. DINCAUZE
1977   Paleo-Indians and Paleo-Lakes: New Data from the Connecticut Drainage. In *Amerinds and Their Paleoenvironments in North America*, edited by Walter S. Newman and Bert Salwen, pp. 333-348. Annals of the New York Academy of Sciences, Vol. 288, New York.

CUNNINGHAM, ROGER M.
1973   Paleo-Hunters Along the Ohio River. *Archaeology of Eastern North America* 1:118-126.

DANIEL, I. RANDOLPH, JR.
1982   *Test Excavations at the Deerstand Site (8Hi483A) in Hillsborough County, Florida.* Interstate 75 Highway Phase II Archaeological Reports No. 2. Bureau of Historic Sites and Properties. Florida Division of Archives, History and Records Management, Tallahassee.
1985   A Preliminary Model of Hunter-Gatherer Settlement in Central Florida. *Florida Anthropologist* 36:67-80.

DANIEL, I. RANDOLPH, JR., and MICHAEL WISENBAKER
1981   *Test Excavations at 8Hi450D: An Inland Archaic Occupation in Hillsborough County, Florida.* Interstate 75 Highway Phase II Archaeological Reports Number 1, Bureau of Historic Sites and Properties. Florida Division of Archives, History and Records Management, Tallahassee.
1983   A Preliminary Report on the Excavations at Harney Flats, Hillsborough County. *Florida Anthropologist* 36:67-80.

DAVIES, W. E., and H. E. LEGRAND
1972   Karst of the United States. In *Karst*, edited by M. Herakand, and V. T. Stringfield, pp. 467-505. Elsevier Publishing, Amsterdam.

DAVIS, JOHN H.
1967   *General Map of Natural Vegetation of Florida.* Institute of Food and Agricultural Services, University of Florida, Gainesville.

DAVIS, MARGARET B.
    1969   Palynology and Environmental History During the Quaternary Period. *American Scientist* 57(3):317-332.

DeJARNETTE, DAVID L., EDWARD B. KURJACK, and JAMES W. CAMBRON
    1962   Stanfield-Worley Bluff Shelter Excavations. *Journal of Alabama Archaeology* 8(1&2):1-124.

DEETZ, JAMES
    1967   *Invitation to Archaeology*. The Natural History Press. Garden City, New York.

DEUERLING, RICHARD J., and PETER L. MacGILL
    1981   *Environmental Geology Series: Tarpon Springs Sheet, Florida*. Bureau of Geology Map Series 99, Tallahassee.

DEW, A. D., and J. W. STEWART
    1980   *Hydrogeologic Data for Eureka Springs Landfill and Adjacent Areas North Central Hillsborough County, Florida*. 1969-1973, U.S. Geological Survey Open File Report 70-80.

DILLON, LAWRENCE S.
    1956   Wisconsin Climate and Life Zones in North America. *Science* 123:167-176.

DILLON, W. P., and R. N. ODALE
    1978   Late Quaternary Sea-Level Curve: Reinterpretation Based on Glaciotectonic Influence. *Geology* 6:56-60.

DOLAN, EDWARD M., and GLEN T. ALLEN, Jr.
    1961   *Investigations at Darby and Hornsby Springs, Alachua County, Florida*. Florida Geological Survey Special Publication No. 7.

DRAGOO, DON W.
    1973   Wells Creek—An Early Man Site in Stewart County, Tennessee. *Archaeology of Eastern North America*, 1(1):1-56.

DUNBAR, JAMES S., and BEN I. WALLER
    1983   A Distribution Analysis of the Clovis/Suwannee Paleo-Indian Sites of Florida—A Geographic Approach. *Florida Anthropologist* 36:18-30.

DUNNELL, ROBERT C.
    1978   Style and Function: A Fundamental Dichotomy. *American Antiquity* 43:192-202.

EDWARDS, ROBERT L., and K. O. EMERY
    1977   Man on the Continental Shelf. In *Amerinds and Their Paleoenvironments in Northeastern North America*, edited by Walter S. Newman and Bert Salwen, pp. 245-256. Annals of the New York Academy of Sciences, Vol. 288, New York.

EDWARDS, ROBERT L., and ARTHUR S. MERRILL
    1977   A Reconstruction of the Continental Shelf Areas of Eastern North America for the Times 9,500 B.P. and 12,500 B.P. *Archaeology of Eastern North America* 5:1-43.

EMERY, K. O.
    1967   The Continental Shelves. *Scientific American* 221(3):106-122.

EMERY, K. O., and R. L. EDWARDS
    1966   Archaeological Potential of the Atlantic Continental Shelf. *American Antiquity* 31:733-737.

EMILIANI, C.
    1966   Isotopic Paleotemperatures. *Science* 154:851-857.

EMILIANI, C., S. GARTNER, K. ELDRIDGE, T. C. HUANG, J. J. STIPP, and M. T. SWANSON
  1975   Paleoclimatological Analysis of Late Quaternary Cores from the Northeastern Gulf of Mexico. *Science* 189:1083-1087.
EVANS, JOHN G.
  1978   *An Introduction to Environmental Archaeology*. Elek Books Ltd., London.
FERNALD, EDWARD A. (EDITOR)
  1981   *Atlas of Florida*. F.S.U. Foundation, Inc., Tallahassee.
FITTING, JAMES E.
  1968   Environmental Potential and the Post-Glacial Readaptation in Eastern North America. *American Antiquity* 33:441-445.
FITTING, JAMES E., JERRY DEVISSCHER, and EDWARD J. WAHLA
  1966   *The Paleo-Indian Occupation of Holcombe Beach*. Anthropological Papers No. 27, Museum of Anthropology, University of Michigan, Ann Arbor.
FLORIDA DEPARTMENT OF NATURAL RESOURCES
  1975   *Florida Environmentally Endangered Lands Plan*.
FORD, JAMES A.
  1954   The Type Concept Revisited. *American Anthropologist* 56:42-54.
FRISON, GEORGE C., and BRUCE BRADLEY
  1980   *Folsom Tools and Technology at the Hanson Site, Wyoming*. University of New Mexico Press, Albuquerque.
FRISON, GEORGE C., and GEORGE M. ZEIMENS
  1980   Bone Projectile Points: An Addition to the Folsom Cultural Complex. *American Antiquity* 45:231-237.
FUNK, ROBERT E.
  1967   A Paleo-Indian Site in the Hudson Valley. *Eastern States Archaeological Federation Bulletin* 26:9-10.
  1972   Early Man in the Northeast and the Late-Glacial Environment. *Man in the Northeast* 4:7-39.
  1977   Early Cultures in the Hudson Drainage Basin. In *Amerinds and Their Paleoenvironments in Northeastern North America*, edited by Walter S. Newman and Bert Salwen, pp. 316-332. Annals of the New York Academy of Sciences, Vol. 288, New York.
GAGEL, KATHERINE
  1981a *Archaeological Excavations at Site (8Hi483B): An Archaic Habitation Site in Hillsborough County, Florida*. Interstate 75 Highway Phase II Archaeological Reports No. 6. Bureau of Historic Sites and Properties. Florida Division of Archives, History and Records Management, Tallahassee.
  1981b Archaeological Excavations at Site 8Hi393C: An Archaic and Deptford Habitation Site in Hillsborough County, Florida. Manuscript on file, Florida Bureau of Archaeological Research, Tallahassee.
  1984   Archaeological Excavations at Site 8Hi510A, An Early to Middle Archaic Habitation Site, Hillsborough County, Florida. Manuscript on file, Florida Bureau of Archaeological Research, Tallahassee.
GAGEL, KATHERINE, and RANDOLPH I. DANIEL, JR.
  1985   Archaeological Excavations at the Titus Church Site (8Hi521) and the

Two Horse Site (8Hi522): Two Archaic Sites in Hillsborough County, Florida. Manuscript on file, Florida Bureau of Archaeological Research, Tallahassee.

GARDNER, WILLIAM M.
1972   Some Thoughts Concerning Paleo-Indians in the Eastern Woodlands, Including a Proposed Model Based on Excavations at the Thunderbird Site. *Eastern States Archaeological Federation Bulletin* 32:11.

1974   The Flint Run Complex: Pattern and Process During the Paleo-Indian to Early Archaic. In *The Flint Run Paleo-Indian Complex: A Preliminary Report 1971-1973 Season*, edited by W. M. Gardner, pp. 5-47. Catholic University of America Archaeology Laboratory, Department of Anthropology. Occasional Publications No. 1.

1977   Flint Run Complex and Its Implications for Eastern North American Prehistory. In *Amerinds and Their Paleoenvironments in Northeastern North America*, edited by Walter S. Newman and Bert Salwen, pp. 257-263. Annals of the New York Academy of Sciences, Vol. 288, New York.

GATES, W. C.
1976   Modeling the Ice Age Climate. *Science* 191:1138-1144.

GIDLEY, J. W.
1926   Fossil Man in Florida. *Bulletin of Geological Society of America* 37:240.

GOGGIN, JOHN M.
1949   Cultural Traditions in Florida Prehistory. In *The Florida Indian and His Neighbors*, edited by John W. Griffin, pp. 13-14. Rollins College, Winter Park.

1950   An Early Lithic Complex from Central Florida. *American Antiquity* 16:46-49.

1952   *Space and Time Perspective in Northern St. Johns Archaeology, Florida.* Yale University Publication in Anthropology No. 47.

GOODYEAR, ALBERT C.
1973   Archaic Hafted Spokeshaves with Graver Spurs from the Southeast. *Florida Anthropologist* 26:39-44.

1974   *The Brand Site: A Techno-Functional Study of a Dalton Site in Northeast Arkansas.* Arkansas Archaeological Survey Research Series No. 7.

1979   *A Hypothesis for the Use of Cryptocrystalline Raw Materials Among Paleo-Indian Groups of North America.* Research Manuscript Series No. 156, Institute of Archaeology and Anthropology, University of South Carolina.

1982a   The Chronological Position of the Dalton Horizon in the Southeastern United States. *American Antiquity* 47:382-395.

1982b   Tool Kit Entropy and Bipolar Reduction: A Study of Interassemblage Lithic Variability Among Paleo-Indian Sites in the Northeastern United States, Manuscript on File, Institute of Archaeology and Anthropology, University of South Carolina, Columbia.

GOODYEAR, ALBERT C., W. THOMPSON, and L. O. WARREN
1968   Suwannee Style End Scrapers from Pinellas County. *Florida Anthropologist* 21:91.

GOODYEAR, ALBERT C., JOHN H. HOUSE and NEAL W. ACKERLY
    1979   Laurens-Anderson: An Archeological Survey of the Inter-Riverine Piedmont. *Anthropological Studies* 4, *Occasional Papers of the Institute of Archaeology and Anthropology*, University of South Carolina.

GOODYEAR, ALBERT C., S. B. UPCHURCH, and M. J. BROOKS
    1980   Turtlecrawl Point: An Inundated Early Holocene Archaeological Site on the West Coast of Florida. In *Holocene Geology and Man in Pinellas and Hillsborough Counties, Florida*, edited by S. B. Upchurch, pp. 24-33. Southeastern Geological Society Guidebook No. 22, Tallahassee.

GOODYEAR, ALBERT C., SAM B. UPCHURCH, MARK J. BROOKS, and NANCY N. GOODYEAR
    1983   Paleo-Indian Manifestations in the Tampa Bay Region, Florida. *Florida Anthropologist* 36:40-66.

GOULD, RICHARD A.
    1980   *Living Archaeology*. Cambridge University Press, Cambridge.

GOULD, RICHARD A., DOROTHY A. KOSTER, and ANN H. L. SONTY
    1971   The Lithic Assemblage of the Western Desert Aborigines of Australia. *American Antiquity* 36:149-169.

GRAHAM, RUSSELL W., C. VANCE HAYNES, DONALD LEE JOHNSON, and MARVIN KAY
    1981   Kimmswick: A Clovis-Mastodon Association in Eastern Missouri. *Science* 213:1115-1117.

GRAMLY, RICHARD M.
    1980   Raw Materials Source Areas and "Curated" Tool Assemblages. *American Antiquity* 45:823-833.
    1981   Eleven-Thousand Years in Maine. *Archaeology* 34:32-39.
    1982   *The Vail Site: A Palaeo-Indian Encampment in Maine*. Bulletin of the Buffalo Society of Natural Sciences, Vol. 30, Buffalo, New York.

GRIFFIN, JAMES B.
    1952   Culture Periods in Eastern United States Archaeology. In *Archaeology of the Eastern United States*, edited by James B. Griffin, pp. 352-364. University of Chicago Press, Chicago.
    1964   The Northeastern Woodland Area. In *Prehistoric Man in the New World*, edited by Jesse D. Jennings and Edward Norbeck, Chicago, pp. 223-258. The University of Chicago Press.
    1977   A Commentary on Early Man Studies in the Northeast. In *Amerinds and Their Paleoenvironments in Northeastern North America*, edited by Walter S. Newman and Bert Salwen, pp. 3-15. Annals of the New York Academy of Sciences, Vol. 288, New York.

GRIFFIN, JOHN W.
    1952   Prehistoric Florida: A Review. *Archaeology of the Eastern United States*, edited by James B. Griffin, pp. 322-334. University of Chicago Press, Chicago.
    1974   *Investigations in Russel Cave: Russel Cave National Monument*. National Park Service. Publications in Archaeology No. 13. U.S. Department of the Interior, Washington, D.C.

HAVISER, J.
    1983   Test Excavations at the Wetherington Ridge Site (8Hi472), A Paleo-

Indian through Transitional Period Base Camp Occupation in Hillsborough County, Florida. Manuscript on file, Florida Bureau of Archaeological Research, Tallahassee.

HAYDEN, BRIAN
- 1977 Stone Tool Functions in the Western Desert. In *Stone Tools as Cultural Markers: Change, Evolution and Complexity*, edited by R. V. S. Wright, pp. 178-188. Australian Institute of Aboriginal Studies, Canberra.
- 1980 Confusion in the Bipolar World: Bashed Pebbles and Splintered Pieces. *Lithic Technology* 9:2-7.
- 1982 Interaction Parameters and the Demise of Paleo-Indian Craftsmanship. *Plains Anthropologist* 27:109-125.

HAYNES, C. VANCE, JR.
- 1980 The Clovis Culture. *The Canadian Journal of Anthropology* 18:115-121.

HEALY, HENRY G.
- 1974 *Potentiometric Surface and Areas of Artesian Flow of the Floridan Aquifer*. Florida Bureau of Geology Map Series No. 73, Tallahassee.
- 1975 *Terraces and Shorelines of Florida*. Florida Bureau of Geology Map Series No. 71, Tallahassee.

HEMMINGS, E. THOMAS
- 1972 Early Man in the South Atlantic States. *Eastern States Archaeological Federation Bulletin* 31:10-11.
- 1975 The Silver Springs Site, Prehistory in the Silver Springs Valley, Florida. *Florida Anthropologist* 28:141-158.
- 1980 Man-Animal Interactions with a Substantive Example: Man and Dog in the Prehistoric Southeast. *Southeastern Archaeological Conference Bulletin* 17:3-5.

HESTER, JAMES J.
- 1972 *Blackwater Locality No. 1: A Stratified Early Man Site in Eastern New Mexico*. Fort Burgin Research Center, Southern Methodist University, Dallas.

HESTER, JAMES J., and JAMES GRADY
- 1977 Paleo-Indian Social Patterns on the Llano Estacado. In *Paleo-Indian Lifeways*, edited by Eileen Johnson, pp. 78-96. West Texas Museum Association, Lubbock.

HESTER, THOMAS R.
- 1979 Early Populations in Prehistoric Texas. *Archaeology* 32(6):26-33.
- 1980 A Survey of Paleo-Indian Archaeological Remains Along the Texas Coast. In *Papers on the Archaeology of the Texas Coast*, edited by Lynn Highley and Thomas R. Hester, Center for Archaeological Research, University of Texas, San Antonio.

HESTER, THOMAS R., GILBOW DELBERT, and ALAN D. ALBEE
- 1973 A Functional Analysis of "Clearfork" Artifacts from the Rio Grande Plains, Texas. *American Antiquity* 38:90-96.

HIBBARD, C. W., D. E. RAY, D. E. SAVAGE, D. W. TAYLOR, and J. E. GUILDAY
- 1965 Quaternary Mammals of North America. In *The Quaternary of the United States*, edited by Herbert E. Wright, Jr. and David G. Frey, pp. 509-525. Princeton University Press, Princeton.

HILL, J. N., and R. K. EVANS
1972   A Model for Classification and Typology. In *Models in Archaeology*, edited by D. L. Clarke, pp. 231-273. Methuen, London.
HILL, RALPH G., and JAMES H. PLEDGER
1939   *The Railroads of Florida*. Florida Railroad Commission, Tallahassee.
HOFFMAN, CHARLES
1983   A Mammoth Kill Site in the Silver Springs Run. *Florida Anthropologist* 36:83-87.
HOUSE, JOHN H.
1975   A Functional Typology for Cache Project Surface Collections. In *The Cache River Archaeologist Project: An Experiment in Contract Archaeology*, assembled by Michael B. Schiffer, and John H. House, Arkansas Archaeological Survey, Fayetteville.
HOUSE, JOHN H., and DAVID L. BALLENGER
1976   *An Archaeological Survey of the Interstate 77 Route in the South Carolina Piedmont*. Institute of Archeology and Anthropology Research Manuscript Series 104. University of South Carolina, Columbia.
HRDLICKA, ALES
1922   *The Anthropology of Florida*. Publications of the Florida State Historical Society, No. 1.
HUDSON, CHARLES
1976   *The Southeastern Indians*. University of Tennessee Press, Knoxville.
HUGHES, G. H., E. R. HAMPTON, and D. F. TUCKER
1971   *Annual and Seasonal Rainfall in Florida*. Florida Bureau of Geology Map Series No. 40, Tallahassee.
HUNT, C. B., and A. P. HUNT
1957   Stratigraphy and Archaeology of Some Florida Soils. *Bulletin of the Geological Society* 68:797-806.
IRWIN, HENRY T., and H. M. WORMINGTON
1970   Paleo-Indian Tool Types in the Great Plains. *American Antiquity* 35:24-34.
JACKSON, L. J.
1983   Geochronology and Settlement Disposition in the Early Paleo-Indian Occupation of Southern Ontario Canada, *Quaternary Research* 19:388-399.
JEFFERSON DAVIS WAR DEPARTMENT MAP
1856   Map on file in the Florida Section of the State Library of Florida, Tallahassee.
JELINEK, ARTHUR J.
1976   Form, Function, and Style in Lithic Analysis. In *Culture, Change, and Continuity, Essays in Honor of James Bennett Griffin*, edited by Charles E. Cleland, pp. 19-76. Academic Press, New York.
JENNINGS, J. D.
1957   *Danger Cave*. Memoir of the Society for American Archaeology No. 14, Salt Lake City.
JOCHIM, MICHAEL A.
1976   *Hunter-Gatherer Subsistence and Settlement: A Predictive Model*. Academic Press, New Yok.

1981 *Strategies for Survival.* Academic Press, New York.
JOHNSON, ROBERT E.
    1985 Archaeological Excavations at the Wetherington Ridge Site (8Hi472B) in Hillsborough County, Florida. Manuscript on file, Florida Bureau of Archaeological Research, Tallahassee.
JONES, B. CALVIN
    1981 Phase III Proposal for Salvage Investigations of Site 8Hi507 (Project No. 10075-3425 and 3416). Manuscript on file at the Division of Archives, History and Records Management, Tallahassee.
JONES, B. CALVIN and LOUIS D. TESAR
    1982 An Update on the Highway Salvage Program in Florida. *The Florida Anthropologist* 35:59-62.
JONES, EMRYS
    1966 *Human Geography.* Praeger, New York.
JUDGE, JAMES W.
    1973 *Paleo-Indian Occupation of the Central Rio Grande Valley in New Mexico.* University of New Mexico Press, Albuquerque.
KEELEY, LAWRENCE H.
    1974 Technique and Methodology in Microwear Studies: A Critical Review. *World Archaeology.* 5:322-336.
    1980 *Experimental Determination of Stone Tool Uses.* University of Chicago Press.
    1982 Hafting and Retooling: Effects on the Archaeological Record. *American Antiquity* 47:798-809.
KENNER, W. E.
    1969 *Seasonal Variation of Streamflow in Florida.* Florida Bureau of Geology Map Series No. 31, Tallahassee.
KINTIGH, KEITH W., and ALBERT J. AMMERMAN
    1982 Heuristic Approaches to Spatial Analysis in Archaeology. *American Antiquity* 47:31-63.
KNAPP, MICHAEL S.
    1980 *Environmental Geology Series: Tampa Sheet, Florida.* Bureau of Geology Map Series No. 97, Tallahassee.
KOHOUT, F. A., H. P. HENRY, and J. E. BONKS
    1977 Hydrogeology Related to Geothermal Conditions of the Floridan Plateau. In *Hydrogeology Related to Geothermal Nature of the Floridan Plateau*, edited by Douglas L. Smith and George M. Griffin, pp. 1-38. Florida Bureau of Geology Special Publication No. 21, Tallahassee.
KRAFT, HERBERT C.
    1977 Paleo-Indians in New Jersey. In *Amerinds and Their Paleoenvironments in Northeastern North America*, edited by Walter S. Newman and Bert Salwen, pp. 264-281. Annals of the New York Academy of Sciences, Vol. 288, New York.
KUNZ, MICHAEL
    1969 The Paleo-Indian Big Game Hunter: A Misconception. *The Anthropological Journal of Canada* 7:27-29.
KVAMME, KENNETH L.
    1982 Methods for Analyzing and Understanding Hunter-Gatherer Site Location as a Function of Environmental Variation. Paper presented at

the 47th Annual Meeting of the Society for American Archaeology, Minneapolis, Minnesota.
LAKELA, OLGA, ROBERT W. LONG, GLENN FLEMMING, and PIERRE GENNELLE
1976 *Plants of the Tampa Bay Area.* Banyan Books, Miami.
LAWRENCE, BARBARA
1968 Antiquity of Large Dogs in North America. *Tebiwa* 11(2):43-49.
LAZARUS, WILLIAM C.
1965 Effects of Land Subsidence and Sea Level Changes on Elevation of Archaeological Sites on the Florida Gulf Coast. *Florida Anthropologist* 28:49-58.
LEE, RICHARD B.
1968 What Hunters Do for a Living, or How to Make Out on Scarce Resources. In *Man The Hunter*, edited by Richard B. Lee and Irven Devore, pp. 30-48. Aldine, Chicago.
LEE, RICHARD B., and IRVEN DEVORE
1968 *Man The Hunter*, edited by Richard B. Lee and Irven Devore, Aldine, Chicago.
LEGRANDE, H. E.
1973 Hydrological and Ecological Problems of Karst Regions. *Science* 179:859-864.
LEIGHTY, R. F., V. W. CARLISLE, O. E. CRUZ, J. H. WALKER, J. BEAN, R. E. CALDWELL, J. B. CROMARTIE, J. L. HUBER, E. D. MATTHEWS, and Z. T. MILLSAP
1958 *Soil Survey of Hillsborough County, Florida.* U.S. Department of Agriculture, Washington.
LEONHARDY, FRANK C. (EDITOR)
1966 *Domebo: A Paleo-Indian Mammoth Kill in the Prairie-Plains.* Contributions of the Museum of the Great Plains No. 1, Lawton, Oklahoma.
LITTLE, ELBERT L., JR.
1978 *Atlas of United States Trees*, Vol. 5, Miscellaneous Publications No. 1361. U.S. Department of Agriculture, Forest Service, Washington.
LONG, ROBERT W.
1974 Origin of the Vascular Flora of Southeastern Florida. In *Environments of South Florida: Present and Past*, edited by P. J. Gleason, pp. 28-36. Miami Geological Society Memoir 2, Miami.
MacDONALD, GEORGE F.
1968 *Debert: A Palaeo-Indian Site in Central Nova Scotia.* Anthropology Papers No. 16, National Museums of Canada, Ottawa, Ontario.
1971 A Reunion of Research of Paleo-Indians in Eastern North America. *Arctic Anthropology* 8:32-41.
MacINTYRE, I. G., B. BLACKWELDER, L. S. LAND, and R. STUCKENRATH
1975 Carolina Shelf Edge Sandstone: Age, Environment of Origin and Relationship to Pre-Existing Sea Levels. *Geological Society of America Bulletin* 86:1973-1978.
MacNEIL, F. STEARNS
1949 Pleistocene Shore Lines in Florida and Georgia. *U.S. Geological Survey Professional Paper* 221-F:95-107.

MARSHALL, S. B.
1982   Aboriginal Settlement in New Jersey during the Paleo-Indian Cultural Period ca. 10,000 B.C.-6,000 B.C. In *New Jersey's Archaeological Resources from the Paleo-Indian Period to the Present: A Review of Research Problems and Survey Priorities*, edited by Olga Chester, pp. 10-51. Trenton.

MARTIN, ROBERT A., and S. DAVID WEBB
1974   Late Pleistocene Mammals from the Devil's Den Fauna, Levy County. In *Pleistocene Mammals of Florida*, edited by S. David Webb, pp. 114-145. University Presses of Florida, Gainesville.

MASON, RONALD J.
1962   The Paleo-Indian Tradition in Eastern North America. *Current Anthropology* 3:227-246.

MATO, GUY R., and JOEL GUNN
n.d.   *A Study of Late Quaternary Environments and Early Man*, Vol. III. Benham Blair and Affiliates, Cultural Resource Management.

McMILLAN, R. BRUCE
1976   The Dynamics of Cultural and Environmental Change at Rodgers Shelter, Missouri. In *Prehistoric Man and His Environments: A Case Study in Ozark Highland*, edited by W. Raymond Wood and R. Bruce McMillan, pp. 111-122. Academic Press, New York.

McNETT, CHARLES W., JR., and BARBARA McMILLAN
1974   Initial Season of the Upper Delaware Early Man Project. Manuscript on file, The American University, Washington, D.C.

McNETT, CHARLES W., JR., BARBARA McMILLAN, and S. B. MARSHALL
1977   The Shawnee-Minisink Site. In *Amerinds and Their Paleoenvironments in Northeastern North America*, edited by Walter S. Newman and Bert Salwen, pp. 282-296. Annals of the New York Academy of Sciences, Vol. 288, New York.

MELTZER, DAVID J.
1983   *Variations in Eastern Fluted Projectile Points*. Paper presented at the 48th Annual Meeting of the Society for American Archaeology, Pittsburgh.

MELTZER, DAVID J., and BRUCE D. SMITH
1986   Paleoindian and Early Archaic Subsistence Strategies in Eastern North America. In *Foraging, Collecting, and Harvesting: Archaic Period Subsistence and Settlement in the Eastern Woodlands*, edited by Sarah W. Neusius, pp. 3-31. Center for Archaeological Investigations Occasional Paper No. 6, Southern Illinois University.

MENKE, C. G., E. W. MEREDITH, and W. S. WETTERHALL
1961   *Water Resources of Hillsborough County, Florida*. Florida Geological Survey Report of Investigations No. 25, Tallahassee.

MILANICH, J. T., and CHARLES H. FAIRBANKS
1980   *Florida Archaeology*. Academic Press, New York.

MILLER, ALBERT, and JACK C. THOMPSON
1979   *Elements of Meterology*. Charles E. Merrill Publishing Company, Columbus.

MILLER, CARL F.
1956   Life 8,000 Years Ago Uncovered in an Alabama Cave. *National Geographic* 110:542-558.

MILLER, ROBERT M.
    1965   Quaternary Freshwater Fishes of North America. In *The Quaternary of the United States*, edited by H. E. Wright, Jr. and D. G. Frey, pp. 569-581. Princeton University Press, Princeton.
MILLIMAN, J. D., and K. O. EMERY
    1968   Sea Levels During the Past 35,000 Years. *Science* 162:1121-1123.
MOELLER, ROGER W.
    1980   *6LF21: A Paleo-Indian Site in Western Connecticut*. Occasional Paper No. 2, American Indian Archaeological Institute, Washington, CT.
    1984   Regional Implications of the Templeton Site for Paleo-Indian Lithic Procurement and Utilization. *North American Archaeologist* 5(3): 235-245.
MORSE, DAN F.
    1971   The Hawkins Cache: A Significant Dalton Find in Northeast Arkansas. *Arkansas Archaeologist* 12:9-20.
    1973   Dalton Culture in Northeast Arkansas. *The Florida Anthropologist* 25:28-38.
    1975   Paleo-Indian in the Land of Opportunity: Preliminary Report on the Excavations at the Sloan Site (36E94). In *The Cache River Archeological Project: An Experiment in Contract Archeology*, assembled by Michael B. Schiffer and John H. House, pp. 135-143. Arkansas Archeological Survey, Fayetteville.
    n.d.   A Paleo-Indian/Early Archaic Cemetery Possibility in Arkansas. Manuscript on file, Arkansas Archeological Survey, Fayetteville.
MOTZ, LOUIS H.
    1975   *Hydrologic Effects of the Tampa Bypass Canal*. Florida Bureau of Geology Report of Investigations No. 82, Tallahassee.
MULLER, JON D.
    1978   The Southeast. In *Ancient Native Americans*, edited by Jesse Jennings, pp. 281-326. N. H. Freeman and Company, San Francisco.
NEILL, WILFRED T.
    1958   A Stratified Early Site at Silver Springs, Florida. *Florida Anthropologist* 11:33-48.
    1964   The Association of Suwannee Points and Extinct Animals in Florida. *Florida Anthropologist* 14:17-32.
    1971   A Paleo-Indian Implement of Ground Stone. *Florida Anthropologist* 24:61-70.
ODELL, GEORGE H.
    1981   The Morphological Express at Function Junction: Searching for Meaning in Lithic Tool Types. *Journal of Anthropological Research* 37:319-342.
ODUM, EUGENE P.
    1971   *Fundamentals of Ecology*. 3rd Edition. W. B. Saunders, Philadelphia.
PALMER, JILL, JIM DUNBAR, and DANNY CLAYTON
    1981   *Phase II Underwater Archaeological Testing at the Fowler Bridge Mastodon Site (8Hi393c/uw)*. Interstate 75 Highway Phase II Archaeological Report, Number 5, Bureau of Historic Sites and Properties, Florida Division of Archives, History and Records Management, Tallahassee.

PIRKLE, E. C., W. H. YOHO, and C. W. HENDRY, JR.
    1970   *Ancient Sea Level Stands in Florida.* Florida Bureau of Geology Bulletin No. 52, Tallahassee.

PURDY, BARBARA A.
    1981a   Investigations into the Use of Chert Outcrops by Prehistoric Floridians: The Container Corporation of America Site. *Florida Anthropologist* 34:90-108.
    1981b   *Florida's Prehistoric Stone Technology.* University of Florida Press, Gainesville.

RAY, CLAYTON E.
    1958   Additions to the Pleistocene Mammalian Fauna from Melbourne, Florida. *American Museum of Comparative Zoology Bulletin* 119:421-451.

RAYL, SANDRA L.
    1974   *A Paleo-Indian Mammoth Kill Site Near Silver Springs, Florida.* Unpublished Master's Thesis, Department of Anthropology, Northern Arizona University, Flagstaff.

REICHENBAUGH, R. C., and J. D. HUNN
    1972   *A Hydrologic Description of Lake Thonotosassa Near Tampa, Florida.* Bureau of Geology Map Series No. 48, Tallahassee.

RICHARDSON, JAMES B., III
    1978   Early Man on the Peruvian North Coast, Early Maritime Exploration and the Pleistocene and Holocene Environment. In *Early Man in America from a Circum-Pacific Perspective*, edited by Alan L. Bryan, pp. 274-289. Occasional Papers No. 1 of the Department of Anthropology, University of Alberta, Edmonton.

RILEY, THOMAS J.
    1974   Constraint on Dimensions of Variance. *American Antiquity* 39:489-490.

RITCHIE, WILLIAM A.
    1953   A Probable Paleo-Indian Site in Vermont. *American Antiquity* 18: 248-258.

ROBINSON, ERNEST L. (EDITOR)
    1928   *History of Hillsborough County, Florida.* The Record Company Printers, St. Augustine, Florida.

ROOSA, WILLIAM B.
    1977   Great Lakes Paleo-Indian: The Parkhill Site, Ontario. In *Amerinds and Their Paleoenvironments in Northeastern North America*, edited by Walter S. Newman and Bert Salwen, pp. 349-354. Annals of the New York Academy of Sciences Vol. 288, New York.

ROPER, DONNA C.
    1979   The Method and Theory of Site Catchment Analysis: A Review. In *Advances in Archaeological Method and Theory* Vol. 2, edited by Michael B. Schiffer, pp. 119-140. Academic Press, New York.

ROSENAU, J. C., G. L. FAULKNER, C. W. HENDRY, JR., and R. W. HULL
    1977   *Springs of Florida.* Florida Bureau of Geology Bulletin No. 31, Tallahassee.

ROUSE, IRVING
    1960   The Classification of Artifacts in Archaeology. *American Antiquity* 25:313-323.

RUPPÉ, REYNOLD J.
    1980   The Archaeology of Drowned Terrestial Sites: A Preliminary

Report. *Florida Bureau of Historic Sites and Properties Bulletin* No. 6:35-45.
SACKETT, JAMES R.
1973   Style, Function, and Artifact Variability in Paleo-Lithic Assemblages. In *The Explanation of Culture Change: Models in Prehistory*, edited by Colin Renfrew, pp. 317-325. Duckworth, London.
SAHLINS, MARSHALL
1972   *Stone Age Economics.* Aldine, New York.
SALWEN, BERT
1962   Sea Levels and Archaeology in the Long Island Sound Area. *American Antiquity* 28:46-55.
SCHIFFER, MICHAEL B.
1972   Archaeological Context and Systematic Context. *American Antiquity* 37:156-165.
1976   *Behavioral Archaeology.* Academic Press, New York.
1979   The Place of Lithic Use-Wear Studies in Behavioral Archaeology. In *Lithic Use-Wear Analysis*, edited by Brian Hayden, pp. 15-25. Academic Press, New York.
1981   Some Issues in the Philosophy of Archaeology. *American Antiquity* 46:899-908.
1983   Toward the Identification of Formation Processes. *American Antiquity* 48:675-706.
SCIENCE APPLICATIONS, INC.
1979   *A Culture Resources Survey of the Continental Shelf from Cape Hatteras to Key West. Vol. II: Prehistoric Archaeology*, Science Applications.
1981   *A Cultural Resources Survey of the Continental Shelf from Cape Hatteras to Key West. Vol. I: Physical Environment*, Science Applications.
SCOTT, THOMAS M., and PETER L. MACGILL
1981   *The Hawthorn Formation of Central Florida.* Florida Bureau of Geology Report of Investigations No. 91, Tallahassee.
SELANDER, ROBERT K.
1965   Avian Speciation in the Quaternary. In *The Quaternary of the United States*, edited by H. E. Wright, Jr. and D. G. Frey, pp. 527-542. Princeton University Press, Princeton.
SELLARDS, E. H.
1916   Human Remains and Associated Fossils from the Pleistocene of Florida. *Florida Geological Survey, Eighth Annual Report*, pp. 123-160. Tallahassee.
1917   Review of the Evidence on Which the Human Remains at Vero, Florida are Referred to the Pleistocene. *Florida Geological Survey, Ninth Annual Report*, Tallahassee.
1952   *Early Man in America.* Greenwood Press, New York.
SEMEONOV, SERGEI A.
1964   *Prehistoric Technology.* Translated by M. W. Thompson. Barnes and Noble, New York.
SERBOUSEK, DON
1983   Explorations of a Paleo-Indian Site on the Aucilla River. *Florida Anthropologist* 36:88-97.

SHAFER, HARRIS J.
    1970   Notes on Uniface Retouch Technology. *American Antiquity* 35:480-487.
    1977   Early Lithic Assemblages in Eastern Texas. In *Paleo-Indian Lifeways*, edited by Eileen Johnson, pp. 187-197. West Texas Museum Association. Lubbock, Texas.
SHEETS, PAYSON D.
    1975   Behavioral Analysis and the Structure of a Prehistoric Industry. *Current Anthropology* 16:369-391.
SIMPSON, CLARENCE
    1948   Folsom-Like Points from Florida. *Florida Anthropologist* 1:11-15.
SIMPSON, GEORGE GAYLORD
    1929   The Extinct Land Mammals of Florida. *Florida Geological Survey 20th Annual Report*, pp. 229-279. Tallahassee.
SODAY, FRANK J.
    1954   The Quad Site: A Paleo-Indian Village in Northern Alabama. *Tennessee Archaeologist* 10:1-20.
SOLLBERGER, J. B.
    1971   A Technical Study of Beveled Knives. *Plains Anthropologists* 16:209-218.
SPAULDING, ALBERT C.
    1953   Statistical Techniques for the Discovery of Artifact Types. *American Antiquity* 18:305-313.
SPURR, STEPHEN H., and BURTON U. BARNES
    1973   *Forest Ecology*. Ronald Press Company, New York.
STEVENSON, HENRY M.
    1976   *Vertebrates of Florida: Identification and Distribution*. University Presses of Florida, Gainesville.
STOCKTON, E. D.
    1973   Shaw's Creek Shelter: Human Displacement of Artifacts and Its Significance. *Mankind* 9:112-117.
STRAHLER, ARTHUR N.
    1971   *The Earth Sciences*. Harper and Row, New York.
    1975   *Physical Geography*, 4th Edition, John Wiley and Sons, New York.
THORNBURY, WILLIAM D.
    1965   *Regional Geomorphology of the United States*. John Wiley and Sons, New York.
TORRENCE, ROBIN
    1983   Time Budgeting and Hunter-Gatherer Technology. In *Hunter-Gatherer Economy in Prehistory: A European Perspective*, edited by G. Bailey, pp. 11-22. Cambridge University Press, Cambridge.
TRINGHAM, R., G. COOPER, G. ODELL, B. VOYTEK, and ANNE WHITMAN
    1974   Experimentation in the Formation of Edge Damage: A New Approach to Lithic Analysis. *Journal of Field Archaeology* 1:186-195.
TUCK, JAMES A.
    1974   Early Archaic Horizons in Eastern North America. *Archaeology of Eastern North America* 2(1):72-80.
UPCHURCH, SAM B.
    1984   Geology and Lithic Materials at the Harney Flats Archaeological Site

(8Hi507), Hillsborough County, Florida. Manuscript on file, Florida Bureau of Archaeological Research, Division of Archives, History and Records Management, Tallahassee.

UPCHURCH, S. B., R. N. STROM, and M. G. NUCKELS
1981   Methods of Provenance Determination of Florida Cherts. Manuscript on file, Florida Bureau of Historic Sites and Properties, Tallahassee.

VERNON, ROBERT O., and H. S. PURI
1964   *Geologic Map of Florida*, Florida Board of Conservation Map Series No. 18, Tallahassee.

VERREY, ROBERT
1986   Methodology for Analysis of Flintknapping Debitage from the Thunderbird Site. *Journal of Middle Atlantic Archaeology* 2:63-78.

VILLA, PAOLA
1982   Conjoinable Pieces and Site Formation Processes. *American Antiquity* 47:276-290.

VILLA, PAOLA, and JEAN COURTIN
1983   The Interpretation of Stratified Sites: A View from Underground. *Journal of Archaeological Science* 10:267-281.

VISHER, F. N., and G. H. HUGHES
1969   *The Difference between Rainfall and Potential Evaporation in Florida*. Florida Bureau of Geology Map Series No. 32, Tallahassee.

WALKER, DANNY N., and GEORGE C. FRISON
1982   Studies on Amerindian Dogs, 3: Prehistoric Wolf/Dog Hybrids from the Northwest Plains. *Journal of Archaeological Science* 9:125-172.

WALLER, BEN I.
1972   Some Occurrences of Paleo-Indian Projectile Points in Florida Waters. *Eastern States Archaeological Federation Bulletin* 31:14-15.
1983   Florida Anthropologist Interview with Ben Waller. *Florida Anthropologist* 36(1-2):31-39.

WALLER, BEN, and JAMES DUNBAR
1977   Distribution of Paleo-Indian Projectiles in Florida. *Florida Anthropologist* 30:79-80.

WARD, DANIEL B. (EDITOR)
1978   *Rare and Endangered Biota of Florida*, Vol. 5 Plants, University Presses of Florida, Gainesville.

WARNICA, JAMES M.
1966   New Discoveries at the Clovis Site. *American Antiquity* 3:345-357.

WARREN, LYMAN O.
1973   Unique Knife or Chisel, Piper-Fuller Airfield, St. Petersburg. *Florida Anthropologist* 26:119-120.

WARREN, LYMAN, and RIPLEY P. BULLEN
1965   A Dalton Complex from Florida. *Florida Anthropologist* 18:29-31.

WATTS, W. A.
1975   A Late Quaternary Record of Vegetation from Lake Annie, South-Central Florida. *Geology* 3:344-346.
1980   The Quaternary Vegetation History of the South-Eastern United States. *Annual Review of Ecology and Systematics* 11:387-409.

WATTS, W. A., and M. STUIVER
    1980   Late Wisconsin Climate of Northern Florida and the Origin of Species-Rich Deciduous Forest. *Science* 210:325-327.

WEBB, S. DAVID (EDITOR)
    1974   *Pleistocene Mammals of Florida*. University Presses of Florida, Gainesville.

WEBB, S. DAVID, JERALD T. MILANICH, ROGER ALEXON, and JAMES DUNBAR
    1983   An Extinct Bison Kill Site, Jefferson County, Florida. *Florida Anthropologist* 36:81-82.

WEIGEL, ROBERT D.
    1962   *Fossil Vertebrates of Vero, Florida*. Florida Geological Survey Special Publication No. 10, Tallahassee.

WEIGEL, ROBERT D., HOLMAN, J. A., and A. A. PALOUMPIS
    1974   Vertebrates from Russel Cave. In *Investigations in Russel Cave*, edited by John W. Griffin, pp. 81-85. National Park Service, Washington, D.C.

WEISBORD, NORMAN
    1973   *New and Little Known Corals from the Tampa Formation*. Florida. Bureau of Geology Report of Investigations No. 56, Tallahassee.

WELSH, JAMES M.
    1983   Mitigative Excavations of the South Prong 1 Site, 8Hi418, and the Cates Site, 8Hi425, Hillsborough County, Florida. *University of South Florida, Department of Anthropology, Archaeological Report No. 13*.

WETTERHALL, W. S.
    1965   *Reconnaissance of Springs and Skins in West-Central Florida*. Bureau of Geology Report of Investigations No. 39, Tallahassee.

WHALLON, ROBERT, JR.
    1973a   Spatial Analysis of Paleolithic Occupation Areas. In *The Explanation of Culture Change: Models in Prehistory*, edited by C. Renfrew, pp. 115-130. Duckworth, London.
    1973b   Spatial Analysis of Occupation Floors I: Application of Dimensional Analysis of Variance. *American Antiquity* 38:266-278.
    1974a   Spatial Analysis of Occupation Floors II: The Application of Nearest Neighbor Analysis. *American Antiquity* 39:16-34.
    1974b   Reply to Riley and Schiffer. *American Antiquity* 39:492-494.
    1978   The Spatial Analysis of Mesolithic Occupation Floors: A Reappraisal. In *The Early Postglacial Settlement of Northern Europe*, edited by Paul Mellars, pp. 27-35. University of Pittsburgh Press, Pittsburgh.

WHARTON, BARRY R.
    1983   Phase II Archaeological Test Excavations at the Diamond Dairy Site (8Hi476A and 8Hi476B), an Archaic Period Site in Hillsborough County, Florida. Manuscript on file, Florida Bureau of Archaeological Research, Tallahassee.

WHARTON, BARRY R., GEORGE R. BALLO, and MITCHELL E. HOPE
    1981   The Republic Groves Site, Hardee County, Florida. *Florida Anthropologist* 34:59-80.

WHEAT, JOE BEN
1971   Lifeways of Early Man in North America. *Arctic Anthropology* 8: 22-31.
WHITE, MAX E.
1980   Early Man and Environment in the Southeastern United States. Paper presented at the Southeastern Archaeological Conference, New Orleans.
WHITE, W. A.
1958   Some Geomorphic Features of Central Florida. Florida Geological Survey Bulletin No. 41, Tallahassee.
1970   The Geomorphology of the Florida Peninsula, Florida Bureau of Geology Geological Bulletin No. 51, Tallahassee.
WHITEHEAD, DONALD R.
1965   Palynology and Pleistocene Phytogeography of Unglaciated Eastern North America. In *The Quaternary of the United States*, edited by Herbert E. Wright, Jr. and David G. Frey, pp. 417–432. Princeton University Press, Princeton.
WHITEHEAD, DONALD R., and MICHAEL V. DOYLE
1969   Late Pleistocene Peats from Long Beach, North Carolina, *Southeastern Geology* 10:1-16.
WILLEY, GORDON R.
1953   *Prehistoric Settlement Patterns in the Viru Valley, Peru*. Bureau of American Ethnology Bulletin No. 155, Smithsonian Institution.
1966   *An Introduction to American Archaeology Part One: North and Middle America*. Prentice-Hall, Englewood Cliffs, New Jersey.
WILLEY, GORDON R., and PHILLIP PHILLIPS
1958   *Method and Theory in American Archaeology*. University of Chicago Press, Chicago.
WILLIAMS, B. J.
1974   A Model of Band Society. *Memoirs of the Society for American Archaeology* No. 29.
WILLIAMS, STEPHEN, and JAMES STOLTMAN
1965   An Outline of Southeastern United States Prehistory with Particular Interest on the Paleo-Indian Era. In *Quaternary of the United States*, edited by H. E. Wright, Jr. and David G. Frey, pp. 669-683. Princeton University Press, Princeton.
WILMSEN, EDWIN N.
1970   *Lithic Analysis and Cultural Inference: A Paleo-Indian Case*. Anthropological Papers No. 16, University of Arizona Press.
1974   *Lindenmeier: A Pleistocene Hunting Society*. Harper and Row, New York.
WILMSEN, EDWIN N., and FRANK H. ROBERTS, JR.
1978   *Lindenmeier, 1934-1974*. Smithsonian Contributions to Anthropology No. 24.
WITTHOFT, JOHN
1952   A Paleo-Indian Site in Eastern Pennsylvania. *Proceedings of the American Philosophical Society* 96:464-495.
WOBST, H. MARTIN
1974   Boundary Conditions for Paleolithic Social Systems. *American Antiquity* 39:147-148.

WOOD, JOHN J.
  1978   Optimal Location in Settlement Space: A Model for Describing Location Strategies. *American Antiquity* 43:258-270.
WOOD, RAYMOND W., and DONALD LEE JOHNSON
  1978   A Survey of Disturbance Processes in Archaeological Site Formation. In *Advances in Archaeological Method and Theory* Vol. 1, edited by M. B. Shiffer, pp. 315-381. Academic Press, New York.
WORMINGTON, H. M.
  1957   *Ancient Man in North America.* Denver Museum of Natural History, Popular Series #4, Denver.
WRIGHT, ALEXANDRA P. (EDITOR)
  1973   *Environmental Geology and Hydrology, Tampa Area, Florida*, Florida Bureau of Geology Special Publication No. 19, Tallahassee.
WRIGHT, H. E., JR.
  1972   Interglacial and Postglacial Climates: The Pollen Record. *Quaternary Research* 2:274-282.
  1981   Vegetation East of the Rocky Mountains 18,000 Years Ago. *Quaternary Research* 15:113-125.
YELLEN, JOHN E.
  1977   *Archaeological Approaches to the Present.* Academic Press, New York.

Index

Illustrations (*f*) and tables (*t*) are indicated in *italics*.

abraders, 16, 90–93, *91f*, 112, 124, 126, 146, 174; dimensions, *90t*; exotic, 126
accessioned, 27
activity areas, 42
adaptation, 42, 167, 172
adzes, 79–81, *79t*, *80f*, 112, 114, 124; bifacial, 79; unifacial, 79
Agate Basin, 159
Alabama, 9, 76, 133
Alachua County, 151
Altonian period, 152
ancient pollen assemblages, 156
animal burrows, 40
anvil, 83, 93, 94, 114, 136, 165
archaeological techniques, 14–27
archaeologists, xi, 41, 42, 43, 99, 100, 102, 131, 132, 134, 140, 144, 146, 149, 150, 162
Archaic: assemblages, 129, 130; cemetery, 92; occupation, 145; periods, 147, 167, 169, 175; settlement patterns, 167; stemmed points, *34f*, 150
Area 1, *20f*, 29, 33, 35, 36, 37, 39, 40, 104–7, 114, 115, 120, 123, 124, 125, 126; artifact provenience, *106f*; cultural sequence, 32; SYMAP, *105f*; test pits, 32, 92
Area 2, 19, 25, 26, 32, 37, 81, 90, 93, 107–12, 114, 115, 120, 123, 124, 125, 126; artifact provenience, *109f*; SYMAP, *108f*
Area 3, 19, 25, *20f*, 26, 31, 32, 92, 112–14, 115, 120, 123, 124, 125, 126; artifact provenience, *113f*; SYMAP, *111f*
Arkansas, 133, 152
Arredondo points, 150
artifact map, 19
artifacts, xi, 14, 15, 16, 19, 26, 27, 31, 37, 38, 39, 40, 41, 42, 55, 68, 69, 79, 92, 99, 102, 103, 104, 107, 110, 112, 114, 129, 133, 135, 136, 137, 138, 139, 140, 145, 146, 147, 162, 168, 175; classification, 41; clusters, 17, 26; collecting, 26; concentrations, 14, 26, 99, 138; counts, *15t*; type, 26, 27, 44, 126
atlatl, 145
Aucilla River, 134, 147
awl, 87
Aziscohos Lake, 138

Bailey, Harry P., 167
Baker Cave, 131
Ballenger, David L., 95
Ballo, George R., xv
Bartolotti, Gene, 12
base camp, 17, 137, 141, 142, 162, 166, 168; aggregate, 175
bases, 53, 57, 60, 62, 104, 133, 138; broken, 55; concave, 44, 51, 55, 150; eared, 53; lanceolate, *60f*, *61f*; square, 57
Beaver Lake: lanceolate form, 62
Beilman, Laurence E., 152
Bellomo, Randy V., xvi
Bierce-Gedris, Katharine, xv
biface, 19, 37, 43, 51, 60, 62, 95, 104, 110, 114, 115, 120, 122, 125, 126, 128, 135, 150, 170; fragments, 97, 110, 112; lanceolates, 57, 62, 150; lozenge-shaped, 57–60, *58–59f*, 62, 120; preform, 44, 110
Bifacial Thinning Flake Model, 95
big-game theory, 130
Big Sandy I, 33
Binford, Lewis R., 37, 98, 100, 101, 102, 103, 122, 162, 164, 165, 167, 173
biogenic activities, 40; bioturbation, 107
bison, 130, 131, 133, 134, 147, 159
Blackwater Draw, 129, 131, 141
Blackwelder, B. W., 154
blade, 53, 55, 72, 87
blanks, 122
Bolen, 102, 161
Bolen Bluff, 74, 150
Bolen points, 33, 35, 36, 37, 38, 55, *56f*, 62, 74, 102, 104, 114, 150, 151; Bolen Beveled, 55, 151; Bolen Plain, 55
bone: artifacts, 92; perforators, 92; pins, 92; points, 92; preservation, 17; tools, 92, 134
Brand site, xi, 63, 68, 69, 70, 77, 85, 152
Broecker, Wallace, 154
Brooks, H. K., 156, 157
Broster, John B., 140
Brown, Ken, xv
Bryan, Alan L., 140
Bull Brook: assemblages, 69; site, 74, 132

Bullen, Ripley P., 33, 34, 44, 55, 148, 150, 151, 152
Burns, Lisa, xv
Butzer, Karl W., 156
Byers, D. S., 74

caches, 125, 126, 166
Caldwell, Joseph R., 167
Calhoun, John C., 11
Callahan, Errett, 44
Cambron, Warren W., 63, 70, 76
Camp Ranch, 74
Cannette, Ed, xv
Cape Hatteras, 154
Carbone, Victor A., 142
caribou, 132, 136, 138
cenotes, 155
Cenozoic era, 159
charcoal, 19, 37
Charleston, 159
chert: exotic, xi, 169, 172; provenance analysis, xv; sources, 124, 169; types, xiii
chopper, 76, 146
chronological sequence, 39
Churchill, Linda, xv
Cleland, Charles E., 167
Clovis: adaptations, 161; material culture, 161; period, 141; site, 131, 142; tool forms, 150
Clovis points, 44, 149, 161; fluted, 130, 149
Clovis/Suwannee point distribution, 143
Coastal Lowlands, 168; Gulf, 168, 169, 175
Coe, Joffre L., 70
Container Corporation of America site, 72
Cooper, Allen, xv
core, 19, 81–83, 84f, 87, 88, 94, 104, 110, 112, 114, 115, 124, 125, 126, 152, 170, 171, 172, 173, 174; bifacial, 63, 81–82, 87, 115, 170, 171, 174; fragments, 16, 81, 104, 110, 112, 115, 125, 126; micro, 83–84, 115; multidirectional, 82–83, 115; polyhedral, 76, 79, 82, 87; unidirectional, 115
Courtin, Jean, 39
Cowhouse Creek, 90
Crystal Springs, 8
culture historic reconstruction, 42
Cumberland points, 150
Cunningham, Roger M., 132, 140
curated: category, 62; gear, 122, 164; tool kit, 170–71; tools, 173, 174
curated unifaces, 107, 122–23, 126, 127, 128, 173, 174

Dalton, 149, 150
Daniel, Becky, xvi

Daniel, Randy, 16
Darby Springs, 147, 151
datum, 38
Debert site, xi, 69, 86, 128, 129, 132, 135–36, 137, 141, 170
debitage, 19, 26, 94, 101, 103, 123, 125, 136; analysis, 94–97, 96f
Department of Anthropology at the University of South Florida, xv, 26
depositional episodes, 37
Devil's Den, 159, 161
discoidal scrapers, 62, 69–70, 107, 110, 112, 114, 125, 170
disturbances, 19, 26, 31, 37, 148; root, 33, 40
Division of Historical Resources History and Records Management (FDHRHRM), 27
Dixie Lime Caves, 151
Dobe Bushmen, 100
Domebo site, 141
Dragoo, Don W., 76, 77
drop zone, 101, 102, 103
Dunbar, James S., 143
Dunnellon, 8

Early Archaic, 37, 76, 148, 149; contexts, 83, 86; levels, 133; period, 134, 146; sites, 137, 144; tool assemblages, 144
Eastern Woodland, 134
effective temperature concept, 167
8Hi393c/uw, 134
8Hi471, 4
8Hi480, 4
8Hi507. See Harney Flats
Elida, 131
Elkins, Cheryl, xv
Emery, K. O., 152, 154, 155
endscrapers, 62, 63–69, 64f, 86, 107, 110, 115, 122, 125, 126, 128, 135, 137, 170, 171; concave, 152; discoidal, 70; hafted teardrop-shaped, xii; plano-convex, 63; snub-nosed, 146; trapezoidal, 63; triangular, 63
ethnoarchaeology, 42–43, 63, 100–102, 162, 168
expedient unifaces, 123, 128, 173, 174

Fairbanks, Charles H., 33, 144, 147, 151, 152
faunal remains from selected sites in Peninsular Florida, 160t
features, 16, 26, 125, 135, 140, 162, 175; cultural, 19, 31
Federal Highway Administration, xv
Fitting, James E., 136, 137
flakes, 42, 44, 63, 68, 70, 72, 74, 76, 77, 79, 81, 82, 94, 95, 104, 135, 171, 174; bifacial, 53; blade-like, 82, 87,

88f, 97, 112, 114, 124; uniface retouch, 77, 87, 95, *96f;* utilized, 76, 97, 112, 146
flaking: bifacial, 53
Flint Run complex, 137, 143
Florida, xi, 7, 8, 9, 10, 11, 16, 17, 35, 57, 70, 72, 85, 86, 92, 102, 131, 132, 133, 134, 143, 145, 146, 147, 149, 150, 151, 152, 154, 155, 156, 157, 158, 159, 161, 169, 173, 175; early man chronologies, *148t;* sequence, 148; site locations in peninsular, *146f;* stratigraphic sequence, 151
Florida Bureau of Archaeological Research, xv
Florida Department of Transportation, xv
Florida Gulf Coast, 169
Florida State Museum, 86
Folsom point: fluted, 130; without flutes, 150
Folsom sites, 141
forager-collector model, 165–67
Forked Deer River, 140
Fort Brooke, 11, 12; Military Preserve, 11; Military Reserve, 12
fossilized shark's tooth, 145
fossils, 159
Funk, Robert E., 140

Gadsden, James, Colonel, 11
Gardner, William M., 131, 137
Georgia, 9, 94, 158
Gidley, J. W., 145
Girard, Greg, xv
Goggin, John M., 146
Goodyear, Albert C., xvi, 51, 57, 61, 68, 85, 86, 148, 149, 169, 172, 173, 174
Gould, Richard A., 63
Graham Cave, 133
Gramly, Richard M., 87, 138
Grange, Roger T., xv
gravers, xii, 42, 62, 69–70, 85–87, 137
Great Plains, 132
Greenbriar point, 145, 147, 151
Green Swamp, 8
Griffin, John W., 145
grinding stone, 131
Gulf Coast lowlands, 4
Gulf of Mexico, 169, 175

hafting, 55, 62, 68, 79, 81, 85, 121–22, 170
Half Mile Rise, 134
hammerstone, 16, 19, 88–90, *89f,* 107, 110, 112, 114, 115, 136, 171, 173, 174; fragments, 88, 112, 115; personal gear, 88
hand-axe, 81, 82, 93, 171

Hardaway: points, 151; site, 63
Hardman, Jay, xv
hardpan, 7, 16, 28, 29, 31, 32, 33, 39
Harney Flats: archaeological site, 1, 4, 7, 11, 12, 14, 16, 17, 18, 28, 31, 32, 33, 34, 39, 40; climate, 9; fauna, 11; flora, 9–10; historical impacts, 11–13; hydrology, 8, 31–32; I-75 By-Pass (Right of Way), *3f;* physiography, 4, *6t;* shematic map of spatial structure, *127f;* site location map, *5f;* site stratification, 28–29, *36f;* soil analysis, 29
Hayden, Brian, 43, 129
Haynes, C. Vance, Jr., 142
Healy, Henry G., 152
Hemmings, E. Thomas, 146, 151
Hernando County, 8
Hillsborough County, 4, 7, 8, 9, 28, 76, 83
Hillsborough River, 8, 11, 13, 134, 168; Valley, 168
Hillsborough River State Park, 8
Holcombe Beach, 132, 136–37
Holocene, 140, 157; early, 156, 158–59, 167
Hopkins, Charles, 11
horizontal: displacement, 102; post depositional displacement, 103
Hornsby Springs, 147, 151
House, John H., 95
Hrdlicka, Ales, 145
Hulse, David C., 63, 70, 76
human remains: Paleo-Indian, 4; skeletal, 145, 147
hunters and gatherer, xi, 100, 102, 128, 141, 162, 163, 164, 165; adaptations, 163, 175; settlement model, 167–69; sites, 128, 163, 174, 175, 171
Huser, Bill, xv

I-75 project, 1, *2f,* 13–17, 26, 33
Idaho, 159
Illinois, 133
Indians: Seminole, 11
inter-area analysis, 103
intra-area: analysis, 102–14; comparisons, 114–28
Itchetucknee River, 145, 150

Jaguar Cave, 159
Jochim, Michael A., 141, 163
Johnson, Bill, xv
Jones, B. Calvin, xvi, 14, 17
Jones, Emyrs, 139
Judge, James W., 141, 142

Kalahari desert, 100
karst: areas, 175; erosion, 155; terrain, 157
Keeley, Lawrence H., 42, 122

kill sites, 139, 141, 145
Kimmswick site, 133
King, John, xv
Kirk serrated points, *34f*; occupation, 36; projectile point, 35, 36, 37
Kunz, Michael, 131, 139

Lake Annie, 157
Lakela, Olga, 10
Lake Thonotosassa, 158
Lake Weohyakapka, 152
Late Pleistocene/Early Holocene sea level, *153f*; sea level stands, *154t*
Laurentide ice sheets, 156, 158
Lett, Roy, xvi
Levi site, 131
Lindenmeier, Colorado, 130
lithic: analysis, xi, xiii; artifact, xiii, 43, 175; assemblage, xiii, 63, 165, 171, 175; material, 4, 129, 131, 143, 147, 173; reduction, 44; sources, 173; technology, 144, 169; tools, 130
Little Salt Spring, 134, 145, 147, 155, 157, 158, 159, 161
Llano: complex, 131; Estacado, 141
logistical strategy, 165, 166
lozenge-shaped bifaces, 57–60, *58f, 59f*
Lytle, Mindy, xv

MacDonald, George F., 86, 135, 136, 137, 141
Maine, 138, 141
mammoth, 130, 133, 141, 145
Marion County, 72, 146
Mason, Ronald J., 150
Massachusetts, 132, 134
mastodon, 133, 145; teeth, 147
McDonough, Susan, xv
McKay Bay, 8, 13
McKinney, Curtis, xv
Meadowcroft Rockshelter, 133
Meer II site, 40
megafauna, 130, 131, 133–34
Megalloway River, 138
Melbourne, 145; bone bed, 159
methodology: phase I survey, 14; phase II testing, 14–16; phase III excavation, 16–27
Michigan, 132, 136
microlith, 83; tool complex, 152
Middle Archaic, 16, 33, 37, 38; tool assemblages, 144; traditions, 133
Middle Shenandoah Valley, 137
Milanich, J. T., 33, 144, 147, 151, 152
Miliman, J. D., 152, 154

Miliman and Emery curve, 154
Miocene epoch, 28; upper Miocene, 152
Misner, Elizabeth J., xvi
Missouri, 133
Mitchell, John, xv
Modoc Rock Shelter, 133
Moeller, Roger W., xvi

Nalcrest site, 70, 86, 152
Naskapi dwellings, 135
Neill, Wilfred T., 146, 149, 150
New Jersey, 154
New Mexico, 129, 134, 140, 141
Newnan: Area 1, 33; components, 36, 102; points, 33, 35, *35t*, 102
New York, 141
Norton, Michael, xv
Nova Scotia, 129, 132, 134, 135, 141
Nuckels, M. G., 169
Nunamiut Eskimo, 164, 167

Obarka, Mark, xv
oblong scrapers, 62, 70–74, *71f, 72f, 73f*, 107, 110, 114, 115, 123, 125, 170, 171
Ocala, 145, 151
Odell, George, H., 42, 43
Ohio Valley, 140
Oklahoma, 141
Ontario, 132

paleoenvironment, 152–61, 175
Paleo-Indian, xi, 13, 14, 15, 16, 31, 36, 72, 76, 129, 131, 132, 133, 134, 135, 138, 139, 140, 142, 157, 169; assemblages, 74, 87, 92, 93, 130, 134; lithic raw material, xiii; period, 37, 57, 134, 139, 147, 148, 154, 168, 169, 170; projectile point, 134, 143, 145, 146, 175; settlement patterns, 139–44, 167, 169; Southeast, xi, xii, 86; stone tool assemblages, 172; subsistence, 130–35; technologies, 172, 174
Pamlico shoreline, 4
Parkhill, 132
Pasco County, 8
Pennsylvania, 133
personal gear, 88, 164, 165, 170, 174
phase I: survey, 1
phase II: excavations, *1t*, 4, 12; results, 16, 17; testing, 4, 16; test units, 12, 32
phase III: artifact processing, 26–27; contingencies, 26; excavations, xvi, *1t*, 4, 7, 16, *18f*, 26, 32, 40; excavation techniques, 19–26; field procedures, 14–19; fieldwork, 16, 19; research problems, 14; testing, 4

phosphate: analysis, 19, 30f; concentration, 29; content, 29
pieces esquillees, 170
Pierce site, 140
Pinellas County, 154
Plainview: occupation, 131; points, 150
plant remains, 131; carbonized, 131; dessicated, 131
playas, 140
Pleistocene, xi, 4, 7, 140, 145, 155, 159, 167; fossils, xi; temperatures, 156
Pleistocene: megafauna, 130–31, 133–34, 159, 161
Poe, Charles, xvi, 16
Pohl, Dave, xv
Polk County, 8, 152
Polk Upland, 168, 169, 175
postdepositional: artifact movement, 40; events, 39, 40
pot hunting, 26
preforms, 120, 136
pre-Suwannee horizon, 149
primary forest efficiency, 167
prismatic blades, 44
profile: unit, 19, 21f, 22f, 23f, 24f; wall, 37
projectile point, 19, 35, 35t, 36, 37, 42, 62, 129, 133, 135, 146, 171; chert, 134, 147; fluted, 132, 133, 138, 139; fossilized ivory, 145; functions, 62; lozenge-shaped, 62; manufacture, 60; preform, 51, 53; refitted, 35, 36, 37, 39, 40; socketed antler, 147; stemmed, 151; types, 35, 55. *See also* Bolen points; lozenge-shaped bifaces; Simpson points; Suwannee: points
provenience, 14, 17, 31; general level, 19, 35, 36; horizontal, 16, 19; vertical, 16, 19
Purdy, Barbara A., 33, 72, 151

Quad: points, 150; site, 133
Quarternary period, 158

radiocarbon dates: Florida, 147
raw materials, xi, 43, 70, 79, 83, 93, 126, 127, 128, 136, 163, 165–66, 169, 170, 171, 172, 173; access, 169; exotic, 93, 129; lithic, 165, 166, 172, 174
reciprocal exchange, 164
refuse: primary, 102, 103; secondary, 102
regional mobility, 163
residential: area, 17, 101; base, 122, 132, 137, 165–67, 174
Ring Model, 100
Robinson, Ernest L., 12
rock: metamorphic, 92, 93, 94, 125; quartzite, 130; rhyolite, 130; sandstone, 114
Rodgers shelter, 133

Rossman, Randi, xv
Rouse, Irving, 145
Russel cave, 63, 133
Rutt, Gary, xv

S. L. EDCO: production staff, xvi
Safety Harbor period, 32
Santa Fe: lanceolate form, 62; points, 151; river, 150
Sarasota County, 147
Schiffer, Michael B., 39, 99, 100, 102
Schneider, Jane, xv
scrapers. *See* discoidal scrapers; endscrapers; oblong scrapers; thick unifaces; thin unifaces
Sellards, E. H., 145
Semenov, Sergei A., 42
Seminole Treaty of 1823, 11
Seminole Wars, 11
Serbousek, Don, 134
settlement: activity, xi; behavior, xi; patterns, 139, 144; system, xiii, xiv, 168–75
settlement map, 99
Shafer, Harris J., 95
Shawnee-Minisink site, 133
Sheelar Lake, 157
Sheets, Payson D., 42
Shenandoah River, 137
Shepaug River, 139
sherds, 32t, 33; limestone tempered Pasco, 32; punctuated sand-tempered, 32; sand-tempered plain, 32; St. Johns, 32
Shoop site, 74, 133
sidescraper, Coe's: I, 76; II, 76; III, 77
Silver Springs: assemblage, 146; site, 146
Silver Springs Run, 145, 150
Simpson, Clarence, 145, 150
Simpson points, 33, 45f, 51, 52f, 57, 62, 150; measurement of bifaces, 46–50t; preform, 37, 54f; preform base, 104
site assemblage patterns, 100
site catchment analysis, 142
site formation processes, 39, 114
situational gear, 62, 165, 170, 174
Sixmile Creek, 8, 12
Sloan site, 17
soil: analysis, 29; Blanton fine sand, 7, 29; clay, 8, 72; descriptions, 19; Lakeland fine sand, 7, 29; Leon, 31; Leon fine sand, 7, 28, 32, 33; Plummer fine sands, 32; quartz sand, 7; sand, 72; sandy, 10, 31; sandy zone, 15, 28; surface sand, 7; unconsolidated sand, 7
soil samples, 19, 29

South Carolina, xi, 9, 150, 159
spatial analysis, xiv, 16, 98–128, 175
spokeshave, 76, 81; hafted, 85–86, 85f, 86t, 107, 112, 114
springs: artesian, 9, 155, 157; nonartesian, 8; saline, 141; water table, 8
St. Petersburg, 72
Stanfield-Worley Bluff Shelter, 63, 133, 148
stratified sequence, xiii
statistical techniques, 98–100; statistical methods, 100
Stevenson, Henry M., 11
Stockton, E. D., 39
Stoltman, James, 150
stone: chalcedonies, 129; chert(s), xi, 81, 90, 94, 124, 129, 136, 144, 169; cryptocrystalline, xiii, 92, 93, 94, 169, 172, 173; exotic, 125; Florida, xi–xii, xiii, 43; jasper, 143; limestone, xiii, 8, 10, 90, 143, 155, 157, 169; quartz, 7, 90
stone tools, xi, xiii, 16, 43, 44, 169, 171, 172; refitting, 128
stratigraphy: profiles, 21–24f, 36f; sequence, 35–36
Strom, R. N., 169
structure: site, 99, 101, 103, 126, 174, 175
Suarez, Joy, xv
subsistence, 144; activities, 102; adaptations, 134; strategies, 142, 165
Suwannee, xi, 35t, 149, 150, 161; blank type, 44, 51; components, 36, 102, 161; fluting, xii, 44; measurement of bifaces, 46–50t; points, xi, xii, xiii, 14, 33, 35, 36, 37, 38, 44–53, 45f, 52f, 55, 60–61f, 62, 74, 102, 104, 114, 146, 149, 150, 151, 154, 170, 171; preform, 51, 53, 104; technology, 173
Swofford, Paul, xv
SYMAPS, xvi, 103, 104, 105f, 108f, 111f

Tallahassee, 27
Tallahassee points, 151
Tampa, 9, 11, 13
Tampa Bay, xi, 8, 9, 10, 11, 26, 32, 92, 94, 158, 161, 162, 169, 175
Tampa Bypass Canal, 8, 9, 12, 13, 14
techno-functional: analysis, xi, xiii; stone tool study, 175
technological organization, 43, 164, 171, 173–75
Templeton-6LF21, 139
Tennessee, 140
Tertiary age limestone outcrops, 143
Tertiary Limestones, 155
test: culturally sterile, 136; pits, 4, 14, 15, 16, 17, 19, 26, 28, 29, 98
Texas, 131

thermoluminescent dating, 19
thick unifaces, 74–77, 75f
thinning: basal, 53, 57; lateral, 53, 57
thin unifaces, 77–79, 78f
Thunderbird, 137–38
tool: analysis, 42–94; discard patterns, 43; edge angles, 43; form, xiii, 19, 36, 42, 43, 62, 63, 74, 92, 170, 173, 175; fragments, 19, 26, 95, 128; function, xiii, 42, 43, 92, 173, 175; haft elements, 43, 55; handheld, 63, 70; kit, 72, 98, 126, 128, 132, 137, 138, 171, 172, 174, 175; manufacture, 43, 51, 53, 83, 93, 95, 115, 124, 126, 135, 136, 168, 170; refitting, xiv, 128; repair/rejuvenation, 43; type, 85, 112, 114, 124, 152, 174; unifacial, 95, 129, 150, 173
topographic features, 1
trade, 94
Transitional Period, 33, 151
trenches, 14, 15, 26, 104
trianguloid endscraper, 63
Tringham, R., 42
Tuck, James A., 33
Turtlecrawl Point site, 154
Two Creeks ice recession, 152
typology, 41, 43; morphological, 42

U.S. Army Corps of Engineers, 13
unifaces, 16, 19, 43, 62–81, 65–67t, 95, 107, 110, 114, 123, 151, 170, 173, 174; flexibility, 62; maintenance, 62; manufacture, 62, 81; portability, 62; uniface fragments, 110, 112. See also discoidal scrapers; oblong scrapers; thick unifaces; thin unifaces
United States: eastern, xi
unscreened excavation units, 25f
Upchurch, Sam B., xiii, xvi, 169
Upper Delaware Valley, 133
use-wear: analysis, xi, 42–43, 62, 70, 74, 76, 77, 81, 171; studies, xiv, 175

Vail site, 87, 138, 141, 170
vandalism, 26
variability: morphological, 44; size, 62
variation, 44
Vero, 134, 145, 159, 161
vertical displacement, 37, 38, 39, 102; vertical artifact mixing, 39; vertical disposition, 40; mechanism of, 40
Villa, Paola, 39
Virginia, 133, 137, 143

Wacissa Bison Kill site, 134
Wacissa River, 134

Waller, Ben, 143
Waller knives, 152
Warm Mineral Springs, 145, 147, 155, 158, 159, 161
water table pond, 9, 31, 32
Watts, W. A., 157, 158
Weeden Island, 32
Welch, John, xv
Wells Creek site, 76, 77, 82
West Athens Hill, 141
Westphal, Jerry, xv
Whallon, Robert, Jr., 98, 99, 100
Willey, Gordon R., 130, 139
Williams, Stephen, 150
Williamson site, 133
Wilmsen, Edwin N., 129
Wiocomico terrace, 7

Wisconsin glaciation, 159; Farmdalian interstade of, 152
Wisconsin period, 156
Wisenbaker, Mike, 16
Withlacoochee River, 8
Witthoft, John, 74
Wogaman, Ronald, 95
Wood, John J., 141, 142
Woodfordian stade, 152
Worthen, Mark, xv
Wright, H. E., Jr., 157
Wyoming, 159

Yellen, John E., 100, 102

Zephyrhills Gap, 168

I. Randolph Daniel Jr., professor of anthropology at East Carolina University, is the author of *Hardaway Revisited: Early Archaic Settlement in the Southeast*.

Michael Wisenbaker is archaeology supervisor for public lands archaeology at the Florida Department of State.

Ripley P. Bullen Series
FLORIDA MUSEUM OF NATURAL HISTORY

Tacachale: Essays on the Indians of Florida and Southeastern Georgia during the Historic Period, edited by Jerald T. Milanich and Samuel Proctor (1978)
Aboriginal Subsistence Technology on the Southeastern Coastal Plain during the Late Prehistoric Period, by Lewis H. Larson (1980)
Cemochechobee: Archaeology of a Mississippian Ceremonial Center on the Chattahoochee River, by Frank T. Schnell, Vernon J. Knight Jr., and Gail S. Schnell (1981)
Fort Center: An Archaeological Site in the Lake Okeechobee Basin, by William H. Sears, with contributions by Elsie O'R. Sears and Karl T. Steinen (1982)
Perspectives on Gulf Coast Prehistory, edited by Dave D. Davis (1984)
Archaeology of Aboriginal Culture Change in the Interior Southeast: Depopulation during the Early Historic Period, by Marvin T. Smith (1987)
Apalachee: The Land between the Rivers, by John H. Hann (1988)
Key Marco's Buried Treasure: Archaeology and Adventure in the Nineteenth Century, by Marion Spjut Gilliland (1989)
First Encounters: Spanish Explorations in the Caribbean and the United States, 1492–1570, edited by Jerald T. Milanich and Susan Milbrath (1989)
Missions to the Calusa, edited and translated by John H. Hann, with an introduction by William H. Marquardt (1991)
Excavations on the Franciscan Frontier: Archaeology at the Fig Springs Mission, by Brent Richards Weisman (1992)
The People Who Discovered Columbus: The Prehistory of the Bahamas, by William F. Keegan (1992)
Hernando de Soto and the Indians of Florida, by Jerald T. Milanich and Charles Hudson (1993)
Foraging and Farming in the Eastern Woodlands, edited by C. Margaret Scarry (1993)
Puerto Real: The Archaeology of a Sixteenth-Century Spanish Town in Hispaniola, edited by Kathleen Deagan (1995)
Political Structure and Change in the Prehistoric Southeastern United States, edited by John F. Scarry (1996)
Bioarchaeology of Native Americans in the Spanish Borderlands, edited by Brenda J. Baker and Lisa Kealhofer (1996)
A History of the Timucua Indians and Missions, by John H. Hann (1996)
Archaeology of the Mid-Holocene Southeast, edited by Kenneth E. Sassaman and David G. Anderson (1996)
The Indigenous People of the Caribbean, edited by Samuel M. Wilson (1997; first paperback edition, 1999)
Hernando de Soto among the Apalachee: The Archaeology of the First Winter Encampment, by Charles R. Ewen and John H. Hann (1998)
The Timucuan Chiefdoms of Spanish Florida, by John E. Worth: vol. 1, *Assimilation*; vol. 2, *Resistance and Destruction* (1998)
Ancient Earthen Enclosures of the Eastern Woodlands, edited by Robert C. Mainfort Jr. and Lynne P. Sullivan (1998)

An Environmental History of Northeast Florida, by James J. Miller (1998)
Precolumbian Architecture in Eastern North America, by William N. Morgan (1999)
Archaeology of Colonial Pensacola, edited by Judith A. Bense (1999)
Grit-Tempered: Early Women Archaeologists in the Southeastern United States, edited by Nancy Marie White, Lynne P. Sullivan, and Rochelle A. Marrinan (1999)
Coosa: The Rise and Fall of a Southeastern Mississippian Chiefdom, by Marvin T. Smith (2000)
Religion, Power, and Politics in Colonial St. Augustine, by Robert L. Kapitzke (2001)
Bioarchaeology of Spanish Florida: The Impact of Colonialism, edited by Clark Spencer Larsen (2001)
Archaeological Studies of Gender in the Southeastern United States, edited by Jane M. Eastman and Christopher B. Rodning (2001)
The Archaeology of Traditions: Agency and History Before and After Columbus, edited by Timothy R. Pauketat (2001)
Foraging, Farming, and Coastal Biocultural Adaptation in Late Prehistoric North Carolina, by Dale L. Hutchinson (2002)
Windover: Multidisciplinary Investigations of an Early Archaic Florida Cemetery, edited by Glen H. Doran (2002)
Archaeology of the Everglades, by John W. Griffin (2002; first paperback edition, 2017)
Pioneer in Space and Time: John Mann Goggin and the Development of Florida Archaeology, by Brent Richards Weisman (2002)
Indians of Central and South Florida, 1513–1763, by John H. Hann (2003)
Presidio Santa Maria de Galve: A Struggle for Survival in Colonial Spanish Pensacola, edited by Judith A. Bense (2003)
Bioarchaeology of the Florida Gulf Coast: Adaptation, Conflict, and Change, by Dale L. Hutchinson (2004)
The Myth of Syphilis: The Natural History of Treponematosis in North America, edited by Mary Lucas Powell and Della Collins Cook (2005)
The Florida Journals of Frank Hamilton Cushing, edited by Phyllis E. Kolianos and Brent R. Weisman (2005)
The Lost Florida Manuscript of Frank Hamilton Cushing, edited by Phyllis E. Kolianos and Brent R. Weisman (2005)
The Native American World Beyond Apalachee: West Florida and the Chattahoochee Valley, by John H. Hann (2006)
Tatham Mound and the Bioarchaeology of European Contact: Disease and Depopulation in Central Gulf Coast Florida, by Dale L. Hutchinson (2006)
Taino Indian Myth and Practice: The Arrival of the Stranger King, by William F. Keegan (2007)
An Archaeology of Black Markets: Local Ceramics and Economies in Eighteenth-Century Jamaica, by Mark W. Hauser (2008; first paperback edition, 2013)
Mississippian Mortuary Practices: Beyond Hierarchy and the Representationist Perspective, edited by Lynne P. Sullivan and Robert C. Mainfort Jr. (2010; first paperback edition, 2012)
Bioarchaeology of Ethnogenesis in the Colonial Southeast, by Christopher M. Stojanowski (2010; first paperback edition, 2013)
French Colonial Archaeology in the Southeast and Caribbean, edited by Kenneth G. Kelly and Meredith D. Hardy (2011; first paperback edition, 2015)

Late Prehistoric Florida: Archaeology at the Edge of the Mississippian World, edited by Keith Ashley and Nancy Marie White (2012; first paperback edition, 2015)

Early and Middle Woodland Landscapes of the Southeast, edited by Alice P. Wright and Edward R. Henry (2013)

Trends and Traditions in Southeastern Zooarchaeology, edited by Tanya M. Peres (2014)

New Histories of Pre-Columbian Florida, edited by Neill J. Wallis and Asa R. Randall (2014; first paperback edition, 2016)

Discovering Florida: First-Contact Narratives from Spanish Expeditions along the Lower Gulf Coast, edited and translated by John E. Worth (2014; first paperback edition, 2015)

Constructing Histories: Archaic Freshwater Shell Mounds and Social Landscapes of the St. Johns River, Florida, by Asa R. Randall (2015)

Archaeology of Early Colonial Interaction at El Chorro de Maíta, Cuba, by Roberto Valcárcel Rojas (2016)

Fort San Juan and the Limits of Empire: Colonialism and Household Practice at the Berry Site, edited by Robin A. Beck, Christopher B. Rodning, and David G. Moore (2016)

Rethinking Moundville and Its Hinterland, edited by Vincas P. Steponaitis and C. Margaret Scarry (2016)

Handbook of Ceramic Animal Symbols in the Ancient Lesser Antilles, by Lawrence Waldron (2016)

Paleoindian Societies of the Coastal Southeast, by James S. Dunbar (2016)

Gathering at Silver Glen: Community and History in Late Archaic Florida, by Zackary I. Gilmore (2016)

Cuban Archaeology in the Caribbean, edited by Ivan Roksandic (2016)

Archaeologies of Slavery and Freedom in the Caribbean: Exploring the Spaces in Between, edited by Lynsey A. Bates, John M. Chenoweth, and James A. Delle (2016)

Setting the Table: Ceramics, Dining, and Cultural Exchange in Andalusia and La Florida, by Kathryn L. Ness (2017)

Simplicity, Equality, and Slavery: An Archaeology of Quakerism in the British Virgin Islands, 1740–1780, by John M. Chenoweth (2017)

Fit For War: Sustenance and Order in the Mid-Eighteenth-Century Catawba Nation, by Mary Elizabeth Fitts (2017)

Water from Stone: Archaeology and Conservation at Florida's Springs, by Jason M. O'Donoughue (2017)

Mississippian Beginnings, edited by Gregory D. Wilson (2017)

Harney Flats: A Florida Paleoindian Site, by I. Randolph Daniel Jr. and Michael Wisenbaker (2017)

www.ingramcontent.com/pod-product-compliance
Lightning Source LLC
Chambersburg PA
CBHW021855230426
43671CB00006B/400